Advance praise for *Althusser: A Critical Reader*:

'Assembled by the foremost authority on Althusser in the English-speaking world, Gregory Elliott's *Althusser: A Critical Reader* is a timely and valuable addition to the critical literature on the late French philosopher's work. Judiciously combining classic essays with recent assessments, including Elliott's own distinguished piece on Althusser's autobiography, this volume will be an indispensable companion to any serious engagement with the Althusserian corpus.'

Michael Sprinker, Professor of English and Comparative Literature, State University of New York at Stony Brook

ALTHUSSER

A Critical Reader

EDITED BY

GREGORY ELLIOTT

First published 1994

First published in USA 1994

Blackwell Publishers
108 Cowley Road
Oxford OX4 1JF
UK

238 Main Street
Cambridge, Massachusetts 02142
USA

British Library Cataloguing in Publication Data

A CIP catalogue record for this book is available from the British Library.

Library of Congress Cataloging-in-Publication Data

Althusser: A Critical Reader / Gregory Elliott.
p. cm.
Includes bibliographical references and index.
ISBN 0–631–18806–1 (alk. paper) – ISBN 0–631–18807–X (alk. paper)
1. Althusser, Louis. 2. Philosophy, French – 20th century.
3. Marxist criticism. I. Elliott, Gregory.
B2430.A474A65 1994
194—dc20

93–38739
CIP

Typeset in 10 on 12 pt Sabon
by Graphicraft Typesetters Ltd., Hong Kong
Printed in Great Britain by T. J. Press, Padstow, Cornwall

This book is printed on acid-free paper

CONTENTS

PREFACE

Towards the end of his *Cool Memories*, Jean Baudrillard scornfully reflects as follows:

> Human rights, dissidence, antiracism, SOS-this, SOS-that: these are soft, easy, *post coitum historicum* ideologies, 'after-the-orgy' ideologies for an easy-going generation which has known neither hard ideologies nor radical philosophies. The ideology of a generation which is neo-sentimental in its politics too, which has rediscovered altruism, conviviality, international charity and the individual bleeding heart. Emotional outpourings, solidarity, cosmopolitan emotiveness, multi-media pathos: all soft values harshly condemned by the Nietzschean, Marxo-Freudian age. . . . A new generation, that of the spoilt children of the crisis, whereas the preceding one was that of the accursed children of history.[1]

Were it necessary to identify the thinker who best symbolizes the 'Marxo-Freudian age', a strong contender -would surely be the Communist philosopher, Louis Althusser, whose 'ideology' (to borrow Baudrillard's casual obscenity) pertains to the *coitum historicum* between the French intelligentsia and Marxism after the Liberation.

That Althusser was the accursed child of more than one history is by now well-known; the posthumous publication of his 'autobiography', *L'avenir dure longtemps*, affords sufficient, if deceptive, testimony. Yet he not only figures among the intellectual progeny of a dramatic French history, punctuated not by the tribulations of *le franc fort* and Euro-Disney, but by fascist leagues and Popular Front; by defeat and occupation, collaboration and resistance; by 'savage wars of peace' abroad (Vietnam, Algeria) and undeclared civil war at home (the overthrow of the Fourth Republic and installation of the Fifth, the 'Generals' putsch' and the OAS, May '68 and March '78). He was not only a contemporary of *Les Temps Modernes* and *Tel Quel*, of existentialism and (post-)structuralism, of *le nouveau roman* and *la nouvelle vague*. He was a progenitor of intellectual developments – one of which, by an unintended consequence of Althusserian action, was his own eventual effacement from the scene. Althusser was an agent, as well as a reagent (and victim). In elaborating a version of Marxism which Francis Mulhern has aptly described as 'a critical classicism',[2] he occupies a crucial – and ineradicable – position in modern French intellectual culture.

To begin with, his endeavour to salvage historical materialism as an explanatory science, both from its ossification under Stalinist auspices and its demotion or denigration at Western-Marxist hands, renders him a central figure in the anti-existentialist and anti-phenomenological turn in French philosophy in the 1960s. Just as, after reading Feuerbach's *Essence of Christianity*, Engels and his contemporaries 'all became at once Feuerbachians', so, upon the appearance of *Pour Marx* and *Lire le Capital*, a cohort of young French intellectuals turned Althusserian: where Sartre had been, Althusser would be. Or rather – and more accurately in one crucial respect – where Sartre had not been, Althusser would be: in the French Communist Party. Refusing the available models of the independent intellectual – Sartre – and the compliant ideologue – Garaudy – Althusser took advantage of the Khrushchevite thaw in the international Communist movement to propound his critique and reconstruction of actually existing Marxism from within its ranks. He articulated Marxist philosophy and Communist politics in a manner that stilled, if it did not altogether dispel, the doubts of a generation instructed by the counter-examples of Zhdanovism and Lysenkoism. As his comrade and collaborator, Etienne Balibar, remarked at his funeral:

> To be *at once* totally a philosopher and totally a Communist, without sacrificing, subordinating, or subjecting the one to the other: such is the intellectual singularity of Althusser, such was his wager and the risk he took. . . . Because Althusser won that wager, Marxism . . . and Communism are inscribed in the history of French philosophy in the second half of the twentieth century. And no-one can dislodge them without leaving a gaping hole.[3]

There is, however, a further – profoundly paradoxical – reason for Althusser's salience in post-war French intellectual history: namely, the unwitting pilot role he played in the widespread transfer of Parisian allegiances from versions of Marxism to varieties of 'post-Marxism'. Expelling *homo dialecticus* and the Hegelian heritage, renouncing autarky and restoring dialogue with non- (or even anti-) Marxist traditions, assimilating 'Nietzscheo-Heideggerian', as well as Spinozist-Bachelardian, motifs, the Althusserian 'renovation' of historical materialism intersected with broader currents in Gallic philosophical culture, associated with the names of Claude Lévi-Strauss or Jacques Lacan, Michel Foucault or Jacques Derrida, and assembled under the flag of convenience, 'theoretical anti-humanism', by those who spoke *in verba magistri*.[4] Source and component part of *la pensée 68*, 'structural Marxism' may be seen in retrospect as a transitional theoretical problematic – a vulnerable compromise-formation, in effect, between the Marxist legacy and non-Marxist modes, whose (auto-) deconstruction signalled the eclipse of one ascendant star of the 'Nietzschean, Freudo-Marxist age'.

Whether or not the contemporary disenchantment with historical materialism is justified, is a question beyond the remit of this Preface and Critical Reader (although it is touched upon in Francis Mulhern's essay). It could be that its agents (and patients) find themselves in the unenviable condition diagnosed by Sartre in *Words*: 'Like all dreamers, I mistook disenchantment for truth.' However that may be, an appreciation of what one of its best analysts has dubbed 'the rise and fall of structural Marxism'[5] is indispensable to an understanding of the renaissance and obsolescence alike of historical materialism in recent decades, not only in France but in the Anglophone world. Without pretending to exhaustivity, *Althusser: A Critical Reader* aims to contribute to that task.

A few words about the principles guiding its compilation are in order. First, although it will be for the Critical Reader on Critical Readers doubtless in the offing to judge, I have (I hope) taken the publisher's rubric literally: what follows is a *critical* anthology, composed in the belief that critique is a more genuine form of intellectual commemoration than apologia. Accordingly, it comes neither to praise, nor to bury, Althusser. Hence – with the possible exception of my own – each of the articles published here refutes (which is not to say merely repudiates) quintessential Althusserian propositions. Second, rather than reprinting and commissioning a host of shorter pieces, I have opted for a combination of the terse and synoptic, on the one hand, with the detailed and discursive, on the other: quantitative quality, as it were. Third, I have given preference to authors who treat Althusser's texts in various of their contexts, locating them, *sub specie temporis*, in one or more of the wider histories and cultures to which they belong. Fourth, I have selected contributions to the debate which are either less readily accessible, or less familiar, than other items in the secondary literature.[6] Fifth, whilst it is a matter for regret that the budget allowed me did not permit of more than a single translation,[7] I have tried to provide some indication of the continental reaction, Marxist and non-Marxist, to Althusser, by giving over virtually half of the volume to material which has for the most part been neglected by Anglophone commentators.

Inevitably partial and ultimately arbitrary in its selections, in addition to any sins of commission for which it is culpable, the Reader must confess at least one of omission: the highly regrettable absence of any feminist contribution. This was not for want of solicitation. However, of those approached to offer a feminist balance-sheet of the Althusserian moment, none, for a variety of reasons, found herself both willing *and* able to accept the commission. Consequently, apart from passing references by David Macey and Francis Mulhern, the volume is bereft of any reflection on a key dimension of the Althusserian impact upon intellectual work, and I can only refer the reader elsewhere.[8]

Each of the ensuing texts speaks more than adequately for itself; and I do not propose to paraphrase their content. It may, however, be helpful briefly to situate them, indicate their focus, and note any editorial interventions.

The Reader opens with E. J. Hobsbawm's review of *Pour Marx* and *Lire le Capital*, originally published in the *Times Literary Supplement* in 1966 and then reprinted in *Revolutionaries* (1973). Hobsbawm – an almost exact contemporary of Althusser's – should need no introduction to prospective readers; he is quite simply one of the foremost Marxist historians of the twentieth century. In the space of a mere five thousand words, he brings his immense, cosmopolitan erudition, and more than three decades' experience (at time of writing) of European Communism, to bear upon the advent of Althusserian Marxism in Thorez' Parti Communiste Français and de Gaulle's France. Better than any comparable essay in English, Hobsbawm both contextualizes Althusser's initiative and tactfully sketches the main lines of much subsequent criticism of it. In order to preserve the flavour of the original, I have retained Professor Hobsbawm's own translations of Althusser's French and his citations from the first edition of *Lire le Capital*.

Seven years after Hobsbawm introduced the name of Althusser across the Channel, Althusserianism was in full florescence not only in Britain and Western Europe generally, but in Latin America, eliciting eulogy and obloquy in equal measure. As Hobsbawm had foreseen, and as E. P. Thompson's broadside of 1978, *The Poverty of Theory*, would demonstrate, Marxist historians were especially sceptical of, or inimical to, what Althusser himself described as 'the very summary (and therefore unilateral) character of the few paragraphs devoted to "history" in the polemical context of *Reading Capital*'.[9] The second text printed here revolves around the blanket Althusserian condemnation of 'empiricism' and 'historicism' in the practice of mainstream and Marxist historiography alike. A leading member of the second generation of the *Annales* school of French historians, Pierre Vilar, who from 1962 until his retirement held the chair in social history at the Sorbonne whose previous tenants had been Marc Bloch and Ernest Labrousse, is the author of *La Catalogne dans l'Espagne moderne* (1962) and *A History of Gold and Money* (1969). His article – originally published in *Annales* (January/February 1973), translated in *New Left Review* that summer, and explicitly sub-titled 'Towards a Dialogue with

Althusser'[10] – is remarkable for its equanimity in the face of Althusser's provocations. By turns generous in its admissions and firm in its rebuttals, Vilar's wideranging *tour d'horizon* has been moderately abridged by the removal of two introductory sections (pp. 65–72 of the original, dealing with Marx as historian and the status of economic theory), and the sacrifice of some explanatory notes added by the English editors.

While still largely unknown outside of the French academy, Althusser had in 1955 crossed swords with Paul Ricoeur over the philosophy of history. Thirteen years later, Ricoeur would be one of his interlocutors at the stormy session of the Société française de Philosophie at which Althusser read his celebrated lecture, 'Lenin and Philosophy'.[11] A leading post-war French philosopher, for many years based at the University of Paris X (Nanterre), and then resident at Chicago University, Ricoeur is the author of a voluminous oeuvre, ranging from *Freud and Philosophy* (1964) to the three volumes of *Time and Narrative* (1983–85). He is unique among the contributors to this volume in that he is not now, and never has been, a Marxist. *Au-dessus de la mêlée marxiste*, the exponent of an innovative blend of phenomenology and hermeneutics, Ricoeur is committed, resolutely against the Parisian current, to a certain humanism. These affiliations are evident in his attentive probing of Althusser's account of the conjoint subjectification/subjection of social agents via the mechanisms of ideology. Ricoeur's text derives from three lectures on Althusser delivered as part of a series at Chicago in autumn 1975, and eventually published by Columbia University Press in 1986 as *Lectures on Ideology and Utopia*. The extract below essentially comprises the second and third lectures (pp. 124–57), specifically focused on the theory of ideology, whereas the first interrogates Althusser's postulate of an 'epistemological break' in Marx's theoretical development. In preparing them for publication, I have cut Ricoeur's résumés of previous lectures, anglicized spelling, punctuation and references, and slightly amended the page reference system.

In an interview released in 1985 Jürgen Habermas remarked, with unwonted hauteur, that '[h]aving rejected the orthodoxy of the philosophy of history, I had no wish to lapse back either into ethical socialism, or into scientism, or indeed into both at once. This explains why I hardly read Althusser.'[12] Fortunately, the same has not been true of all members of the second or third generations of the Frankfurt School. In 1971 Alfred Schmidt published a careful response to what he regarded as the 'structuralist attack on history', which was translated a decade later as *History and Structure*. The long text by Axel Honneth translated here originally appeared in German in 1977, in an anthology of writings on historical materialism edited by him in collaboration with Urs Jaeggi.[13] Currently Professor of Philosophy at the Free University, Berlin, and author of *The Critique of Power* (1985) and *The Struggle for Recognition* (forthcoming in English translation), Honneth criticizes, *inter alios*, Vilar (whose essay appeared in the same collection) for undue indulgence towards Althusser. Arguing that Althusser conflates quite distinct philosophical and political projects under the catch-all of 'historicism', and misconstrues Marx's anatomy of the peculiar logic of capital as the paradigm for a general structural theory of history, Honneth lucidly articulates the main areas of contention between the principal rival schools of Western Marxism in the 1960s and 70s. To facilitate publication of the article in its entirety, the notes – in particular, those referring to the details of contemporary West German debates and their accompanying literature – have, with Professor Honneth's consent, been considerably abridged.

A prominent British exponent of the Habermasian brand of Critical Theory is Peter Dews, whose collection of interviews with Habermas has already been cited, and whose *Logics of Disintegration: Post-Structuralist Thought and the Claims of Critical Theory*, published by Verso in 1987, was widely received as the most balanced assessment to date of Derrida, Foucault, et al. In the course of the research which formed the basis of that book, in 1980 Dews drafted a sixty-page chapter on 'Structuralism and the French Epistemological Tradition', a little over half of which is published below. (Excisions, made at points where Dews embarks upon detailed discussion of Foucault, are signalled by ellipses.) Locating *For Marx* and *Reading Capital* in their national philosophical conjuncture, Dews investigates Althusser's attempt to resolve the controversy between Lévi-Strauss and Sartre over the status of historical knowledge, arguing that his Spinozist inflection of the Bachelardian tradition of French historical epistemology reproduces the very vices he reproves in Lévi-Straussian structuralism. Contrasting Althusser's subsequent development with that of his former pupil, Foucault, Dews indicates how the incoherence of Althusser's 'self-criticisms' helped to open the way for the relativist turn of the emergent post-Althusserianism.

1980 was the year in which Althusser's murder of his wife, Hélène, sealed more than one of his fates. In their various fashions, the remaining contributions to the Reader are retrospects, from the vantage-point (if such it be) of the 1990s, on the invariably dramatic, and occasionally anguished, history associated with the name of Louis Althusser.

In an essay written specially for this volume, David Macey, author of *Lacan in Contexts* (Verso, 1988) and an acclaimed recent biography of Foucault (*The Lives of Michel Foucault*, Hutchinson, 1993), casts a sceptical eye over the *de facto* 'Rejection Front' formed between Althusser and Lacan in opposition to Marxist and Freudian 'revisionism'. Macey acknowledges the part played by Althusser's essay of 1964, 'Freud and Lacan', in resuming the dialogue between historical materialism and psychoanalysis brutally interrupted in the PCF by the *Gleichschaltung* of the Cold War in theory. And yet he reckons both it, and subsequent Althusserian endeavours in this field, to have been based upon readings of Lacan that are arguably matched in their tendentiousness only by Lacan's interpretation of Freud. Conceptual loans have to be repaid – and sometimes at compound interest.

Like Macey an actor in the theoretical history he surveys, Francis Mulhern is more inclined to accentuate the positive dimensions of the Freudo-Marxist encounter staged by Althusser, at least as regards its salutary impact upon literary studies in an Anglo-Saxon culture largely innoculated by the experience of the 1930s against any 'materialist' tampering with things of the spirit. In a new overview of the English inductions of Gallic constructions, the author of a classic study of Leavism, *The Moment of 'Scrutiny'* (New Left Books, 1979), explores the diversity of Anglophone 'Althusserianism', isolates the aporias which smoothed the passage from euphoria to disenchantment, and concludes with a reassessment of Althusser's central theses that finds them fit neither for some arc de triomphe, nor the nearest oubliette. As messges in bottles go, Althusser's once fared well – possibly too well – but now deserve better.

My own piece – a considerably revised and expanded version of a review article[14] – is devoted to the 'return of the repressed', in the shape of *L'avenir dure longtemps*, in the spring of 1992. Responding to the patently malevolent or merely credulous readings to which the philosopher's 'wild analysis' of his own case history had been subjected, I took the opportunity of Althusser's own observations on his theoretical formation, as well as the invaluable detail supplied by Yann Moulier Boutang, to adumbrate themes – of Althusserian heterodoxy and non/contemporaneity – which I intend to develop at length in a forthcoming intellectual biography for Blackwell, provisionally entitled *Althusser's Solitude*.

Finally, at the publisher's suggestion, a bibliography of Althusser's published writings is, with due disclaimers, appended for the seriously curious.

In the conception and realization of this Reader, I have incurred various debts: to my editor, Simon Prosser, for his encouragement and patience; to David Macey and Francis Mulhern for once again gratuitously adding to their workloads; to Gordon Finlayson for undertaking the translation of the Honneth article; and to Michael Gane, who invited me to write on Althusser's 'traumabiography'. I am grateful to all of them.

NOTES

1 *Cool Memories*, Verso, London, 1990, pp. 223–24.
2 Introduction to Mulhern, ed., *Contemporary Marxist Literary Criticism*, Longman, London, 1992, p. 12.
3 'Adieu', in Balibar, *Ecrits pour Althusser*, La Découverte, Paris, 1991: here p. 122.

4 See Luc Ferry and Alain Renaut, *La Pensée 68*, Gallimard, Paris, 1985 and cf. Alex Callinicos, 'What is Living and What is Dead in the Philosophy of Althusser', in E. Ann Kaplan and Michael Sprinker, eds, *The Althusserian Legacy*, Verso, London, 1993.
5 See Ted Benton's excellent book of that title, Macmillan, London, 1984. Other full-length treatments in English are Miriam Glucksmann, *Structuralist Analysis in Contemporary Social Thought: A Comparison of the Theories of Claude Lévi-Strauss and Louis Althusser*, Routledge and Kegan Paul, London, 1974; Alex Callinicos, *Althusser's Marxism*, Pluto Press, London, 1976; E. P. Thompson, 'The Poverty of Theory', in his *The Poverty of Theory and Other Essays*, Merlin, London, 1978; Steven B. Smith, *Reading Althusser: An Essay on Structural Marxism*, Cornell University Press, Ithaca, 1984; Gregory Elliott, *Althusser: The Detour of Theory*, Verso, London, 1987; and Robert Paul Resch, *Althusser and the Renewal of Marxist Social Theory*, University of California Press, Berkeley and Los Angeles, 1992. To these should be added Perry Anderson's extended arbitration of Thompson's indictment in *Arguments within English Marxism*, Verso, London, 1980 and the conference papers collected in Kaplan and Sprinker, eds, *The Althusserian Legacy*.
6 This explains, for example, exclusion of Norman Geras, 'Althusser's Marxism: An Account and Assessment', *New Left Review* 71, January/February 1972 (reprinted in NLR, ed., *Western Marxism: A Critical Reader*, New Left Books, London, 1977 and in Geras, *Literature of Revolution*, Verso, London, 1986); of André Glucksmann, 'A Ventriloquist Structuralism' (1967), *New Left Review* 72, March/April 1972 (reprinted in *Western Marxism*); of Jacques Rancière, 'On the Theory of Ideology (The Politics of Althusser)' (1973), *Radical Philosophy* 7, Spring 1974 (reprinted in Roy Edgley and Richard Osborne, eds, *Radical Philosophy Reader*, Verso, London, 1985); of Paul Hirst, 'Althusser's Theory of Ideology', *Economy and Society*, vol. 5, no. 4, 1976 (reprinted in his *On Law and Ideology*, Macmillan, London, 1979); or of any extract from Thompson, 'The Poverty of Theory'.
7 As a result, two insightful early critiques – both from within the Althusserian milieu – remain unavailable in English: Nicos Poulantzas, 'Vers une théorie marxiste', *Les Temps Modernes* 240, 1966 and Alain Badiou, 'Le (re)commencement du matérialisme dialectique', *Critique* 240, 1967. Other candidates for translation from the French (to look no further) would have been Henri Lefebvre, 'Sur une interprétation du marxisme', *L'Homme et la Société* 4, 1967, or 'Les paradoxes d'Althusser', *L'Homme et la Société* 13, 1969 (both reprinted in his *Au-delà du structuralisme*, Editions Anthropos, Paris, 1971); Lucien Goldmann, 'L'Idéologie Allemande et les Thèses sur Feuerbach', *L'Homme et la Société* 7, 1968 (reprinted in his *Marxisme et sciences humaines*, Gallimard, Paris, 1970); and Jean Hyppolite, 'Le "scientifique" et l' "idéologique" dans une perspective marxiste', *Diogène* 64, 1968 (reprinted in his *Figures de la pensée philosophique*, Presses Universitaires de France, Paris, 1971).
8 To Michèle Barrett's overview of Marxist feminism, *Women's Oppression Today*, Verso, London, 1980 and to Benton, *The Rise and Fall of Structural Marxism*, pp. 134–40. For a judicious critique of Althusser by a feminist sympathetic to elements of humanist Marxism, see Kate Soper, *Humanism and*

Anti-Humanism, Hutchinson, London, 1986. The main protagonist in the feminist reception of Althusser in Britain was, of course, Juliet Mitchell: see especially 'Women: The Longest Revolution', *New Left Review* 40, November/Decmember 1966 (reprinted in her collection of that title, Virago, London, 1984), and *Woman's Estate*, Penguin, Harmondsworth, 1971. A representative text of feminist post-Althusserianism is Rosalind Coward's 'Rethinking Marxism', *m/f* 2, 1978.

9 In a letter of 28 March 1979 to the editor of *New Left Review*, declining the invitation to respond to Thompson in the pages of that journal. Less ruffled by Thompson than his correspondent had anticipated, Althusser stated that he had found *The Poverty of Theory* 'interesting'.

10 As Vilar underlined to an interviewer – the German historian, Peter Schöttler – in *Kommune*, vol. 5, no. 7, 1987, pp. 62ff., where he recalls that in the early 1970s 'the first thing I was asked, from Athens to Grenada, and from Lima to Berkeley, was to talk about Althusser.' For some fascinating observations on the issues raised by Vilar's counter-critique, see Schöttler's paper, 'Althusser and *Annales* Historiography – An Impossible Dialogue?', in Kaplan and Sprinker, eds, *The Althusserian Legacy*. That Vilar still regarded some of Althusser's questions as valid, even if he rejected his answers, is perhaps attested by the fact that the volume in which he reprinted his 1973 essay is entitled *Une histoire en construction: Approche marxiste et problématiques conjoncturelles*, Paris, 1982.

11 See, respectively, Althusser, 'Sur l'objectivité de l'histoire (Lettre à Paul Ricoeur)', *Revue de l'Enseignement Philosophique*, vol. 5, no. 4, 1955, and *Bulletin de la Société française de Philosophie* 4, October/December 1968, pp. 127–81.

12 'A Philosophico-Political Profile', in Peter Dews, ed., *Autonomy and Solidarity: Interviews with Jürgen Habermas*, revised edn, Verso, London 1992: here p. 149.

13 'Geschichte und Interaktionsverhältnisse. Zur strukturalistischen Deutung des Historischen Materialismus', in *Theorien des Historischen Materialismus*, Suhrkamp Verlag, Frankfurt/M., 1977. Honneth discusses the circumstances in which he composed his critique in a recent interview, 'Critical Theory in Germany Today', *Radical Philosophy* 65, Autumn 1993.

14 Published in *Economy and Society*, vol. 22, no. 1, February 1993.

ACKNOWLEDGEMENTS

For permission to publish texts contained in this Reader the Editor and publishers wish to thank the following copyright-holders:

E. J. Hobsbawm for 'The Stucture of *Capital*'.

New Left Review, London, for Pierre Vilar, 'Marxist History, a History in the Making: Towards a Dialogue with Althusser'.

Paul Ricoeur and Columbia University Press, New York, for extracts from Paul Ricoeur, *Lectures on Ideology and Utopia*.

Suhrkamp Verlag, Frankfurt/M., for Axel Honneth, 'History and Interaction: On the Structuralist Interpretation of Historical Materialism'.

Peter Dews for extracts from his 'Structuralism and the French Epistemological Tradition'.

1

THE STRUCTURE OF *CAPITAL*

E. J. Hobsbawm

A few years ago an able and acute observer of Marxism could suggest that the history of its evolution as a theory was virtually at an end; or at all events at a standstill. It is plainly not possible to take such a view today. The cracking of the apparently smooth and firmly frozen surface of Stalinism in the Soviet Union and of the unified and apparently integrated international Communist movement has not merely produced, or revealed, equivalent cracks in the systematic compendium of dogma elaborated in the 1930s, and brilliantly simplified for pedagogic purposes in the *Short History of the CPSU*. The thaw of the ice-cap also watered the numerous plants of heterodoxy, schism or mere unofficial growth which had survived on the margin of, or under, the giant glacier. The hundred flowers bloomed, the schools began once again to contend, in a manner unfamiliar to all except the elderly who could throw their minds back to the 1920s or the old who recalled the days before 1914. Marxism, which had apparently aspired to turn itself – and by *force majeure* had largely turned itself – into a closed system, communicating with the outside world chiefly by a series of operations designed to show that it had no need to do so, was opened up again.

If we leave aside, as lacking much theoretical interest, the attempts to retain something like the old orthodoxy unchanged (as in China or among some groups of sectarians in other countries), and the moves to accept useful theories and techniques from the 'bourgeois' world without integrating them into the nominally unmodified Marxist system (as happened to some extent in the Soviet Union), the Marxist re-thinking of the past ten years has, broadly speaking, followed four paths. First, it has attempted something like an archaeological operation, by identifying the strata of theoretical thinking which had gradually accumulated on top of Marx's original thought, and for that matter pursuing the evolution of the great man's ideas themselves through its various stages. Second, it has sought to identify and to pursue the various original theoretical developments made from time to time on the basis of Marxism, but for various reasons officially expelled from, or never absorbed into, the main corpus of its ideas. Third, it has attempted to come to terms, where this seemed apposite, with the various intellectual developments which had taken place outside Marxism, and once again were deliberately extruded from it in the Stalinist period. Last, it has tried to return to an analysis of the world (i.e., primarily of its social, economic and political developments) after a long period when the official interpretation had become increasingly remote from reality.

Among the pre-Stalinist currents of Marxism, one has long proved to be particularly fruitful and attractive to the re-thinkers, the 'central European' strain, to use George Lichtheim's convenient term. Most of the rare Communist writers who retained any reputation as independent minds in the 1940s and early 1950s belonged to this tradition, e.g., Georg Lukács, Henri Lefebvre or, nourished in the Italian rather than German version of Hegelianism, Gramsci. The central Europeans formed part of that passionate reaction against the evolutionist positivism and mechanical determinism to which the theoretical leaders of the Second International had tended to reduce Marxism, and which, in one form or another, provided the intellectual base for a return to revolutionary ideology in the year preceding and following the October Revolution. For a brief period after the collapse of syndicalism (which had absorbed part of this left-wing revulsion against the Kautskys of the pre-1914 era) virtually all the rebel currents flowed together into the single cataract of Bolshevism. After Lenin's death they began to diverge again, or rather the gradual and systematic construction of a single channel of official theory called 'Leninism' forced the rest out of the main stream. Yet though Lenin's own thought was one of the forms of this reassertion of revolutionary theory against 'revisionism' and 'reformism', and by far the most important in practice, it had been by no means the only one. Luxemburg and Mehring in Germany, the central-European Hegelians, and others, converged with Lenin in practice as revolutionaries, but were in no sense Leninist in origin or intellectual procedures.

Politically the central European strain was revolutionary, not to say ultra-left. Socially, it was not so much a collection of intellectuals – all ideological schools are that – as one of men and women whose taste ran to agitation, writing and discussion rather than organization and the (Bolshevik) executive life. In theory it was above all hostile to the Darwinian and positivist versions of Marxism *à la* Kautsky, and suspicious even of those aspects of the mature Marx and Engels which might have encouraged determinism rather than voluntarism. Even the young Gramsci in Turin reacted to the October Revolution by calling for a 'revolt against Marx's *Capital*'. Philosophically it tended to stress – against the more official theorists of social democracy and the revisionists – the Hegelian origins of Marx and such of his youthful writings as were then available. The publication of the *Fruehschriften* by Landshut and Mayer in 1932 was to provide the central Europeans with what has turned out to be their basic text, the 1844 Manuscripts, and their basic operational tool, 'alienation'. By this time, however, the political situation had changed. The central Europeans no longer stood on the extreme left of the movement, a place now occupied by the Trotskyists (though in the west most of these, as J. P. Nettl has pointed out, were in fact Luxemburgians). Their passionate voluntarism, their own contempt for bourgeois science and their idealization of proletarian consciousness had been selectively absorbed into, even exaggerated by, the official Soviet doctrine. The main advantage the central Europeans retained was the capacity to combine the passion for social revolution, even the readiness to accept the Jesuit discipline of the Communist parties, with the interests of mid-twentieth-century western intellectuals – such as *avant-garde* culture and psychoanalysis – and a version of Marxist theory which, against the apparent trend of events in the Soviet Union itself, reaffirmed the humanist Utopia of Marx. War and resistance brought them political reinforcements, especially in France, from revolutionary intellectuals to whom the discovery of German philosophy (in this instance not mediated by Marxism) gave a justification for the assertion of human liberty, the act of this assertion and struggle, and therefore the function of the 'engaged' intellectual. Via the phenomenologists Sartre moved into something like a position as honorary central European, and eventually into what he at any rate considered Marxism. The collapse of Stalinism relieved what had become an increasingly intolerable pressure on the central Europeans within the Communist movement – Stalinist theory had shown a diminishing toleration for the Hegelian or pre-1848 elements in Marx – and left them as the most obvious ideological nucleus for critical Communist thought. Paradoxically a strain of ideas which began on the ultra-left ended on the right wing of the revolutionary movement.

Sooner or later a reaction was to be expected. It has now emerged under the leadership of Louis Althusser, a philosopher who has left the shadows of the great École Normale Supérieure of the rue d'Ulm for the limelight of Parisian intellectual celebrity; or at any rate celebrity in the fifth and sixth *arrondissements*, which is even harder to achieve. His rise has been curiously sudden. Before 1965 he was virtually unknown even to the left-wing public, except as the author of an essay on *Montesquieu* and a selection from Feuerbach. In that year no fewer than three volumes came out as the first offerings of a series called *Théorie* under M. Althusser's direction: a collection of papers under the title *Pour Marx*[1] and two volumes essentially recording the papers presented at an intensive seminar by M. Althusser and his followers called *Lire le Capital*.[2] (The laconic titles are part of the Althusserian trademark.) Their success has been startling. It is no reflection on the very considerable gifts of the author – not least his

Gallic combination of evident intelligence, lucidity and style – to observe that he has been lucky in the moment of his emergence. The atmosphere of the Althusserian Quartier Latin is the one in which every self-respecting left-wing secondary schoolboy or student is a Maoist or at least a Castroite, in which Sartre and Henri Lefebvre are ancient monuments and the self-lacerations of the intellectual ex-Communists of 1956 as incomprehensible as the 'opportunism' of Waldeck-Rochet and Roger Garaudy. A new generation of rebels requires a new version of revolutionary ideology, and M. Althusser is essentially an ideological hard-liner, challenging the political and intellectual softening around him. It is typical that, though a member of the Communist Party, he should choose as his publisher François Maspero, the mouthpiece of the ultra-left.

This does not make him into a 'neo-Stalinist' as his detractors have suggested. The eloquent and rather moving pages of intellectual autobiography with which *Pour Marx* opens show no indulgence to Stalinism, but their target is not so much 'le contagieux et implacable système de gouvernement et de pensée [qui] provoquait ces délires' – the Althusserian prose is in the classic tradition – but the 'conditions of theoretical void' in which French Communism grew up and which Stalinism helped to conceal behind that 'primacy of politics' which was in any case congenial to the French. It led those philosophers who were not content to 'confine themselves to commentaries and meagre variations on the theme of Great Quotations' in sheer intellectual self-defence either to deny the possibility of any philosophy, or to maintain some sort of dialogue with their professional colleagues by 'disguising themselves – dressing up Marx as Husserl, as Hegel, as the humanist and ethical Young Marx – at the risk of sooner or later confusing the mask with the face'. The end of Stalinist dogmatism did not 'give us back Marxist philosophy in its integrity'. It merely revealed its absence. Yet – and here M. Althusser leaves a moderately well-beaten track and at the same time allows himself scope for a good deal of private innovation – its absence was not due merely to the defects of the French intellectual left. It was not there because Marxist philosophy, 'founded by Marx in the very act of founding his theory of history, has still largely to be constructed'; M. Althusser's ambitious purpose is to construct it.

In one sense this position has similarities with some tendencies of thought in the Stalin era, for one of the characteristics of that period was the systematic assertion of the absolute originality of Marx: the sharp cut which sundered him from Hegel and his own Hegelian youth, and from the utopian socialists (Roger Garaudy was obliged to revise his *Sources françaises du socialisme scientifique* on these grounds in the late 1940s). M. Althusser also talks of the *coupure* in Marx's evolution, and, while placing it, with most students, around 1845, seems reluctant to accept anything as fully 'Marxist' before the *Poverty of Philosophy* and the *Communist Manifesto*.[3] But of course the Stalinist theories had no doubt about what Marxist philosophy was. M. Althusser is just prepared to admit that certain thinkers in the past began to ask the crucial question how, e.g., the purpose of *Capital* differs from that of political economy – Lenin, Labriola, Plekhanov, Gramsci and various Italian scholars following the underestimated Galvano Della Volpe, the Austro-Marxists (who fell into neo-Kantianism), and some Soviet commentators (who were incompletely aware of the implications of their analyses). But he denies that there is as yet a satisfactory answer.

For there is none in Marx himself. Just as classical political economy did not quite see the point of what it observed, and what Marx formulated for it, so that Adam Smith gives, as it were, the right answer to questions he had not consciously asked, so Marx himself surpassed his own insight, leaving us to recognize where it was he was going:

> What political economy does not see is not something pre-existing which it might have seen but did not, but something it has itself produced in its operation of knowing [*connaissance*], and which did not exist before this operation. It is precisely the production [of knowledge] which is identical with that object. What political economy does not see is what it makes: its production of a new answer without question, and at the same time its production of a new latent question carried within that new answer (*Lire le Capital* I, pp. 25–26).

Marx himself suffers from the same weakness, which is the inevitable concomitant of the process of understanding. He was a far greater man than Adam Smith, because, while unable to emerge fully into his own novelty, he reaches out for 'his' question, formulating it somewhere or other, perhaps in a different context, searching for the answer 'by multiplying the images suitable for its presentation'. We, however, can know what he lacked: 'le concept de l'Éfficace d'une structure sur ses effets' pp. 33–34). In discovering this lack we can not only begin to grasp Marxist philosophy – the philosophy which Marx founded but did not construct – but also advance beyond it. For

> a science progresses, that is to say lives, only by paying extreme attention to its points of theoretical fragility. In this respect it holds its life less by what it knows than by what it does not know; on the absolute condition of circumscribing that non-known, and of formulating it rigorously as a problem.

It will be evident that the core of M. Althusser's analysis is epistemological. The nature of his exercise is the exploration of Marx's process of understanding and his main method an intensely detailed critical reading of the works, using all the resources of linguistic, literary and philosophical discipline. The first reaction of his own critical readers may well be that the methods and concepts he applies are not necessarily those emerging by his own favourite process of epistemological advance, from Marx himself. To say that 'along other roads contemporary theory in psychoanalysis, in linguistics, in other disciplines like biology and perhaps in physics has confronted the problem without realizing that Marx had "produced" it much earlier', may be true; but it is not impossible that the problem has been discovered in Marx because of the new and considerable vogue for linguistic 'structuralism' and Freud in France. (Indeed, while structural-functionalist elements are easily recognized in Marx, it is by no means so clear what Freud has to contribute to the understanding of *Capital*.) But if in fact these are to some extent insights from the outside ('nous devons ces connaissances bouleversantes . . . à quelques hommes: Marx, Nietzsche et Freud') it may be wondered whether the critical effort is merely confined to 'making manifest what is latent' in Marx.

A second reflection is that the Althusserian type of analysis finds it difficult, if not impossible, to get outside the formal structure of Marx's thought. M. Althusser is aware of this characteristic ('at no point do we set foot on the absolutely uncrossable frontier which separates the "development" of specification of the concept from the development and particularity of things') and appears to justify it by abstract argument ('we have demonstrated that the validation of a scientific proposition as knowledge in a given scientific practice was assured by the interplay of particular forms, which guarantee the presence of scientificity [*scientificité*] in the production of knowledge, in other words by specific forms which confer the character of – true – knowledge upon an act of knowledge'). Yet even if this is true and this method of validation can be applied as easily to *Capital* as to mathematical propositions (which is not obvious) all mathematicians know that a considerable gap still remains between their demonstrations and such real life phenomena – for instance, the evolution and operation of the capitalist system – as may be found to correspond to their discoveries. One can agree with M. Althusser's profound and persistent dislike of empiricism, and still feel uneasy about his apparent dismissal of any exterior criterion of practice such as actual historical development, past or future ('nous considérons le résultat sans son devenir'). For in fact Marx did get down to the difficult problem of the concrete. If he had not, he would not have written *Capital* but would have remained within the sphere of generality which dominates that marvellous and neglected *Introduction to the Critique of Political Economy*, which is in many respects the key work of the Althusserian Marx, as the 1844 Manuscripts are the key work of the Hegelian-humanist Marx whom he rejects.

And indeed, as soon as M. Althusser descends from the level where Marxism establishes what history or economics can or cannot do ('the mathematical formalization of econometrics must be subordinate to conceptual formalization') and turns to its actual subject matter, he says little that is new or interesting. He produces a brilliant critique of the vulgar-Marxist views on 'base' and 'superstructure' and a satisfying formulation of their interaction. But such practical applications of the general principle as are used to illustrate it are taken from Marxists who have used a more direct and less intellectually self-contained route.

While students like M. Godelier[4] face the concrete problems of historic periodization raised by Marx, and have, for instance, taken a leading part in the rediscovery and re-analysis of the 'Asiatic mode of production' which is one of the more interesting intellectual results of the revival of original thought among Communist intellectuals since Stalin, E. Balibar's long discussion of historical materialism (*Lire le Capital*, vol. 2) remains resolutely on the heights of what one might call meta-history.

Moreover, M. Althusser's type of approach, valuable though it is, simplifies away some of Marx's problems – for instance, that of historic change. It is right to show that the Marxian theory of historical development is not 'evolutionist' or 'historicist' in the nineteenth-century sense, but rests on a firm 'structuralist' foundation: development is the totality of all combinations, actual or possible, of the limited number of the different elements of 'production' which analysis defines; those actually realized in the past make up the succession of socio-economic formations. Yet one might object to this, as to the not dissimilar Lévi-Straussian view, that by itself it does not explain how and why one socio-economic formation changes into another but merely establishes the limits outside which it is senseless to speak of historic development. And also that Marx spent an extraordinary amount of his time and energy trying to answer these questions. M. Althusser's work demonstrates, if demonstration be still needed, the remarkable theoretical power of Marx as a thinker, his status and originality as a 'philosopher' in the technical sense of the word, and argues persuasively that he is far from a mere Hegel transposed from idealism to materialism. Yet even if his reading of Marx is correct, it is only a partial reading.

This does not diminish the force of his analysis as a tool of negative criticism. Whatever we may think of the polemical formulation of his contentions ('from the point of view of theory Marxism is no more an historicism than it is a humanism'), the strength of his objections to the Hegelian and 1844 Manuscripts interpretation of Marx is substantial, the acuteness of his analysis of certain weaknesses of the thought of Gramsci (and their reasons) or of Sartre is impressive, the critique of 'model-building' including that of Weberian ideal types, is to the point. This is due to some extent to the personal abilities of the man whom *Le Monde* (reporting the special session of the French Communist Party's Central Committee devoted to the discussion of his and M. Garaudy's views) calls a 'philosophe de grande qualité', a quality revealed among other things in the intellectual respect he thinks he owes to some of those he criticizes. Nevertheless, it is also due to the thinker and the cause who so evidently inspire his passionate study.

One reads him with attention, even with excitement. There is no mystery about his capacity to inspire the intelligent young, and though it may be feared that the Althusserian school whom he will certainly gather round him will be more scholastic than sparkling, the net effect of his irruption into Marxist theoretical debate may be positive. For his procedure is, almost by definition, that of asking rather than answering questions: of denying that the right answers have merely to be re-established even by the closest textual scrutiny of authority, because they have as yet to be worked out. For M. Althusser the relation between Marx and his readers is one of activity on both sides, a dialectical confrontation which, like reality, has no end. It is curious and characteristic that the philosopher (who has also, as in one essay of *Pour Marx*, doubled as a dramatic critic) chooses the metaphor of theatre – needless to say that of Brechtian theatre – to describe both Marx's process of exposing what lies beyond him (the *Darstellung* of 'ce mode de présence de la structure dans ses effets, donc la causalité structurale elle-même') and the readers' relation to him:

> C'est alors que nous pouvons nous souvenir de ce terme hautement symptomatique de la '*Darstellung*', le rapprocher de cette 'machinerie', et le prendre au mot, comme l'existence même de cette machinerie en ses effets: la mode d'existence de cette mise-en-scène, de ce théâtre qui est à la fois sa propre scène, son propre texte, ses propres acteurs, ce théâtre dont les spectateurs ne peuvent en être, d'occasion, spectateurs, que parce qu'ils en sont d'abord les acteurs forcés, pris dans les contraintes d'un texte et de rôles dont ils ne peuvent en être les auteurs, puisque c'est, par essence, un théâtre sans auteur (*Lire le Capital*, vol. 2, p. 177).

But the pleasure of reading an intelligent and original thinker ought not to blind us to his weaknesses. M. Althusser's approach to Marx is certainly not the most fruitful. As the above discussion has suggested tactfully, it may even be doubted whether it is very Marxist, since it plainly takes no interest in much that Marx regarded as fundamental, and – as his subsequent writings, few though they are, make increasingly clear – is at loggerheads with some of Marx's most cherished arguments. It demonstrates the new-found post-Stalinist freedom, even within Communist parties, to read and interpret Marx independently. But if this process is to be taken seriously, it requires genuine textual erudition such as M. Althusser does not appear to possess. He certainly seems unaware both in *Pour Marx* and *Lire le Capital* of the famous *Grundrisse*, though they have been available in an excellent German edition since 1953, and one may even suspect that his interpretation has preceded his reading of some of the texts with which he is acquainted. To this extent he still suffers from the after-effects of the Stalinist period, which created a gap between the older generation of enormously learned Marx-scholars and both the political activists and the younger neo-Marxists.

Moreover the revival of Marxism requires a genuine willingness to see what Marx was trying to do, though this does not imply agreement with all his propositions. Marxism, which is at once a method, a body of theoretical thinking, and collection of texts regarded by its followers as authoritative, has always suffered from the tendency of Marxists to begin by deciding what they think Marx ought to have said, and then to look for textual authority for their chosen views. Such eclecticism has normally been controlled by a serious study of the evolution of Marx's own thought. M. Althusser's discovery that the merit of Marx lies not so much in his own writings, but in allowing Althusser to say what he ought to have said, removes this control. It is to be feared that he will not be the only theorist to replace the real Marx by one of his own construction. Whether the Althusserian Marx or other analogous constructs will turn out to be as interesting as the original is, however, quite another question.

NOTES

1 Louis Althusser, *Pour Marx*, François Maspero, Paris, 1965.
2 Louis Althusser, Jacques Rancière and Pierre Macherey, *Lire le Capital I*, François Maspero, Paris, 1965; Louis Althusser, Etienne Balibar and Roger Establet, *Lire le Capital II*, François Maspero, Paris, 1965.
3 Althusser has since pushed the frontiers of the 'pre-Marxist' Marx steadily further forward, until little before 1875 is acceptable as properly non-Hegelian. Unfortunately, this eliminates the bulk of Marx's writings.
4 Maurice Godelier, *Rationality and Irrationality in Economics* (1966), New Left Books, London, 1972.

2

MARXIST HISTORY, A HISTORY IN THE MAKING: TOWARDS A DIALOGUE WITH ALTHUSSER

Pierre Vilar

[. . .] While stressing the purely philosophical (that is, *theoretical* character) of his work, Althusser himself believes it should interest historians and economists. Indeed, the very legitimacy of their disciplines is called in question when Marx is simultaneously exalted as the *first* discoverer of the *scientific foundations* of these subjects, and then respectfully but firmly convicted of not knowing that he was, and not saying so either. Here too the term 'new' is employed with particular insistence, as in '*new* quantitative history' or '*New* Economic History'. The reference back to over a hundred years ago in discussing Marx does not alter this, since (precisely) a century ago his novelty was so 'new' that even he could not understand it. The point is (I imagine) that it answered too far in advance certain criteria which recent 'histories of knowledge' have suggested to the philosopher.

Like Caesar's wife, scientific knowledge must be above all suspicion of (i) ideology, (ii) empiricism. Althusser shows easily enough (although by allusion rather than by example, unfortunately) how non-Marxist economists erect naïve anthropology into theory through their appeals to the concrete, the 'historical facts'. No less easily (though again allusively) he shows how historians, with their traditional care for 'exact' facts and their relish for proud resurrections from the dead, have never formulated the theoretical object of their science. *Time*, in particular, remains for them a simple linear 'datum'.

We shall examine below, at the appropriate moment, the constructive and useful elements in Althusser's powerful contribution to the building of Marxist science. More immediately, and no less usefully, let us try and establish the limitations of a project which liquidates somewhat too easily (in a way Marx was careful to avoid) the various 'habitable storeys' built at different phases of scientific advance, of which none deserves to be made an object of worship.

If one is a Marxist, or simply anxious to achieve coherence, then there is a preliminary question one must put to Althusser. Given that he accepts the basis of a critique of knowledge drawn from Marx, and suspects all ideas which depart from it as 'pre-critical', 'empirical', or 'ideological', given that in this way he claims the right to suspect Marx himself to the extent to which the latter's revolution remained unfinished – how then, can he fail to be equally suspicious vis-à-vis what he calls 'those studies in the history of knowledge now available to us' (he lets the reader guess what these are, but this is not hard)? Why is he not as vigilant towards that 'necessary philosophical formation' which is indispensable, so he claims, in order to read Marx profitably? I fear that one can detect here an attitude like that of Joan Robinson and similar economists, who certainly enjoy 'reading Marx' but do so in the light of a 'necessary formation in economics': their own, of course. Let it be clearly understood that I am not advocating *ignorance* of 'modern' economists or 'today's' epistemologists, in the name of Marxism. Only, it does not seem to me that it is fidelity to Marx to see *Capital* as an anticipation of Foucault or a forerunner of Keynes; it means rather subjecting Foucault and Keynes to the sort of systematic doubt Marx would have felt about them.

In the field of economics, Althusser knows this so well that he envelops both the greatest of old classics and the most learned young econometricians in the same utter disdain; somewhat hastily it must be said. Whereas on the other hand he is quite ready to borrow from 'histories of knowledge' the themes of a 'philosophy' whose mission, he says, is to 'watch over' (*veiller*) dialectical materialism as Lenin did from 1900 onwards, after the first theoretical crisis in physics. However, Lenin had nothing against physicists, he was attacking their interpreters. What would he have had to say – one can at least pose the question – of those trends in epistemology which for several decades now have so constantly opposed an anti-humanist neopositivism to Marx's systematic *prise de parti* and an anti-historicist and neo-idealist structuralism to what Althusser recognizes quite rightly as a 'theory of history'? Not to speak of a critique of empiricism and common sense executed in the name of the scientific spirit, which bases itself deliberately upon individual psychoanalysis and neglects the existence of classes, class struggles and class illusions?

A Marxist study of these intellectual trends must be tempting to both historians and philosophers. They bear witness to the (existential) ideological reaction of a threatened class. All spontaneous 'anti-historicism', every 'critique of historical reason' is a carefully cultivated antidote to Marx's true discovery, his *historical critique of reason*.

Nevertheless, the indubitable Marxist sincerity of Louis Althusser and his disciples forces us to classify them among the victims of this trap, rather than among those who set it – and so, to explore Marx side by side with them, although not in their fashion. On some points the historian can do for them what they have done for him – indicate certain possibilities and pitfalls. If they have quite properly pointed out to us that the concept of history has yet to be constructed, we should point out to them in return that it cannot be defined without historians, and above all without the prodigious historian that Marx could sometimes be, whether he was 'doing history' *implicitly* or in an explicit and traditional way.

I willingly grant that the object Marx is constructing in *Capital* is a 'theoretical' one; indeed, this seems more self-evident to me than it does to Althusser. I admit that one ought neither to mistake thought for reality nor reality for thought, and that thought bears to reality only a 'relationship of knowledge', for what else could it do? Also that the process of knowledge takes place entirely within thought (where else on earth could it take place?) and that there exists an order and hierarchy of 'generalities' about which Althusser has had really major things to say. But on the other hand I fail to see what 'astounding' mistake Engels was committing when he wrote (in a letter, incidentally, as a casual image) that conceptual thought progressed 'asymptotically' towards the real, while (according to Althusser) the law of value to which Engels' image referred is 'a concept perfectly adequate to its object since it is the concept of the limits of its variation and therefore the adequate concept of the field of its inadequacy'.[1]

Such subtlety suggests, I concede, the genuine difficulties we experience in the definition of our procedures and the practice of our research as historians, in which it is easy to 'fall into empiricism' by adhering too closely to the object described, to the 'example'. However, the abyss of empiricism is only separated by a hair's breadth from the abyss of idealism. Too great a revulsion from 'examples', too strong a wish to isolate the 'Holy of Holies of the Concept' (I came across this expression in a recent 'Althusserian' thesis on Marx's notion of economic laws) and one risks being 'precipitated' (or catapulted) into a world which is no longer that of Marxism. For, when reading the 1857 *Introduction*, if one should 'hear its silences', one should also take care not to silence its words: 'The totality as it appears in the head, as a totality of thoughts, is a product of a thinking head, which appropriates the world in the only way it can, a way different from the artistic, religious, practical and mental appropriation of this world. The real subject retains its autonomous existence outside the head just as before; namely as long as the head's conduct is merely speculative, merely theoretical. Hence, in the theoretical method too, the subject, society, must always be kept in mind as the presupposition'.[2] The whole of Marx is here. The world remains 'autonomous' only if the mind remains 'speculative'. *The subject is society*. The theorizer 'appropriates' it only if it remains always 'present' to him.

Althusser may tell us that in this *Introduction* (from which everyone takes what suits him, unfortunately), Marx failed to discern the hierarchy of abstractions. But Marx points out different ways of 'appropriating the world' in it: the empirical mode (the 'practical mind'), the religious mode (myths and cosmogonies), the artistic mode (of which Bachelard, Foucault and even Althusser make ample use). The scientific mode *proceeds out of* and *differs from* these. It proceeds out of them because it cannot do without the 'practical mind' (in its 'techniques') and it progressively 'rectifies' cosmogonies and traditions. But it *differs* from them, and this is why all serious epistemological studies are useful in indicating the 'thresholds' between the different types of knowledge. If by contrast one type of abstraction is labelled 'good' and another 'bad' (as Ricoeur has done with different 'subjectivities'),[3] then the very choice of vocabulary tends to lead to a slide towards philosophical dogmatism, and the slightest distraction results in ill-considered ideological condemnations.

Ultimately, this dispute between empirical observation and theoretical construction comes down to the same *Methodenstreit* between the 'historical school' and the mathematical economists, that was contemporary and akin to the controversy between Engels and Schmidt. Now if this dispute can be said to have been resolved and surpassed today, it is in the direction which Althusser describes as 'new' – that is, in terms of the now familiar imagery of theoretical objects, combinatory games and logical matrices. Hence if Marx's innovation (which, it is true, did herald *all that*) is taken as heralding *only* that, then it could well be argued that it has achieved its fulfilment in the recent development of economic science. After all the latter defends itself against well-worn objections about the gap between model and reality or the unfathomable 'richness' of the world, in the same way as Althusser legitimately defends Marx – by answering that the 'object' in question is not the same. To this sort of economics, the utility-scarcity game is a theoretical game quite adequate for its object. In addition, macro-economics has proceeded beyond such premises nowadays: is not its operational concept of 'capital formation' perhaps only another name for 'surplus value'? Some economists will not hesitate to admit therein a belated triumph of Marxian discoveries. But would it be 'Marxist' simply to join them in accepting this claim? No. Because the essence of Marx's discovery was not a matter of economics, of pure theory; it was *socio-historical* in nature. It consisted in the exposure of the *social contradiction* which the free spontaneous formation of surplus value (the 'accumulation of capital') generated within the coherent totality of the mode of production which sustains it, and which it conversely defines.

At this point we can rejoin Althusser. Marx's theoretical object, his central concept and coherent whole, is certainly the mode of production, seen as a structure both determinate and determinant. But its originality does not lie in its being a theoretical object. It lies rather in the fact that this was the first theoretical object which expressed a *social whole*, where earlier attempts at theory in the human sciences had been confined to the economy and had perceived social relations either as immutable (like the physiocrats' conception of landed property) or else as ideals to be attained (like the juridical liberty and equality of liberal thought). The second originality of the mode of production as a theoretical object is that it is a structure *of functioning development*, and as such is neither formal nor static. Its third originality is that such a structure itself implies the (economic) *principle* of the (social) *contradiction* which bears with it the necessity of its destruction as a structure, of its own *destructuration.*

Inversely, this acknowledgement does not allow one to liquidate all non-Marxist economic theory with contempt (which would be ridiculous). It enables one to see that the latter can perfectly well *exist as theory*, without thereby possessing the status of 'science' (except for its upholders, and Althusser), and at the same time *be an ideology*, not out of incoherence or empiricism but because it *claims universality* for laws *of only one level* (the economic) *within only one mode of production* (capitalism). Marx's critique of Ricardo, which Althusser considers insufficient, is in this sense exemplary. One can and one should acknowledge and make use of the genius of other minds and the logic of other systems, provided one sees clearly: (i) the logical field within which their hypotheses are valid; (ii) the barriers which no bourgeois theorist may cross without denying his own nature (Walrus, Keynes, Schumpeter were perfectly aware of them); (iii) the practical domains where the true limitations of the theory's area of judgement are revealed (not the distance between model and reality, which is a feature of all knowledge). Here the limitations are: modifications in the structure of capitalism, politico-social problems, the treatment of pre-capitalist societies, and the historical appearance of forms of socialism.

The analysis of these questions is a task for historians. In it lies the hope of a 'construction of the concept of history'. However, to work in Marx's way it is not sufficient to say, with Althusser, that 'classics' and 'moderns' have 'different problematics', that notions like the 'optimum' or 'full employment' are of the same kind as physiocratic harmonies or socialist utopias, or that the 'needs/scarcity' dualism is utilized as an 'empirical-ideological datum' when it is actually an archetypal 'theoretical' dualism or 'constructed' object. On the contrary, what we must strive to think out *historically* (if we want to 'understand the facts' as Marx likes to say) is how a *theory*, because it is *partial* (the theory of *one* level of *one* mode of production) *yet claims universality*, may serve simultaneously as a *practical* and as an *ideological* tool, *in the hands of one class*, and for *one period of time*. This time has to be 'constructed', it is true, since it consists of alternating defeats and successes, movements of pessimism and optimism, moments when even appearances (profits) have to be camouflaged, and moments when the reality itself (surplus value) can be exalted, if only when it is rediscovered during phases of expansion, as investment, as the basis of enlarged reproduction. But what matters most is the perception of what is *invariably* disguised, because it is given the status of an untouchable hypothesis – the equivalent of landed property for the physiocrats, which for the capitalist mode of production is: (i) *the private appropriation of the means of production*; (ii) *the determination of value by the market*.

Once these 'relations of production' are taken for granted, there is of course no reason why one may not theorize effectively on the economic level or elucidate the 'economic history' of the lands and epochs where such relations have prevailed. But this is just why the historian who wants to be a Marxist will refuse to confine himself within 'economic history' (except to study this or that case empirically). I have said on other occasions and I will maintain that so-called 'quantitative histories' are nothing but retrospective econometrics, and that the 'New Economic History' cannot measure the realm of Clio. As Colin Clark has stated, history stands 'higher up' in the hierarchy of the sciences than economics, *because it contains* the latter.[4] Fidelity to Marx demands that one add: and *because it cannot be divided*.

In my own case (this is why it is clear to me) this conviction arose from a convergence between the lessons of Lucien Febvre and the lessons of Marx. For Febvre, the chief vice in the historical practice of his own time, and the chief object of his fierce attacks, lay in its very academic respect for 'fixed boundaries': you take economics, you politics, and you, ideas. So I owe it to Louis Althusser to express my astonishment and disappointment at finding that his theses on the 'Marxist conception of the social totality' conclude by stating not only the 'possibility' but the 'necessity' of returning to a division of history into so many different 'histories'. If anything does have the odour of empiricism, it is precisely this plurality. In historical knowledge it sanctions all the old pretensions of the 'specialist'. In social practice – this is one of the dramas of socialist construction – it solicits the world of science, the world of economic technocracy, the world of politics, the world of ideas, and the world of the arts all to live according to their own 'levels' and specific 'tempos'. Meanwhile, beneath them, in spontaneous processes, a symphony is orchestrated underground.

I refuse to admit that one can affirm the 'specific dependence' of levels on each other and then proclaim the relative independence of their histories. 'Independence within interdependence' – is not the fate of verbal games of this kind well known, when the content of the two terms is not fixed ? Perhaps we should conclude that our task is to fix their definition. But the example given (for once) by Althusser scarcely reassures one as to what the distinction of 'histories' has in store for Marxism. It is that of the history of philosophy. According to chronology, we are told, philosophers succeed one another. This succession is not the history of philosophy. Who would disagree? What work, what manual, still confuses them? It might, perhaps, be as well if some of them did. A reference book is always useful. The same cannot be said of all constructions. But what are the distinguishing marks of 'history' here? Althusser demands that there be rigorous definitions of: (i) the philosophical (= the theoretical); (ii) its appropriate 'time'; (iii) its 'differential relations', its distinctive 'articulations' with the other levels.

Excellent proposals. But we have seen above how the isolation of the economic from the social led necessarily to an *ideological* definition of the former. How is this result to be avoided in defining the philosophical? Ideology is a superstructure. Science should not be. But where is the 'theoretical' to be situated? What is its degree of independence at each instant vis-à-vis the other 'levels'? To pass judgement on this would require, as well as the necessary *philosophical formation, a historical information* capable of 'mastering' the whole relevant material, of the sort Marx had acquired before he talked about economics.

Now Althusser's procedure is the inverse: he wants to derive from his particular 'relatively autonomous' history, a supposedly 'rigorous' definition of 'facts' or 'events'. A 'philosophical event' is that which 'effects a mutation of the existing theoretical problematic'. The 'historical fact' is whatever 'causes a mutation' in the existing structural relationships. He even speaks of 'philosophical events of historical scope',[5] thus testifying to the persistent weight of the dramatization of 'naïvely gathered' history upon the language of theory.

There is in fact no event which is not in one sense anecdotal. Except in idealist historiography, even the appearance of a Spinoza or a Marx has 'historical scope' only through and for the (more or less distant) time which will heed their thoughts. Otherwise, it may even be the *repression* of their thought which constitutes *history*. Furthermore, have 'structural relations' ever been modified by 'a fact'? The most conscious of revolutions have so far modified them only very imperfectly. Not to speak of techniques. Papin 'sees' the power of steam, and Watt tames it, but his 'innovation' must be 'implanted' in order to become a true 'force of production'. Amongst other factors, in one limited world. Where is the 'break'?

Professional sensationalists like to multiply 'events'. 'Historic facts' are all the rage on a day of lunar landings or barricades. It may be objected: exactly, the theorist has to choose. But choose what? The housewife who cannot or will not pay ten francs a kilo for beans, or the one who does buy, the conscript who joins his draft, or the one who refuses? They are all acting 'historically'. Conjunctures depend on them, they are reinforcing or undermining structures. However imperfect its interpretation may still be, it is the *objectification of the subjective through statistics* which alone makes materialist history possible – the history of *masses*, that is both of *massive, infrastructural facts*, and of those human 'masses' which theory has to 'penetrate' if it is to become an effective force.

One is led to wonder if the theorist of the concept of history has not spent so much energy attacking a type of history that is now outmoded, that he has unwittingly become its prisoner. Having allowed history to be divided up among 'specialists' he then sets out in search of 'historical facts' and 'events'. An event certainly has its importance, above all its place – fortuitous or integrable – within the series of which it forms a part. But although he will mistrust the excesses of the 'anti-eventful' historiography which has transformed historical practice in the last forty years, the Marxist historian remains loyal to its central principle, which was that of Marx. He can have nothing to do, even verbally, with the myth of 'the days which made France' or even with 'the days that shook the world'. Eisenstein's *October* ends with the declaration: 'The revolution is over.' We know very well that it was just beginning.

The difficulty cannot be evaded by extending the sense of the word 'event', after using the term 'mutation' to suggest the idea of a 'break'. Today science and theory are ill with words. They invent esoteric words for ideas which are not; and they give familiar names to esoteric contents. 'Event' and 'chronicle' pass into the language of mathematics, while they become suspect to historians. Genes start to 'take decisions' just as it is agreed that heads of state enjoy only the illusion of doing so. 'Overdetermination' and 'the effectivity of an absent cause' come to us from psychoanalysis, as 'mutation' comes from biology.

But will a term invented for one structure do for all others? Even Marx and Engels were not always fortunate in their use of this type of comparison. Schumpeter wrote of Marx that he effected a 'chemical' blend between economics and history, not a mechanical mixture.[6] For long I found the image a seductive one, since I had learned at school a very long time ago that in a mixture the elements remain separate while in a chemical compound a new entity is formed (in this case, the Marxist totality). But what is such a comparison worth for modern science? And what does it teach me in my trade? Balibar would very much like to replace 'combination' with the mathematical 'combinatory'. Yet he hesitates: 'pseudo-combinatory', 'almost a combinatory', a 'combinatory, though not in the strict sense . . .'[7]

Would it not be better, since Marx is still 'new', to decide to keep the words which he did invent, and invent new ones where these are needed, without borrowing from other sciences which cannot in any case speak for our own – if they could, why should we have to 'construct' the latter? In short, the theoretical commentary on *Capital* seems to me to have had the very great merit of showing how history had always been written without 'knowledge' of exactly what 'history' was (but the same could be said of so many things!). However, once again, while it was good of Althusser and Balibar to pose the question, they may have been imprudent to think they possessed the answer to it (this is not said with any intention of reviving the positivistic scepticism of old Seignobos).

It is not possible to answer the question 'what is history?' by theory any more than by practice alone. One can only try to answer, in Marx's fashion, by a passionate dual effort at making a complex subject-matter 'one's own', which always demands a minimum of theory, and to 'construct' the object of thought corresponding to that matter, which demands that the thinker both escapes from the latter yet holds it 'present' to his mind. No research without theory – and here the historian's complacency about theory often rightly irritates the philosopher. But also, no theory without research, or else the theorist will soon find himself accused (as the economist used to be) of merely juggling with 'empty boxes'.

Looked at more closely, the boxes may appear less empty than was thought, because historians are less empiricist than imagined. Instead of taking idle pleasure in negative pronouncements – which are part of an ideological trap – would it not be more reasonable to take note of some of the steps forward that historians have made? In the same way, it might be *more scientific* to attempt an *historical balance-sheet* of Marxism in the manner of *historians*, not 'judging' it according to our political or moral preferences, but 'thinking' it as a phenomenon to be re-situated in time.

Our philosophers are gladly anti-humanist in their theoretical requirements; yet they appear irked by the fact that – Lenin placed religiously apart – far too many Marxist thinkers and political leaders were ignorant enough of the great heritage to try and live it as an 'ideology' rather than as 'science', in a 'historicist' perspective rather than as an absolute. Above all, they feel that compared to the accelerating rhythm of the forces of production, the mutation of the world appears a slow process filled with errors and horrors; while on the other hand there exists a theory which would make history reasonable, if only it were better understood. Althusser writes: 'On the day that history exists as theory in the sense defined, its dual existence as theoretical science and empirical science will pose no more problems than does the dual existence of the Marxist theory of political economy as theoretical science and empirical science.'[8] 'No more'? Is that not enough? The victory of socialist economics lies in the fact that it exists – many believed it was impossible – not in its absence of problems. The same may be said of socialism *as a totality*, as a *nascent mode of production* – which incidentally perhaps invalidates the term 'totality' which means a global structure truly in place. Its constitution within a hostile world is certainly no less dramatic and imperfect – possibly more so – after a century of thought and fifty years of action, than was the installation of the capitalist world or of the feudal world. They took *centuries* to think out their meaning, centuries to be born. The logic of the Napoleonic wars must have seemed very tricky to contemporaries.

Impatience is not a virtue of theorists. Nicos Poulantzas is indignant at the successive and contradictory interpretations which the Third International gave of fascism. Well! Before interpreting one has to study, to see.

Struggles do not always leave time for this. The victories of 'science' are won in the long-run.

These considerations go somewhat beyond the aims of this study. But they are not unrelated to them. Economics, sociology and history (Marxist and non-Marxist alike) have always been subjected to the 'over-determining' pressures of the present. Today they are more so than ever. In the age of positivism they defended themselves against such pressures, angrily and naïvely. Nowadays, they have all become *applied* sciences, *practical* sciences, whether as politicology, empirical sociology, or various prospectuses, whether they accept the existence of the class struggle or believe in 'consensus'. History is following their example. It is as important to it to explain Fidel Castro as Hernan Cortés. Our journals show this well enough.

This presence of the present in the past and the past in the present is in no way contrary to the *spirit* of Marx. It is even one of the latter's main characteristics. But this is true only *under certain conditions*, which return us to our argument. Does our way of looking at the past accord with Marx's epistemological innovations, consciously or unconsciously? On several important points, and on one in particular – that of *historical time* – Louis Althusser's studies give us a clear consciousness of our various lacunae, our loyalties and our infidelities, but also of certain of our gains.

In his discourse on 'historical time', Althusser warns of two related abysses: the 'homogeneous and continuous' time of common sense and historical research; and the time of Hegel – 'essential sections', the 'historical present', the continuity of time and the unity of the moment.[9]

As for the second of these – what historian takes his business so unseriously as to accept these 'absolute horizons' the philosophers have brought to life again? As for the first, there are various sorts of continuity. The time of physicists is counted in millionths of a second; the time of sportsmen in tenths. Lived time has traditionally been that of day and night, winter and summer, sowing and harvest, the lean years and the fat ones, the intervals between births, the expectation of deaths. Historical demography is a great schoolteacher, as far as differential temporality is concerned. The time of men who have seventy years ahead of them is no longer that of men who had thirty. Any more than the time of the Carib Indian is that of the Eskimo.

If the mistake of mechanical periodization has been committed, it has been made by economists, who, in their anxiety to oppose an 'objective' time to that of historians, have cut their temporal series up into decades or half-centuries without realizing that they were destroying the meaning of the series, even from the point of view of simple mathematical probability.

Let me go even further. It was traditional history which 'constructed' time – even the old 'Annals', even the scholastic Chronicles. Events, reigns, eras: these were ideological constructions, but not homogeneous ones.

Thus, when chronological preoccupation became a *critical* one, how many myths it demolished, how many texts it desacralized! This too is part of the 'history of knowledge', of the 'production of knowledge'? On the other hand, when Michel Foucault loses his way in the economic domain, both in his own chronology and in chronology *tout court*, he ends up writing neither archaeology, nor history, nor science, nor epistemology, but literature.

To date for the sake of dating is only a (useful) scholarly technique. To 'date intelligently' remains a duty for historians. For the *consciousness of successions in time and of relative durations is anything but a naïvely given datum*. It does not arise out of nature and myths, but *against them*. Why is it that Althusser, who concludes that the concept of history is to be identified with that of a time, has not felt to the full the content of the term *chrono-logy*?

By contrast, having read Hegel, he overestimates the significance of the notion of *periodization:* 'On this level, then, the whole problem of the science of history would consist of the division of this continuum according to a *periodization* corresponding to the succession of one dialectical totality after another. The moments of the Idea exist in the number of historical *periods* into which the time continuum is to be accurately divided. In this, Hegel was merely thinking in his own theoretical problematic the number one problem of the historian's practice, the problem Voltaire, for example, expressed when he distinguished between the age of Louis XIV and the age of Louis XV; it is still the major problem of modern historiography.'[10] Let us say that after disengaging it from myths, history tends spontaneously to *systematize* chronology. It is curious that it should be reproached for so doing. From the Revolution onwards, French historiography tried to do this on the basis of the concept of *social classes*. Even our school-room periodization (Antiquity, Middle Ages, Modern Times, the Contemporary Period) translates the succession of the three main *modes of production*, 'modern' times corresponding to the preparation of the third mode through the triumph of the mercantile economy. This schema is Eurocentric, poorly conceptualized, and naïvely divided according to the 'mutation-events' of the sort dear to Althusser, like 1492 or 1789. However, it does reassure us to some degree about the convergence to be expected between 'practical' approaches and theoretical 'constructions'.

It is true that in *Capital* Marx gave us a 'construction of time' in the economic field, and that this is complex and not linear: a 'time of times' not measurable against everyday clock time, but adapted to each thoroughly conceptualized operation (labour, production, the rotation of different forms of capital). People have often affected not to notice this discovery. However, who has taken this temporal construction – the time of capitalism – to its logical conclusion, if not modern economists? Once again, if this was the essential Marxian innovation, it would have to be declared accepted, perfected, surpassed. But it was not. It was, rather, Marx's demonstration that 'rotations' and 'cycles' (and naturally 'revolutions' too, in spite of certain plays on the double meaning of the word) never lead back to their point of departure again, but *create new situations not only in the economy but in the social whole.* This is the difficulty, which the philosophers will seize upon. To speak of 'creative time' means nothing (I did it once myself, unwisely). Lévi-Strauss proposes 'cumulative history' and 'hot history' (to evade the problem). It is not easy to name what makes the new emerge out of the old.

To physicists this is unimportant, and biologists may be reduced to philosophizing about it: their subject-matters do not alter with the rhythm of human lives. But the historian's domain is that *of change itself, change at the level of structures as well as on the level of particular 'cases'.* To the historian, the temptation to search for stabilities is an *ideological* temptation, founded upon the anguish of change. There is no way out of it: save for a few fragments on the point of vanishing, men in society no longer live in *pre-history* – a term whose very invention shows that *the concept of history has itself a history*, one less simple than Althusser believes. Six thousand years at the most comprise 'historical times'. A few centuries form our familiar horizons, and two or three of them exhaust our economy and our science. The 'long duration' is not so very long. Between it and the 'event,' it is mean or usual time which is enigmatic.

Althusser agrees that 'historians are beginning to ask questions' about all this, and even doing so 'in a very remarkable way'. But (he goes on) they are content to *observe 'that there are'* long, medium and short times, and to note the interferences resulting from their interaction, rather than perceiving these as the product of one commanding totality: the mode of production. A ten-line critique and three names in parentheses (Febvre, Labrousse, Braudel)[11]: is this really enough to situate contemporary 'historical practice' in relation to (i) historical time, (ii) Marx? To tell the truth, one gets the impression that for Althusser, the evocation of these three names is a *mere scruple.* His criticisms are actually addressed to the *whole* of historiography from its beginnings, up to and including nearly all living historians. Not that this attitude is necessarily unjustified. It suggests a very important investigation: it would be most valuable to know the role of what Althusser splendidly describes as the 'elegant sequences of the official chronicle in which a discipline or a society merely reflects its good conscience, i.e., the mask of its bad conscience'[12] in class culture and popular culture, both academic history and television spectacles.

But this would mean a world-wide inquiry. And a second and more difficult one, into the eventual role and sites of growth of 'true history', *supposing one could define this, and find it being practiced.* On this point Louis Althusser's hopes for the *construction of historical time, a construction in Marx's sense*, differ from our own. We shall set out the latter by considering the three historians Althusser mentions and with some reference to our own personal experience. However, we are perfectly aware of the limitations of the arguments below in relation to the dimension of the two questions to be posed: (i) *what was, what is* the historical function of history *as ideology*? (ii) what is *now*, and what *could be*, the role of history *as science*?

The only historical practice which inspires an approving word from Althusser is that of Michel Foucault. The latter (he claims) is the discoverer of a 'real history' quite invisible within the ideological continuum of linear time – time which it is enough to simply divide up into parts. Foucault has discovered 'absolutely unexpected temporalities', 'new logics' in relation to which Hegelian schemas (here they are again!) possess only a 'highly approximate' value, 'on condition that they are used approximately in accordance with their approximate nature'[13] – in short, he has carried out a work not *of* abstraction but *within* abstraction, which has constructed an historical *object, by identifying it*, and hence also the concept of *its* history.

If, when he wrote these lines, Althusser had known only the Foucault of *L'Histoire de la folie* and *Naissance de la clinique* I might be induced to share his fervour. However, if each 'cultural formation' of this sort must have its 'own time', then what happens to the time of society at large? On reading the first of these two works I experienced an anxious sensation of 'enclosure', appropriate to the subject of course, but due also to the way in which the latter had been *cut off* on its own. I thought that this dissatisfaction was *Marxist*. Since then, Foucault has gone on to generalize his method, in large works which display its vices more prominently than its virtues. At the outset, a few authoritarian hypotheses. As soon as it is a question of demonstration – wherever some light on the topic already exists, one is confronted with jumbled dates, forced readings of texts, ignorance so gross that one must think it deliberate, and innumerable *historical absurdities* (a redoubtable category). Above all, Foucault is always ready to substitute without warning for the 'episteme' he discusses, not thought-out concepts (one would be grateful for that), but *his own private imagery*. Althusser talks of 'delirium' in connection with Michelet. Equal in this respect, Foucault's talent is no different. However, if he has to choose between two forms of delirium, the historian will prefer Michelet. Michel Foucault's modesty will surely forgive this comparison.

Lucien Febvre appears much less distant from Marx. Where does Althusser situate him, however? Among the assemblers of the 'linear time' so ill-adjusted to the historical totality? No description could be less appropriate to the man. Among the promoters of the elegant official sequences? Who has not been guilty of this to some degree? But who has demolished more of them than Lucien Febvre? All things considered, where can one find more 'unexpected temporalities', 'antipodes of empirical history' or 'identified historical objects' than in his work? Is not the unbeliever as good an historical object as the madman? Is Febvre's 'mental equipment' quite useless for the 'production of knowledge'? It is very much a trait of our times to refer to Lucien Febvre in brackets, between a condemnation of Michelet and an exaltation of Foucault, as somebody who 'began to ask the right questions'. That is, of times so concerned with communication that each understands only one language in them – that of his 'training'. It is not by chance that we have come to read so many self-contained 'cultures' into the past. It would be useful to discover which other epochs of crisis have shared this tendency to erect sealed partitions.

Febvre's sixteenth century is not closed: Luther, Lefevre, Marguerite, Rabelais, des Periers: all appear there within the exact limits which the cohesion of the 'over-determining' totality imposes on them. But the latter is *in movement*. 'One cannot judge a revolutionary epoch by the consciousness which it has of itself.' The historian had to demonstrate this *against* the ideology of his own time, of the rulers. If he could do it, it was because he had *first of all* made the sixteenth century 'his own', *at all its levels*, and held it 'present' through a process of research which was *concrete, but not empirical*. His research was systematized by his struggle to determine its problematic, against the historical positivism of the age, his struggle for the massive fact against the minute and precise fact, for true scrupulousness against false erudition. It is a struggle which often yields much the same sounds as Marx's bad-tempered scoldings.

'Real history' may spring in this way out of a *practice* and a *criticism*, not from an affected 'rigour' but from a *correctness* shown by the *absence of any absurdity*. Lucien Febvre never called himself a theorizer or a Marxist. But it would never have occurred to him to enclose Marx in the nineteenth century as in a prison (as Foucault calmly does in *The Order of Things*).[14]

Ernest Labrousse's more evident relationship to Marx does not incline Althusser to give him any special consideration. He apparently wishes to attack *all conjunctural history* as such, through Labrousse. But the latter is unjustly accused by Althusser's critique; especially when this critique neglects the whole immense tradition from Vico to Kondratieff, from Moore to Åkerman, from Levasseur to Hamilton (not forgetting Simiand, if one wants to remain gallocentric), a tradition that pretended to explain the relations between *cycles* and *development*, between *natural, economic* and *historical time* by the observation of statistical *indices*. Claimed, that is, to answer *the real question which has been posed*.

Was this question posed as a function of 'vulgar' time, or of the Marxist 'whole', the 'mode of production'? Here we face a genuine difficulty. Sometimes, in effect, conjunctural history tends – by its expository methods, by hasty commentary or schoolbook vulgarization – to make history seem a product of time (which is meaningless) rather than time (i.e., non-homogeneous, differentiated time) a product of history (i.e., of the moving play of social relationships within certain structures). A Marxist objection to this position has already been made by Boris Porshnev, who, at first glance, extended it (wrongly) to Labrousse's work. The relationship between conjunctural and Marxist treatments of history thus certainly needs to be clarified.

Marx himself can help us in this respect. Consider his characteristic way of treating the boom years of the 1850s ('this society appeared to enter upon a new phase of development after the discovery of the Californian gold mines . . .'), or the hopes he shared with Engels at each sign of capitalist crisis (the pardonable naïvety of a man of action), or his repeated references to the long period of economic expansion after the great Discoveries which served as the launching-pad of bourgeois society, or his interest in Tooke's *History of Prices* and his reproaches to Hume for having talked of the monetary systems of Antiquity without *statistical* evidence, or (lastly) his systematic analysis of the trade 'cycle' – a much more 'modern' analysis than is often thought. All this prevents one from counterposing Marx to conjunctural history or from seeing the latter as an innovation with respect to him. What ought to be contrasted with his work are rather the underlying *theoretical foundations* and the often intemperate *historical conclusions* of the various forms of conjuncturalism.

Observation of the *real rhythms* of economic activity should start from a *strict conceptualization* of what it is that is being observed. For far too long observers have simply registered nominal prices here, money prices there, volumes of production here and stock-exchange quotations elsewhere, long term curves here and short term curves there, and failed to ask themselves what was *index* and what was *object*, and what *theory* made this an index of that object. I criticized Hamilton a long time ago for his ultimate confusion of capital-formation with the distance between nominal prices and wage-aggregates – which does not mean that Marx was ignorant of the category of 'inflationary profits'! A concept or a standard are only valid for one time: in spite of Marczewski (or Fourastié) I continue to reject the belief that it is meaningful to search for the 1970 equivalent of a 1700 income. Finally, by eliminating one movement in order to isolate another, one can create a statistical mirage. There are pitfalls in 'construction' as well. This is why the most classical of conjunctural movements can be questioned, and it is enough to read Imbert in order to measure our theoretical destitution faced with the Kondratieff waves.[15] As the present international monetary crisis shows, while capitalism – since the failure of Harvard empiricism – has learned to tame the shorter-term (intra-decennial) cycle, it has yet to prove able to control middle-range time. Some are already inclined to dismiss the shorter cycle completely. But, as an *economic time* of a long phase in the mode of production, the latter is an integral part of the corresponding *historical* time. The historian cannot escape from the labyrinth of conjuncture.

Althusser does not always help us in our effort to take Marx as a guide. Without examples, it remains purely verbal to substitute 'variations' for 'varieties ', to replace 'interferences' with 'interlacings'; and if we can find only *economic* times in *Capital* where can we grasp the 'different temporalities' of the other 'levels'? He warns us that 'we must regard these differences in temporal structure as, *and only as*, so many objective indices of the mode of articulation of the different elements of structures in the general structure of the whole . . . It is only in the specific unity of the complex structure of the whole that we can think the concept of the so-called backwardnesses, forwardnesses, survivals and unevennesses of development which *co-exist* in the structure of the real historical present: the present of the *conjuncture*.'[16] Structure-conjuncture: in historians' practice has this not become a *typical grid* guaranteeing nothing in itself but distancing research equally from quantitative empiricism and the traditional 'elegant sequences'? We know the location of the 'break' between the conjunctural economism of Simiand and a structural conjuncturalism closer to Marx: it lies in the work of Ernest Labrousse. What has this to tell us about 'temporalities'?

If one interprets Labrousse as saying: the French Revolution was born of a 'fusion' between a *long time* – the economic expansion of the eighteenth century – *a medium time* – the intercycle of depression, 1774–88 – and a *short time* – the price crisis of 1789 which culminated (almost too perfectly) in the *seasonal* paroxysm of July 1789, then it looks as if the demonstration is a mechanistic explanation of the revolution which shuffles together linear times as if they amounted to a causal concatenation. But is this what he says?

In fact, the statistically observable *short cycle* which pulsates in the economic *and social* reality of the French eighteenth century is *the original cycle of the feudal mode of production*, in which: (i) the basis of production remains agricultural; (ii) the basic productive techniques do not yet dominate the stochastic cycle of production; (iii) the dues levied on the producers *should* vary according to the amount produced; (iv) charity and taxation *should* cushion the worst forms of misery, in a bad year. *However*, this pre-capitalist tempo already *co-exists* along with others in the eighteenth century, which though not yet typical of the future mode of production (like the 'industrial cycle', for instance) pave the way for it and are part of it: (i) a *long period* of preparatory accumulation of money-capital, directly or indirectly *colonial* in origin, which creates a moneyed bourgeoisie and 'bourgeoisifies' part of the nobility; (ii) the *medium-term* possibility of *commercial depressions* (market crises, price depressions) affecting and upsetting growing numbers of farmers, proprietors and entrepreneurs whose products have entered the commercial circuit and become 'commodities' – so many social strata interested in legal equality, free markets, and the end of feudal structures; (iii) lastly, the aggravation of 'old-style crises' *in the short run*, since though they are less lethal than in the days of famines, the new speculation on shortages which they provoke is less restrained by administrative taxes and ecclesiastical redistributions, and they therefore pauperize and proletarianize the masses more than ever and turn the poorer peasants against both feudal or royal levies and market freedom.

What better example than this could one find of an 'interlacing of times' as the 'process of development of a mode of production' or even as a transition from one mode to another – this convergence of 'specific temporalities' which in July/August 1789 resulted in the famous 'event' that overthrew the whole juridical and political structure of society?

Althusser is, I know, professionally interested in the times of science and philosophy; while legitimate anxiety about contemporary history makes him even more interested in words like 'backward', 'advanced', 'survivals' and 'under-development'. In his definition of 'conjuncture' he precedes such terms with an ironical 'so-called', hoping in this way to draw attention to the absurdity (and the ideological dangers) of a terminology that takes models and goals for granted, and ends up by reading like a railway timetable. And certainly, many of the graphs dear to statistical annuals justify his irony, with their picture of a dollars-per-capita or rate-of-investment or quantum-of-scientific-journals line where some countries seem to be on the 'Mistral' express and others on a slow-stopping train. However, this necessary criticism of the verbal vainglory of ruling classes and their economies, and of the distorting mirror of certain quantitative criteria, ought not to make us forget essential Marxist principles: (i) the *primacy* of the economic-technical as synthesized in the productivity of labour; (ii) the need to escape from vague descriptions by *quantification*; (iii) the *major reality* constituted by the *inequalities of material development*. Marx always kept 'present' England's advance and the potential of the United States, as did Lenin his concept of 'uneven development'. One must know how to go beyond linear time. But it is not sufficient to condemn it.

Suppose there is a disjuncture between an institutional form, a mode of thought, an economic attitude or a social ethic and the *mode of production which we assume to be operative* (these are all *theoretical* hypotheses). Must we then say that these 'morals', 'attitudes', 'thoughts', etc. are 'advanced' or 'backward', are 'survivals', have an 'autonomous rhythm' and so on? Would it not be better to say: to what extent is this mode of production, taken to be in place, functioning, according to its own model? In what areas does it do so? Over what 'durational scale'? In which sectors is it an effective totality (*already*, if it is developing, and *still*, if it has begun to become destructured)?

It is in this way that the full meaning of 'conjuncture' must be understood (not in Simiand's 'meteorological' sense). Several different 'specific times' enter into it. In my own work on Spain, I have always deciphered *structural contrasts* from the *specificity* of *economic rhythms*. In Catalonia, a small zone, I distinguished up to three different rhythms in the process of modification of the mode of production.[17] During the subsistence crisis of 1766 the rebels, priests and agitators levied popular taxes (*taxations sauvages*) in the name of conceptions of justice, morality and property belonging to the twelth century, while at the same time almost any small shopkeeper's correspondence on free enterprise and true prices is already couched in the language of Samuelson. Here the specificity of time is also a specificity *of class*. Study of the 'industrial cycle' is no less instructive. It is disappearing from the socialist economies, while the slowness of their transformation of agricultural techniques maintains the older 'cycle' still in being in the countryside. But any attempt to restore the market as a 'regulator' soon causes the 'industrial cycle' to reappear, with inflation as its sign. Alternatively, when the same cycle is attenuated under capitalism, the latter is departing from its own model. The *sectoral* location of transformations, the *class* location of superstructures, and the *spatial* location of 'totalities' are all disclosed by so many 'objective indices'.

This kind of analysis allows us to go from the theory to the 'cases'. It may help to build up the theory – above all with regard to processes of transition. It cannot be reproached with conceptualizing time without regard to the concept of the mode of production: it refers constantly to the latter. If, by contrast, one looks for a 'specific time' to attach to each different 'level' then this reference is very likely to be abandoned.

The name of the third historian cited by Althusser was an inevitable one. Because of a rightly famous article.[18] But an article which was doubtless the source of Althusser's misconception. When after thirty years of practice Fernand Braudel takes it into his head to theorize, the philosopher cries out: look, he's *beginning* to ask himself questions! Not at all! In 1958 Braudel *ended* by asking questions *of other people*, provoked and even irritated by their indifference to historians' discoveries: 'The other social sciences know little of the crisis that our historical discipline has undergone during the last twenty or thirty years; they tend to misunderstand our *works*, and in so doing also misunderstand an aspect of social reality of which history is a good *servant* but not always a good *sales-girl* – that is, social duration, or those multiple and contradictory forms of time in the life of man . . . yet another cogent argument for the importance and use of history or rather of the dialectic of duration exhibited in the *profession* and *sustained observation* of historians.'[19]

Profession, observation, works, servant, sales-girl . . . These words must have displeased our theorist. I note also the words which must have persuaded him to range Braudel among the unemancipated slaves of linear time: the addition of days, his *recitatif* of conjunctures, the rotation of the earth, time as a measure, time identical with itself and, in the plural, times which lock into one another without difficulty and are measured by the same standard. All this is quite opposed to Bachelard's sociological time. Yet is it so difficult to perceive the beginnings of a critique, the gleams of irony behind Braudel's insistence? Althusser has not 'situated' the essay. For him, the knowledge of history is no more historical than the knowledge of sugar is sweet. Nonsense! The knowledge of this knowledge is always itself *historically* constituted, whether in Braudel, in Althusser, or in Marx (who knew this well).

In 1958 Braudel wonders about the destiny of his personal contribution to such knowledge: the 'long tempo', 'geo-history' conceived as something imposed by space upon time. This is a weighty question, to which he turns twelve years after writing his *Méditerranée*, in response to *other orientations*, some a matter of 'historical practice', others not. Implicitly ironizing at the expense of the 'récitatif' of conjunctures, Braudel expresses the fear that the latter may lead to a kind of return to 'events'. Labrousse had passed from his own 'long eighteenth century' of 1933 to a subsequent emphasis in 1943 on a pre-revolutionary 'intercycle' of less than fifteen years, and then – in 1948 – to a brilliant summary of revolutions taken in the short term: 1789, 1830 and 1848.[20] This earns him some friendly teasing on the 'tricks of the trade' or the historian as 'film director'. For Braudel the historian should take up a stance *above* the level of 'dramatic news'. If it is objected that the trade of the historian consists, precisely, in situating events within the dynamic of structures, then (he insinuates) by trying to do this the historian will always end by sacrificing structure to events.

When he wrote his essay, he could afford to be less anxious in the other sense, concerning the 'long term'. But here he has since been outflanked. Today, there is an 'anthropology' which seeks its permanent factors in the logical structure of sociological 'atoms', and an economics which has discovered virtues in the qualitative mathematics of 'communication'. Always responsive to the 'latest thing', Braudel is much drawn by such seductions. These novelties go broadly in his direction – that of resistance to changes. Yet he loves his own trade. The historian welcomes 'long tempos'. But if time disappears altogether, then so must he. He therefore proposes the term structure for 'an assemblage, doubtless an architecture, but more importantly for a reality which time wears away only with difficulty, and carries forward only very slowly'. The theorist may still look down his nose at this. 'Doubtless', 'more important', that is not very 'rigorous'. And whatever the reality may be, it is not 'time' which erodes it, but 'something' which wears it away unevenly according to the realities in question. It is this 'something' which is the problem.

If one reality lasts longer than another, however, it will envelop the latter, and it is this term 'envelop' which Braudel selects, stressing its mathematical meaning. For him it designates the geographical and biological constraints, the technical impotences out of which he built up his 'long tempos', and which include (anticipating Foucault) the 'persistent prisons' of 'intellectual constraints' or 'mental frameworks'. Can one fail to situate these statements in relation to Marx, when Braudel refers to him explicitly as the first creator of 'historical models' and indicates in which sectors he has tried to follow his example, if not his method? If the reference is not too persuasive, however, I think this may be because Marx never thought with *partial* models: thus the concept of 'model' as applied to monetary circulation is not Marxist, while concepts such as 'crisis' or 'mental equipment' are much more so, even if they do not claim to be 'models'.

But this does not mean that Marxist theory will be able to ignore the problems posed by Fernand Braudel both in this essay and in his work as a whole. Nature, geographical space, resistant structures, a-historical structures (if there are any such): what will the historian make of these?

(i) First *nature*. In the only text of his which can be considered as the sketch of a possible historical treatise, Marx recalls finally that 'the point of departure' is 'obviously the natural characteristics, subjectively and objectively';[21] his fundamental definition of productivity also mentions 'natural conditions' at the end. Last but not least. For a dialectic between man and nature can scarcely underestimate the importance of 'natural conditions'. Only, one must set over against these conditions *techniques* (and then science). Between any two victories of the latter the mode of production is framed within the *limits* thus marked out. The fifth of the 'points not to be forgotten' in the 1857 *Introduction* – 'dialectic of the concepts productive force (means of production) and relation of production, a dialectic whose boundaries are to be determined, and which does not suspend the real difference'[22] – shows, for example, how one should treat the persistence of 'crises of the old sort' in several modes of production in twentieth-century Europe.

To think history geographically is not therefore contrary to Marxism. It would, however, be more Marxist to think geography historically. Among the 'permanences' how may we distinguish the poles where man's grip is most effective? The Mediterranean is full of them. But they are 'enveloped' by deserts and mountains. This is surely a fine object to be 'identified' and 'constructed' by a (dialectical) history; but Althusser is not sufficiently aware of this even to discuss it.

(ii) Then, *space*. This is equally an *object to be constructed*. Theories of it have been suggested, and then worked out, but while Braudel has paid attention to them, Althusser has not. They refine (and occasionally caricature) the old temptations of geographers, economists and logicians in this respect. Men, villages, towns, fields, factories, were not implanted 'any old how', and we ought to be able to discover a logic to their location. This can give rise to many exercises in mathematics, graphics and cartography, none of which should be disdained. But if the historian can take some lessons from them, he also has his own to give. The organization of space in the service of man, a 'geography of the will', is quite thinkable; this is one of the tasks of the day after tomorrow. One can also imagine a new capitalism upon a new space, installing itself with no overall plan, according to its own internal logic. The United States was almost like this (as Marx often indicated). The impetus of development in this case was very powerful. It is now coming to be perceived as monstrous, so that the mystique of 'ecology' has arisen around it.

In old countries, however, the problem is more complex than this. There history is not only an interlacing of times but of spaces as well. The logic of a Breton village is not that of Nuremberg, which in turn is not that of Manhattan. The nineteenth century eviscerated medieval Paris and ruined the Marais. The twentieth century is saving the Marais, and demolishing Les Halles in Paris. Barcelona took five centuries to move outside its walls, invented the Cerda Plan, then disfigured it almost at once. The Latin American city bears with it the cancer of the *favelas* and the *barriadas*. The periphery of the Mediterranean has become a play-ground, torn between the skyscraper and the tent. The current Vedel Plan offers the vocation of pleasure-park to two-thirds of arable France. In this world there is no more 'long duration'.

But historians of rural landscape or urbanization usually lose their way in prehistory or in collective psychology. While space itself, if it escapes the speculator, falls into the clutches of the empirical sociologist or the technocrat. If divorced from the concept of time, the concept of space is ill-suited to old countries in which every stage of production, every social system, has had its towns and fields, its palaces and cottages, each historical totality nesting down as best it can in the heritage of another. A 'real history' would draw up balance-sheets and display mechanisms and thus help to *construct* – this time in a concrete sense – a properly thought-out combination of past and future. Socialism can count some successes in this domain. It would be interesting to know what (if anything) they owe to the Marxist conception of this combination.

(iii) *Historical times and struggles between groups* are combined in still another fashion. With their terse assimilation of history to class struggle, Marx and Engels gave rise to a long equivocation over their thought. It came to be believed that they despised the ethnic bases of political groupings. And at first this equivocation was a useful weapon in the fight against a conception of history founded ideologically upon the might of monarchs and national wars. But in their correspondence and their journalistic articles Marx and Engels employ the terms German, French, English, Turk and Russian as often as they do 'proletarian' and 'bourgeois'. Class contradictions are the *motor* of history, as technique and economy are *the origin* of these contradictions. However, this 'last instance' exerts its power through many other realities. Again, among the 'points not to be forgotten' of the

1857 *Introduction*, the very *first* place goes to *war*, and the last to *peoples, races*, etc.[23] We are certainly compelled to remember them. Nationalities and supranationalities, fascist nationalisms and revolutionary nationalisms, centralized states against ethnic minorities, the resistance of monetary autonomies to multinational economic bonds – all go to show a second half of the twentieth century at least as sensitive as the first (and possibly more so) to the *existence* or the *demands* of political formations expressing the consciousness of groups. Here too Marxism has a *theory* to propose, decisively formulated by Stalin in 1913, and based upon 'differential tempos' explained in terms of the central concept of *mode of production* (let me add: also of the concept of *class*).

The political type-formation corresponding to competitive capitalism is the *Nation-State-Market* with a bourgeois ruling class, which either develops out of an over-narrow feudal framework (Germany, Italy) or else at the expense of vast and heterogeneous empires (Austria, Russia, Turkey). But the condition of such formations is the pre-existence of 'stable communities', not eternal in character but *historically constituted* by a number of very different factors over *very long periods of time*. In no sense does Marxism accept these communities as absolute ends-in-themselves, or determining factors. They are the *pre-posed framework*, the instruments offered to *one* class with which to forge *its* state. In its own fashion the feudal world had already given examples of this. The mercantilist phase of the bourgeoisie directly prepared the national state in France and England.

Now this projection backward suggests another one forward in time. Other classes can in their turn take such 'stable communities' as the basis for their action. Their success depends upon their ability to create a new mode of production. On the other hand, the role of capitalism as a national instrument has meanwhile been eroded. Rosa Luxemburg unduly anticipated the *long-term* tendency of capital to weave multinational ties and forge super-states (as Lenin's critique of her pointed out). But today this tendency is manifestly asserting itself, and the national bourgeoisies are only feebly resisting it. It is peoples which resist, to the degree to which the class struggle has created revolutionary situations amongst them. Socialism, finally, faces the task of *constructing* the past-future combination in the organization of multinational spaces, as in the organization of economic spaces (*scientifically* if possible and – of course – on the basis of a concept of history). Everything here depends upon its *analytical fidelity to theory*.

This three-fold dialectic between (a) 'long times' and specific times of the mode of production, (b) the small spaces of ethnic groups and the large zones demanded by modern activity, and (c) between class struggles and the consciousness of groups, has served my own historical researches very well and thrown much light on the present for me. Hence I can only regret that it was invoked neither by Fernand Braudel in relation to his 'long tempos' nor by Louis Althusser with regard to his 'interlacing' of specific tempos. Doubtless Marxist theory becomes more opaque, as it penetrates deeper into a history still under construction.

(iv) Some words on *a-historical structures*. The historian (the Marxist historian above all) will distrust this concept. For him, *everything changes*. And nothing is totally independent of a global structure itself in course of modification. Yet if he admits the notions of 'long times' and 'stable communities', why should the resistant networks of the most ancient structures – like the family, or myth – not be integrated in the same categories? Naturally the historian must be grateful to the ethnologist who has reconstructed the logic of these structures when they have observed them in near to their pure state. But what will be of more concern to him are the gradations, modes and functions of such resistant networks inside societies under transformation. Again, the 'interlacing of tempos'.

Two other claims of structuralism (or structuralisms), perhaps inevitable at an early stage and now anyway moderated, demand a different sort of discussion:

Firstly, the autonomy of fields of research. Anxious above all for a self-sufficient explanation in terms of its own internal structures, each field proclaimed any attempt at historical integration of its case-studies to be useless, even scandalous. Quite possibly this impulse represented – in literature, for example – a healthy reaction against *superficial* historical treatment of examples; yet to carry it too far means leaving any concrete case incompletely understood. I have tried to show this myself in the case of Cervantes,[24] but I believe that essays of this kind should ideally come as the *conclusion* of global historical research in depth, rather than as objects studied in their own right and vaguely related to an approximate history. Structuralo-Marxist essays generally suffer from lack of sufficient historical information; and Althusser has given us few particulars concerning his combination of autonomous-dependent 'levels'.

Secondly, there is another and global 'structuralist' pretension: all the human sciences (history and the quantitative 'social sciences' excluded) must be seen as constituting an 'anthropology' based upon their formalizable structures, and in particular upon those of communication, such structures being taken as the revelation of underlying psychological and intellectual mechanisms. Curiously, this 'anthropology' with man as its 'object' declares itself also anti-, or at least a-humanist. Yet to the extent to which it wants to be, or thinks it is, an *exact science*, it would surely be very odd if it did not rapidly become an *applied science* and – consequently – tied to the interests of human beings and their social classes. The project itself rejoins the old metaphysics of 'human nature' and is *ideological* in character: it sets out to study societies on the basis of their 'atoms', before observing them on the macro-economic and macro-social levels.

The assimilation of social relationships to a 'language', and of economics to a 'communication of goods' (neglecting production, and the relationship with nature) refurbishes the 'naïve anthropology' of exchange equilibrium. A theory of games in which all the players take rational decisions always makes it difficult to explain the existence of losers. All this arises from a generalized confusion with the science of linguistics, as renovated by structuralist discoveries after a long period of false historicization. But it is already becoming clear that the autonomy of linguistics is not integral. Above all, while the historian (as in the analogous cases of literature and art) must assimilate enough of the structuralist lesson to avoid conferring a historical meaning on what may only be a common inheritance, he knows that *differentiations* are still his domain. If historical semantics remains an unploughed field, it is because changes in signs, *words*, here represent changes in *things*; if 'stable communities' are separated by linguistic barriers, why do some resist the passage of time and events so much better than others? The questions which interest the historian are *those to which structuralism has no answer*.

It is curious that Marx thought an analogy with language useful, in his discussion of production: 'however, even though the most developed languages have laws and characteristics in common with the least developed, nevertheless just those things which determine their development, i.e., the elements which are not general and common, must be separated out from the determinations valid for production as such, so that in their unity – which arises already from the identity of the subject, humanity, and of the object, nature – their essential difference is not forgotten.'[25] Balibar is quite right to point out that this text does not seek to distinguish between the generality of concepts and the particularity of the real, but rather between two sorts of abstraction, two sorts of liaison between concepts in the theory of history, neither of which is privileged when it comes to constituting the theory of knowledge. This remark is crucial for the debate between history and structuralism. It should be added, though, that Marx warns the reader against any appeal to 'generalities' about man or nature in economics, which rely upon 'commonplaces gone mad'. The commonplace and the tautology are often rediscovered (not always uselessly) in an examination of the logic of things. One must merely make sure that, beneath scholarly guise or vulgar mask, the commonplace is not delirious.

I have deliberately chosen to be optimistic in a time of gloom. I have tried to show that history is better equipped than is imagined by many theoretical Marxists in pursuit of the (quite un-Marxist) goal of absolute knowledge. I have attempted to indicate the possible utilization by Marxist historians of everything in contemporary historical research which seeks for a global view of society, and which has turned away from the piecemeal treatment of fragments of reality – but without falsely attributing to Marx such advances as have been made without major reference to his theories. Finally, I have endeavoured – without taking too seriously that itch for novelty which troubles the epidermis of the younger human sciences – to neglect nothing in them which may serve science in the Marxist sense of the term, like their inter-disciplinary approach to society. Like empiricism, structuralism is only *ideological* to the extent to which it aspires either to an immobile universalism, or to an atomistic solitude.

It remains to try and point out some considerable and persistent difficulties in the way of scientific historical practice; and also some of the many and varied ways forward.

I do not think the problems lie in the direction of that 'theory of transition' for which Althusser yearns, and claims not to find in Marx. Because he is a philosopher, Althusser has remained more of a Hegelian than he would like to be; so he has crystallized and enclosed his concept of the mode of production to such an extent that it becomes an anxious problem for him how one can either get in or out of it. He is right only if it is necessary to erect 'transition' *as such* into a new object of thought. But Marx not only proposed a viable theory of the capitalist mode of production, after regarding and scrutinizing its operation from every possible point of view (a theory which includes a prevision of the system's destruction). He also regarded and scrutinized from every angle the preceding transition from feudalism to capitalism, starting from those days in 1842 when the debates in the Rhineland Diet revealed to him the profound conflict between two different laws, two different conceptions of ethics and the world, even over such an apparently trivial episode as the gathering of dead wood. This is, incidentally, a characteristic starting-point, regularly omitted from its proper place at the head of Marx's *Works* because editors are not sure whether it should be classified as 'economic', 'political' or 'philosophical' (of course its whole interest arises from this unclassifiability).

Given the richness of the suggestions in Marx's own work, and in that of Lenin; given the previous (but by no means outdated) debates among Marxist historians like Dobb, Sweezy and Takahashi; given the advanced state of work on 'modern times' as distinct from the Middle Ages and the contemporary period, I think we may confidently state that we are progressing in the 'real history' of the transition from feudalism to capitalism and that this will in turn help us to theorize other historical transitions. I leave out of account here my own experience of research in this field which, while it is not for me to assess its worth, has at least enabled me to see and assess the work of others.

One regret: at the 1970 International Conference of Economic Historians in Leningrad the vague title of 'modernization' was chosen for what in good Marxist terms ought to have been called the transition from pre-capitalist modes of production (feudal or even earlier), either to some form of capitalism or to the socialist mode of production (even assuming that the latter exists *in the full sense*). On this occasion, which called for the widest-ranging reflection on the countries of Africa, Asia and America, the 'western' historians simply retired into the traditional themes of their assorted 'specialities' ('the eighteenth century', the 'priority of agriculture', 'English leadership' . . . etc.), while the Soviet historians offered an impressive set of *results*, in the shape of collective syntheses on the different areas of their country, but next to nothing on the *processes* involved, and even less on their *theory*. It ill becomes me to condemn this debate, or rather lack of debate, since I presided over it. However, my disappointment makes me less restive in the face of Althusser's demands and rigours. It is thus that the *theoretical abdication of Marxism* takes the form of a *renunciation of the concept of history*.

So it is good that men like Boris Porshnev or Witold Kula have undertaken to construct a 'theory of the political economy of feudalism', in the same way as Marx attempted to build a theory of the determinant economic nexus of capitalism.[26] One can understand, too, the often passionate interest some young historians show for the 'Asiatic Mode of Production', which Marx only referred to in passing, but whose importance and historical originality are beyond doubt. The title is an unfortunate one, however, and does not acquire higher theoretical value by being knowingly shortened to 'AMP'. Occasions like this show one how difficult it is to theorize validly on the basis of too partial an experience, or too limited a knowledge (here the historian has the advantage over Althusser). It will take many years, even decades of research to arrive at any global theory of the very varied forms of the 'AMP'. But in this field there is no hurry.

What is more urgent is the elaboration of methods of passing from theory to the analysis *of cases* (or *frameworks for action*), whose reality generally consists neither in one single mode of production, nor in a 'transition' towards one of them, but in complex and often very stable combinations, not merely of *two*, but of *several* different modes of production. The distinction between the real 'socio-economic formation' and the theoretical object 'mode of production' should be generally familiar by now, although often the vocabulary of Marxist studies remains indecisive in this respect. But what we need to know (it is something I have often asked myself) is whether a complex structure, a 'structure of structures', bears within itself a certain power of determination, an 'efficacity' (as a mode of production does).

In the case of Latin America – where the exception all but makes the rule – Celso Furtado has employed multiple-parameter economic models to build up an interaction of sectors with differentiated 'fundamental laws.'[27] But he confines himself to the economy, and one may wonder if the notion of 'maximization of profit' has any meaning outside the capitalist mode of production. Take another example, nineteenth-century Spain, which I know a little better: it would be absurd to describe it as either 'capitalist' or 'feudal'; 'semi-feudal' is a poor compromise term, and 'bisectoral' evokes the idea of simple juxtaposition. Now even if one does more or less perceive two dominant forms juxtaposed in the same space, one must then ask – are not the solidarities between them sufficient to constitute an original *body*, one characterized by this very juxtaposition, with its contradictions and conflicts, and the consciousness of these conflicts? Should one therefore, for each such 'formation', construct a corresponding theoretical object? This is the normal procedure in chemistry.

The main problem remains *causality*, and it is not resolved by the use of a term like 'effectivity'. I share Althusser's distrust of the facile Marxism which declares that 'necessity is asserting itself' wherever it is short of an argument which will relate its theory to reality. For Althusser, the mistake lies in confronting theory and reality in this fashion. They are different objects. However, if the historian refuses to rally to the throng who declare that 'this is how things happened' (implying that history is not theoretically thinkable), then he will quickly find himself forced in practice to *choose*, or to combine various sorts of causal relationships: linear, alternative, statistical or probabilist. But he should not conclude this suffices to make him a theorist. He remains within empiricism. Often enough within the difficult empiricism of sociologists, as when they try very cautiously to establish correlations among series of different kinds, between quantifiable economic relations, rather less quantifiable social relations and a mental realm which *may* one day be quantifiable . . . Althusser wishes, very understandably, to get away from terrain like this. But through new and tentative methodologies which have carried them far away from their old traditions, today's historians have begun to be conscious of the unity and complexity of their subject-matter; they are aware of its originality, and of the need to seek a *new type of rationality* for it, whose mathematical forms will come much later on.

Althusser proposes a solution: a 'structural causality' internal to the mode of production, founded on the key concept of *Darstellung* (representation) in Marx, designating *the presence of the structure in its effects*. Or (better still) it is *in the effects that the whole existence of the structure consists*. This is a seductive notion, and reinforces my conviction (already stated above) that no global structure can exist unless all its effects are present. Yet I do not like Althusser's arguments. They are too close to images. The image of the *Darstellung* is that of a theatrical representation. It was first proposed by Marx and while I appreciate its suggestive force, I can also see its vagueness and incoherence. Elsewhere Marx compares a mode of production to 'a general illumination which bathes all other colours and modifies their particularity' and then to 'a particular ether which determines the specific gravity of every being which has materialized within it'.[28]

No, this is not the best of Marx, at least on the level of expression (for the idea is a powerful one). Neither are the other Marxian metaphors in which Althusser sees 'almost perfect concepts', in spite of their incompatibility with those just quoted: i.e., mechanism, machinery, machine, montage (what would the reaction be if one were to exploit these terms against Marx!). Marx also employs the word 'metabolism'. While it is above all to psychoanalysis that Althusser himself refers. How unconvincing these comparisons are, I repeat, when after all there is no good reason to expect the social totality to behave like either a physiological or a psychological whole. In fact, Marx like everybody else happened occasionally to choose a word or metaphor for the sake of effect, and to make a more or less happy choice. This is why I prefer to try and grasp his thought *in the whole of his work*, in his *typical forms of analysis*, and in their 'illustrations'.

In their *applications* also. A psychoanalyst is a *practitioner*. If he talks of 'the efficacy of an absent cause', this concept evokes a certain number of *cases* for him. If a creative Marxist (whatever his theoretical contribution may be – Lenin, Stalin, Mao, Ho-Chi-Minh, Fidel Castro) tests the efficacy of the mode of production he wishes to create upon a society long conditioned by some other (or several other) structures, it is then that he tests the validity of its concept. The historian sees similar tests, less conscious but by no means blind, in the England of 1640 or the France of 1789. Here history bears evidence. IMPORTANT

A last difficulty: sometimes Althusser is led by other influences to define structural causality as a simple logic of positions. The 'relations of production' would then flow only from the *place* of men in the system – the latter become the *supports* rather than the *subjects* of these relations. It is true that for Marx social relationships are not *exclusively* inter-subjective, as they are in vulgar economics. First of all because they comprise certain relations *with things* (this is the primacy of *production*). Then too because he was never concerned to denounce *individual* exploiters, but to discern the nature of a *social* exploitation. Marxism can thus never be reduced to a theory of 'human relations' (if so, why not 'public relations'!). However, to try and express all this by declaring such reductionism 'an insult to Marx's thought' is to give way to an *anti-humanism* which risks an insult to his person. To the author of the *Manifesto*, history is no chess-board, and the class struggle is no game. It is not even a 'strategy'. It is a battle.

The difficulties discussed above prove that the field remains quite open to whoever wants to solve them by research. But for a Marxist historian two avenues seem to me excluded: (i) the repetition of theoretical principles combined with criticism of whoever does not know of them, all in the service of skeletal and weightless constructions; (ii) a historical practice, which, however far removed from traditional canons, confines itself to specialist areas, partial problems, and tentative technical innovations, and thereby remains loyal in fact to the least creative kind of empiricism.

'Real' Marxist history, by contrast, must be ambitious in order to advance. It must – and no science can do otherwise – move ceaselessly from patient and ample research to a theory capable of the utmost rigour, but also *from theory to 'cases'*, in order to avoid the risk of remaining useless knowledge.

From research to theory: we have noticed far too many ill-solved theoretical problems not to stress this first way forward for the historian – *comparative history in the service of theoretical problematics.*

If we ask – what is a structure? What is a structure of structures? An interlacing of differential tempos? An articulation of the social with the economic, or of the mental with the social? A class struggle? An ideology in the class struggle? The relationship between an agent's place in production and the human relationships presupposed by that place? The combination between class struggles, and conflicts between ethnic or political groups? Such problems, which are both historical and theoretical, impose one fundamental duty upon us: *research*. They demand we take critical account (as Marx did) of all the economic, political, and social investigations of our own times, but without taking for granted the historical specificity of the last twenty years. One does this by *going back in history*. By thinking about *all countries*. The theoretical validity of any subsequent analysis will depend upon the depth, the precision, and the range of such investigations (whether or not one decides to recount one's inquiry as part of the result). The only danger of this procedure is its slowness. Engels knew that Marx never began to write (still less to publish) anything on a particular subject without having read everything on it. This is one of the reasons why, as Althusser reminds us, *Capital* ends with – 'Social classes. Forty lines, then silence'.[29] *It is this silence which we should strive to break*, rather than the hypothetical 'silences between words'.

Theory will not suffer from research. Here it is worth recalling [. . .] Marx's chapter on money. Only the vast historical information displayed in the diversity of the facts, times, places and thoughts considered there allowed him to attain the *theoretical originality* of the text. Of a text, that is, which, alone among the almost inexhaustible literature on the topic, succeeded in demystifying the false problem of the quantitative theory of money. In two pages it says everything there is to say about what was later to be known as 'Fisher's equation', with the difference that it leaves no doubt in the reader's mind about the reversibility of the relationships involved. All possible hypotheses are mentioned, with the relevant historical examples in the background, so that no room is left for the confusions which mathematical formulations have inspired in later more naïve (or hurried) historians.

It may be objected: but this is economics, not 'history'. Firstly, this is inexact – there is no such thing as 'pure' economics, and monetary questions are ceaselessly intertwined with other sorts of history (political, psychological). Secondly, why not apply the same method to other concepts which are neither more nor less theoretical and neither more nor less historical, than that of money? *Class, nation, war, and state* for example, around all of which there has accumulated such a mountain of ideological fabulation, and so many 'commonplaces gone mad' in the guise of theory.

Yet Althusser, who affirms at one and the same time that there is no 'general history' and that it is necessary to 'construct the concept of history', says nothing at all about these *intermediate concepts* that are so constantly manipulated and so rarely examined. A constructive critique ought surely to have borne upon this point, for which Marxism should assume responsibility (as sometimes it does).

From theory to 'cases': here is the second, no less difficult, obligation. It is a *necessary duty*, for what would a 'theory' be if it did not help the historian to understand *this* country, *this* time, or *this* conflict better – if after, as before, they appeared as mere chaos to him? If it did not help the man of action (any man of action, since all are concerned) to understand *his* country, *his* time, or *his* conflicts better? But it is a *difficult obligation* too, unfortunately. Alongside some massive successes which must indicate some degree of theoretical adaptation to 'cases' – Lenin in revolution, Stalin in construction and war, Mao in the overthrow of a traditional world – it is only too well known how Marxism has tended to alternate between an abstract schematism whose validity depended on its simplicity, much too 'all-purpose' to allow proper application, and (on the other hand) 'revisions' in the name of real complexity that risk falling back into merely empirical treatment of each 'case' – or else, into pure speculation which merely leaves reality 'autonomous'.

But what is the 'treatment' of a historical 'case'? (i) There are certain kinds of 'theoretical cases', which present themselves in a number of different exemplifications at one moment of history and demand a common interpretation. Fascism, for example, or enlightened despotism: forms of authority which, by installing a certain type of state, endeavour to save a mode of production drawing towards its end, while adopting (or pretending to adopt) part of the new mode of production whose advent appears imminent. A theory of modes of production, a theory of transition, a theory of the state are therefore all involved in the analysis of such real cases; but their combination may in turn suggest a theory of the phenomenon itself. (ii) Distinct from these easily grasped cases which seem to invite theory, there are the multiple, dispersed, incoherent 'episodes' of more 'historical' history – the rise and fall of men and governments, parliamentary debates, coups d'états, diplomacy, and (finally and above all else) wars. We know that each such 'event' should become a 'case', whose particularities would appear only as expressions of a wider *ensemble* or historical moment, if not of a model, but we are very far from this goal. It must be admitted that we have no theory of the articulation between the global functioning of societies and the incubation of 'events'.

'Politicology', 'polemology': such terms testify to the *need* for science in this domain, but also to the trend towards fragmentation of what is really unitary. Is a 'political theory' of fascism possible without a theory of war? But can one call a caricatural strategic schema, a 'delirious commonplace' which mixes up Salamis and Hiroshima, a 'theory of war'? A 'polemology' ought to relate together modes of production, types of state, types of army, types of tension, and types of class struggle, so that each conflict (past, present, or possible) will appear within a global framework without the effacement of its particular nature. Lenin was a master of this. (iii) Finally, *the* 'case' *par excellence:* that of *the socio-economic formation within one historically stable framework*, the 'nation' or 'state' (one of the problems being the coincidence or non-coincidence of these two categories). How can the Marxist historian pass from a general sociological *theory* to an *analysis* of a juridically and politically delimited 'body' of this kind, which also depends upon (and is occasionally disrupted by) solidarities of a different type – an analysis which will be explicative of its past and effective in its present?

The nineteenth century gave to written and taught history an ideological role in this regard. Hence the Marxist tradition has for long sought to break with its national, nationalist and nationalitarian (*nationalitaires*) perspectives, and every 'new' history has striven to find other ones. However, this old historiography bears witness to a whole age. It is itself part of its own history. To expose its ideological character is certainly a step forward in the direction of science. But it is impossible to renounce examination of the overall transformations of the world through the prism of national 'cases'. All we can do is think them in a new way, by situating the latter in relation to the former.

One must also keep in mind the *totalizing effects* of each 'case'. We have already observed briefly that, while the global social structure is determinant, the 'regional' structure of a society – as a complex combination, a structure of structures – must equally be recognized through its effects. Here we touch upon the notion of 'total history' which I have often defended, and which arouses some sarcasm. As if one could say *everything* about *everything*! But of course it is a question only of saying *what the whole depends upon*, and *what depends upon the whole*. This is a great deal. But it is less than the useless accumulations formerly made by traditional histories, or by the juxtaposed specialist chapters in today's compendia, which precisely claim to treat *everything*.

Whether in any human group or in a 'nation', the problem is, as usual, to distinguish *appearance* from *reality*. The appearance (which gives rise to ideological history) is that there are 'national characters' and 'power interests', which are *given* factors, and *create* history. The reality is that 'interests' and 'powers' are made and unmade on the basis of successive impulses from the forces and modes of production; and that 'national characters' and 'national cultures' are modelled, over long durations, upon the frame which these successive impulses either create or maintain. The appearance (temperaments, languages, cultures) is, naturally, registered by common sense. During the Middle Ages, the university 'nations' already lampooned each other constantly, and the modern 'nations' have continued to do the same in new circumstances, sometimes good-naturedly, sometimes violently. This is a dimension of the question one must study carefully, since everyone needs to be wary of its influence. The problem remains: why groups? How must one conceive nations?

The answer can only be, once more: by 'penetrating' the subject-matter, by making it 'one's own'. In 1854 Marx received from the *New York Tribune* a request for some articles on a recent Spanish *pronunciamiento* – the very archetype of a banal 'event'. What did he do? *He learned Spanish*, by reading translations of Chateaubriand and Bernardin de St Pierre (which apparently amused him greatly). Soon he was reading Lope and Calderón and at last he could write to Engels – 'Now I'm in the middle of Don Quixote!' The great and good Spanish anarchist militant Anselmo Lorenzo was astonished by Marx's Hispanic culture when he met him in 1871; admiring, if somewhat outclassed, he described it as 'bourgeois'. Nevertheless, in his series of articles of 1854–56, Marx had given an historical vision of Spain of which only the twentieth century has been able to appreciate the full lessons – one which encompassed all the major features of Spanish history, without a single absurdity, and which in certain judgements on the War of Independance has yet to be improved upon.[30] There was a genius at work here, admittedly. But also his method. We asked above if Marx had ever meant to 'write a history'. Here is the answer. In order to write one article about one military escapade he did not write a 'history of Spain'; but he thought it necessary *to think Spain historically*.

To think everything historically, that is Marxism. In relation to this, the problem of whether there is or is not a 'historicism' is (as in the case of 'humanism') a verbal side-issue. I distrust over-passionate denials. It is important to know (we are told) that the object of *Capital* is not England. Of course not: it is capital. But the pre-history of capital is called Portugal, Spain and Holland. History must be thought in terms of spaces, as well as of times: 'World history has not always existed', wrote Marx. 'History as world history is a result.'[31]

Here is another crucial phrase. Born out of colonization and the 'world market', capitalism has *universalized* history. It has not *unified* it, certainly – this will be the task of another mode of production. It is in this perspective that the historian's ultimate ambition must lie. 'Universal history' belongs to yesterday. Its time is not yet over. There is something laughable about these remarks one now hears so frequently: 'We know too much', 'There are too many specialists', the world is 'too big' for any one man, one book, or one teaching-method to tackle 'universal history'. This implicit encyclopaedism is the polar opposite of the notion of 'reasoned history', 'total history' or – simply – the 'concept of history'.

It is possible to dream of three kinds of enterprise: (i) 'treatises of history', an aim no more absurd than 'treatises of psychology' or of 'sociology'; (ii) national histories clearly periodized in relation to the chronology of productive forces, social relationships, differential tempos, and combinations of regional structures; (iii) universal histories sufficiently well informed to omit nothing essential from the fundamental traits of the modern world, yet sufficiently schematic to let the explanatory mechanisms be seen. The latter are bound to provoke cries of dogmatism and ideology. Perhaps one should recall at this point the *Manual of Political Economy of the Academy of Sciences of the USSR*, and the discredit into which it has fallen. Yet what has it been replaced by, except denials of the unity of the social whole, and the historical whole? On every level, Marxist history remains to be made, as does history *tout court*. In this sense, all 'real history' must be 'new history'. And all 'new' history without totalizing ambition will be a history old before its time.

NOTES

1 Louis Althusser and Etienne Balibar, *Reading Capital*, New Left Books, London, 1970, p. 82.
2 *Grundrisse*, Penguin/*New Left Review* edition, London, 1973, pp. 101–02.
3 See Paul Ricoeur, *Histoire et vérité*, Paris, 1955, p. 26.
4 Colin Clark, *The Conditions of Economic Progress*, London, 1957, p. 2.
5 *Reading Capital*, p. 102.
6 *Capitalism, Socialism and Democracy*, London, 1961, p. 44.
7 *Reading Capital*, pp. 216, 226, 241.
8 Ibid., p. 110.
9 Ibid., pp. 94–95.
10 Ibid., p. 94.
11 Ibid., p. 96.
12 Ibid., p. 103.
13 Ibid.
14 Cf. Michel Foucault, *The Order of Things*, Tavistock, London, 1970, pp. 261–62.
15 See Gaston Imbert, *Des mouvements de longue durée Kondratieff*, Aix-en-Provence, 1959.
16 *Reading Capital*, p. 106.
17 See Pierre Vilar, *La Catalogne dans L'Espagne moderne: Recherches sur les fondements économiques des structures nationales*, Paris, 1962, vol. II, pp. 391–400.
18 'La Longue durée', *Annales*, October/December 1958; translated as 'History and the Social Sciences' in Peter Burke, ed., *Economy and Society in Early Modern Europe: Essays from Annales*, London, 1972.

19 *Economy and Society in Early Modern Europe*, pp. 12–13 (translation modified).
20 Respectively, *Esquisse des mouvements des prix et des revenus en France au XVIIIe siècle*, Paris, 1933; *La Crise de l'économie française à la fin de l'ancien régime et au début de la révolution*, Paris, 1944; 'Comment naissent les révolutions', in *Actes du congrès historique du centenaire de la révolution de 1848*, Paris, 1948 (translated as '1848–1830–1789: How Revolutions are Born', in F. Crouzet, W. Challoner and W. Stern, eds, *Essays in European Economic History 1789–1914*, London, 1969).
21 *Grundrisse*, p. 109.
22 Ibid.
23 Ibid., pp. 109–10.
24 Pierre Vilar, 'The Age of Dox Quixote', *New Left Review* 68, July/August 1971.
25 *Grundrisse*, p. 85.
26 Boris Porshnev, *Ocherk Politicheskoi Ekonomii Feodalizma*, Moscow, 1956; Witold Kula, *An Economic Theory of the Feudal System* (1962), New Left Books, London, 1976.
27 Celso Furtado, *Economic Development of Latin America*, Cambridge, 1970.
28 *Grundrisse*, p. 107.
29 *Reading Capital*, p. 193.
30 Marx's writings on Spain are collected in Marx and Engels, *Revolution in Spain*, London, 1936.
31 *Grundrisse*, p. 109.

3

ALTHUSSER'S THEORY OF IDEOLOGY

Paul Ricoeur

In the previous lecture on Althusser, I discussed his concept of the ideological break and its epistemological implications. [. . .] In the present lecture, I shall discuss Althusser's concept of ideology itself. This discussion will proceed in three steps: first, how is the problem of ideology placed in the superstructure-infrastructure framework; second, what can be said about particular ideologies, such as religion or humanism; and third, what is the nature of ideology in general.

As to the first topic, one of Althusser's most important contributions is his attempt to refine and improve the model of infrastructure and superstructure borrowed from Engels. As we recall, the model is summarized both by the efficiency in the last instance of the economic base – this base is the final cause, the prime mover – and by the relative autonomy of the superstructure, a model of the reciprocal action (*Wechselwirkung*) between base and superstructure. For Althusser, the first point we must understand is that whatever the value of Engels' model, it is, contrary to Engels' own beliefs, as far from Hegel's dialectic as possible. [. . .] In *For Marx* Althusser introduces the discussion by quoting the statement in Marx, appearing as late as *Capital*, on which Engels relies: ' "With [Hegel, the dialectic] is standing on its head. It must be turned right side up again, if you would discover the rational kernel within the mystical shell" '.[1] Althusser maintains that this declaration is not as easily interpreted as first appears. Engels falsely believes that there is a common element between Hegel and Marxism, the 'rational kernel', and that there is need to drop only the 'mystical shell'. This argument appeared frequently among Marxists, the thought being that it was possible to keep Hegel's dialectics and apply it no longer to the Hegelian Spirit but to new objects: to society, classes, and so on. The common use of dialectical argument would imply, so the argument goes, at least a formal continuity between Hegel and Marx.

For Althusser, however, this is still to grant too much, and with good reason. We cannot treat the Hegelian dialectic as an empty or formal procedure since Hegel keeps repeating that the dialectic is the movement of the things themselves. Hegel is against any kind of formalism that would allow us first to establish a method of thinking and then to go on to solve the problem of metaphysics. This is what he discards in Kant. The entire preface of the *Phenomenology of Spirit* is written exactly against the claim that we must first have a method and then do philosophy. For Hegel, philosophy is the method, it is the *Selbstdarstellung*, the self-presentation of its own content. It is not possible to separate method from content in order to retain the method and apply it to new content. Therefore, even the structure of the dialectic in Hegel (negation, negation of negation) must be considered as heterogeneous to the structure of the dialectic in Marx. If it is true that we cannot separate method from content, and I am sure that it is, then we must define the Marxist dialectic in terms that leave only the word 'dialectic' in common with Hegel. The question then is: why the same word? In fact we should drop the word or say either that there is no dialectic in Hegel or no dialectic in Marx; but this is another problem.

In place of the Hegelian dialectic Althusser substitutes the concept of overdetermination. This concept is obviously borrowed from Freud, although there is also an implication of Lacan. (The influence of Lacan is permanent in all Althusser's work and increasingly evident in his later essays.) To introduce the concept of overdetermination, Althusser starts from a remark by Lenin, when Lenin raises the question: how was it possible that the socialist revolution occurred in Russia, when Russia was not the most advanced industrial country? Lenin's response is that to claim that revolution should occur in the most industrial country implies that the economic base is not only determinant in the last instance but the sole determinant factor. What we must realize, then, is that the economic base never works alone; it always acts in combination with other elements: national character, national history, traditions, international events, and accidents of history – wars, defeats, and so on. An event like a revolution is not the mechanical result of the basis but something involving all the 'various levels and instances of the social formation' (FM, 101). It is a combination of forces. This nexus is what Althusser calls overdetermination and opposes to the Hegelian contradiction.

It is difficult, though, to locate exactly the difference between Althusser and Hegel on this point. We could say that there is overdetermination in Hegel also. In whatever chapter we read in the *Phenomenology*, each figure has so many conflicting elements that precisely the dialectic must proceed toward another figure. We may say that the instability of the figure is a product of its overdetermination. Althusser's claim, and I am less convinced by this argument, is that there exists in Hegel no real overdetermination involving heterogeneous factors. Instead, Althusser argues, the process is one of cumulative internalization, which is only apparently an overdetermination. In spite of the complexity of a historical form in Hegel, it is actually simple in its principle. Though the *content* of the Hegelian figure may not be simple, its meaning is, because finally it is one figure, whose unity is immanent in its form. In Hegel, says Althusser, an epoch has 'an internal spiritual principle, which can never definitely be anything but the most abstract form of that epoch's consciousness of itself: its religious or philosophical consciousness, that is, its own ideology' (FM, 103). The 'mystical shell' affects and contaminates the supposed rational 'kernel'. For Althusser, therefore, Hegel's dialectic is typically idealistic: even if a historical period has complex elements, it is ruled by one idea, it has a unity of its own. The point, then, is that if we assume with Althusser the simplicity of the Hegelian form, such that it can be encapsulated in a label like the master-slave relation or Stoicism, the contrast is to the complexity of Marxist contradiction. The complexity of the contradictions spawning the Russian Revolution are not an accident in Marxist theory but rather the rule. The argument is that the contradictions are always this complex.

If we put together this notion of overdetermination with Engels' concept of causality in the last instance by the base and the reaction back on the base by the superstructure, we then have a richer concept of causality. We see that in fact the infrastructure is always determined by all the other components. There is a combination of levels and structures. This position was originally developed, we must not forget, to counter the mechanicist trend in Marxism – represented particularly by the German Social Democratic Party. This mechanicism, which endorsed a fatalistic or deterministic view of history, was denounced by Gramsci in an interesting argument reproduced by Althusser. Gramsci says that it is always those with the most active will who believe in determinism; they find in this fatalism of history a confirmation of their own actions. (In a certain sense this is quite similar to the Calvinistic notion of predestination.) Proponents believe that they are the chosen people of history, and therefore there is a certain necessity in history's movement. Althusser quotes Gramsci's strong statement that fatalism has been ' "the ideological "aroma" of the philosophy of praxis" ' (FM, 105 *n.*). The word 'aroma' is an allusion to Marx's early essay on Hegel's *Philosophy of Right.* Just as Marx criticized there the illusions of religion's spiritual aroma, here fatalism is subject to the same censure.

Can we say that Althusser's introduction of the concept of overdetermination in any way displaces the causalist framework of infrastructure and superstructure? In actuality this framework is more reinforced than qualified by this analysis. Althusser repeatedly affirms that the notion of infrastructure and superstructure is what gives meaning to overdetermination, not the contrary. He acknowledges that it is Engels' formula which in fact rules his own concept of overdetermination. Perhaps it is a concession to Marxist orthodoxy, I am not sure, but Althusser is very clear on this point. Speaking of the accumulation of effective determinations (derived from the superstructure) on determination in the last instance by the economic, Althusser says: 'It seems to me that this clarifies the expression overdetermined contradiction, which I have put forward, this specifically because the existence of overdetermination is no longer a fact pure and simple, for in its essentials we have related it to its bases . . .' (FM, 113). The concept of overdetermination does not help to overcome the weakness of the concept of infrastructure and superstructure, since it is only a commentary on the same argument. The framework of causality is affected not at all.

As a sign that this framework is still troublesome for Althusser – there is a great sincerity and modesty in all his texts – Althusser says that when we put together the determination in the last instance by the economy and the reaction back on the infrastructure by the superstructure, we hold only 'the two ends of the chain' (FM, 112). This expression is an allusion to Leibniz' description of the problematic relationship between determinations made by God and determinations made by human free will. Thus, Marxism repeats a paradox that was typically theological, the paradox of the ultimate determination; at issue is the relative effectivity of independent actors in a play decided elsewhere and by someone else.

> [I]t has to be said that the theory of the specific effectivity of the superstructure and other 'circumstances' largely remains to be elaborated; and before the theory of their effectivity or simultaneously . . . there must be elaboration of the theory of the particular essence of the specific elements of the superstructure (FM, 113–14).

The role of overdetermination remains more than a solution. It is a way of qualifying a concept which itself remains quite opaque.

This is why I wonder whether it would not be more helpful to start from the Freudian-Althusserian concept of overdetermination, to take it for itself, and then try to see whether it does not imply another theoretical framework than that of superstructure and infrastructure. My alternative would be a motivational framework; this structure would allow us to understand that it is in fact in terms of motives and motivation that we may speak of the overdetermination of a meaning. Perhaps without a concept of meaning, we cannot speak adequately about overdetermination. The concept of overdetermination, I think, does not necessarily require a causalist framework. What confirms this attempted change is that, according to Althusser himself, we must grant some meaning to the relative autonomy of the superstructural sphere.

> [A] revolution in the structure [of society] does not ipso facto modify the existing superstructures and particularly the ideologies at one blow (as it would

> if the economic was the sole determinant factor), for they have sufficient of their own consistency to survive beyond their immediate life context, even to recreate, to 'secrete' substitute conditions of existence temporarily... (FM, 115–16).

The superstructure is a layer with its own consistency and finally its own history. As the intriguing Marxist theory of 'survivals' attempts to take into account, we must come to understand why, for example, bourgeois morality persists even after a period of social transformation. My claim is that such practices may continue to prevail precisely because a certain strain of motives survives the change in the social framework. To my mind at least, the independence, autonomy, and consistency of ideologies presuppose another framework than that of superstructure and infrastructure.

Let me turn, though, away from this theme to what is the most interesting topic for us in Althusser, the theory of ideologies themselves, ideologies considered for their own sake. Althusser undertakes this treatment in two steps, and this is expressed in my own treatment of the problem: first 2he speaks of particular ideologies, and then he tries to say something about ideology in general. The distinction between these two themes is not made very clearly in *For Marx* but appears rather in a later, very abstract article called 'Ideology and Ideological State Apparatuses'. This article, included in *Lenin and Philosophy*, will be at the centre of our attention when we discuss Althusser's theory of ideology in general, but let me quote it briefly here to indicate how Althusser introduces the distinction in question. '[I]f I am able to put forward the project of a theory of ideology *in general*, and if this theory really is one of the elements on which theories of ideolog*ies* depend, that entails an apparently paradoxical proposition which I shall express in the following way: *ideology has no history*'.[2] Mainly under the influence once more of Freud and Lacan, Althusser says that we need to pursue a theory of ideology in general, just as metapsychology is a theory of the unconscious in general, an inquiry separate from specific treatment of the expressions of the unconscious found in such particular areas as mental illness, art, ethics, religion, and so on. As we shall see, the reason ideology in general has no history is because it is a permanent structure. Freud's metapsychology is Althusser's model for the relation between particular ideologies and ideology in general. For our purposes, examination of the nature of ideology in general is the more interesting question, and so I shall treat the problem of particular ideologies fairly quickly.

The approach to a theory of ideology through analysis of particular ideologies is more or less imposed by the Marxist model, where ideologies are always presented in an enumeration. Those familiar with Marxist texts may have noticed that when Marx himself discusses ideology, he continually opens a parenthesis and refers to specific – that is, religious, ethical, aesthetic, and political – ideologies. It is by enumeration of these forms that Marx builds the more general analysis, a method quite similar to Descartes' analysis of the *cogito*. We should not forget either that Marx also proceeded historically by a similar process: from the critique of religion, to the critique of philosophy, and then to the critique of politics. The dispersion of ideologies is an important aspect of the problem, the fact that there are ideologies, in the plural. We should note, however, that within Marxist texts as a whole the framework of response to this problem is not always the same. In some texts the word 'ideology' is used to cover all that is not economic, while in others differentiation is made between economics, politics, and ideologies. In his own comprehensive concept of ideology in his later work, Althusser himself identifies the political structure as a particular ideology.

Let me offer two examples of Althusser's adoption of this enumerative approach: his treatment of humanism and of the state. In *For Marx* the paradigmatic example of a particular ideology is humanism. Humanism is treated as an ideology and as an ideology that has determinant boundaries. It is defined as a specific anthropological field. It is therefore a cultural pattern, something to which some people belong and others do not. A particular ideology may be contrasted to ideology in general, which is not a historical pattern but a permanent structure, just like the Freudian unconscious. Again, the attraction of Freudian concepts is most important. In spite of the narrowness of the concept of ideology when identified with one problematic among others, this concept is nevertheless quite revealing about the structure of ideology in general, since in fact the general structure of ideology in Althusser repeats the structure of humanism, as we shall discover.

The case of humanism is crucial in another respect, since it gives us the right to put *The German Ideology* within the same anthropological field as the earlier texts. What defines humanism, even that which is called socialist humanism, is a common participation in the same ideology. Therefore, Althusser considers the rebirth of humanism in modern Marxism a return to Feuerbach and the early Marx; it belongs to the same anthropological field. Althusser's analysis of humanism is a central illustration of his uncompromising denial of any conceptual blending between ideology and science. '[I]n the couple "humanism-socialism" there is a striking theoretical unevenness: in the framework of the Marxist conception [Althusser's own, of course], the concept "socialism" is indeed a scientific concept, but the concept "humanism" is no more than an ideological one' (FM, 223). For Althusser, humanist socialism is a monstrous kind of concept. Unfortunately, this position sometimes has severe political implications. During the 1968 invasion of Czechoslovakia, for example, Althusser kept silent; his stance allowed him to argue that purely theoretically, the reform movement was wrong. The Czechoslovak socialists were attempting something that does not exist – humanistic socialism; they relied on an impure concept.

The argument against linking the concept of humanism to that of socialism is that the former 'designates some existents, but it does not give us their essences' (FM, 223). The argument is Platonic, an objection that humanism speaks of existence – human beings, life, and so on – and not conceptual structure. Althusser's perspective is a necessary consequence of the epistemological break, which places both the *Manuscripts*' idealism of consciousness and *The German Ideology*'s concrete anthropology on the same – and wrong – side. In his strongest statement about Marx's theoretical anti-humanism, Althusser says:

> Strictly in respect to theory, therefore, one can and must speak openly of Marx's theoretical anti-humanism, and see in this theoretical anti-humanism the absolute (negative) precondition of the (positive) knowledge of the human world itself, and of its practical transformation. It is impossible to know anything about men except on the absolute precondition that the philosophical (theoretical) myth of man is reduced to ashes. So any thought that appeals to Marx for any kind of restoration of a theoretical anthropology or humanism is no more than ashes, theoretically (FM, 229–30).

Here is perhaps the common side to Althusser, the French structuralist group in general, and others like Michel Foucault: the idea that the 'philosophical . . . myth of man' must be reduced to ashes. On the basis of this orientation, I do not see how it would be possible to build, for example, a protest against the betrayal of rights. Someone like Sakharov must be treated as an ideologist, but Althusser would say that Nobel Prizes are both given to ideologists and, even more surely, given by ideologists.

Nevertheless, we have a hint of something else in this analysis, when Althusser says that knowledge of an object does not replace the object or dissipate its existence (FM, 230). To say that something is *theoretically* no more than ashes means that we do not change its reality by arguing that it does not really exist. To know that an ideology has no theoretical status is not to abolish it. Here again there is a reminiscence not only of Spinoza – that in the second kind of knowledge the first one survives – but also of Freud, when Freud says that it is not enough in a therapeutic process to understand intellectually, if the balance of forces – of repression and so on – has not changed also. To explain to someone that he or she is caught in an ideology is not sufficient; it does not change the situation. The claim that something is 'no more than ashes, theoretically' is only a qualified claim.

We must deal, then, with a strange necessity: we know that humanism has no theoretical status, but yet it has a kind of factual existence. By relating humanism to its condition of existence, Althusser says, we can recognize its necessity as an ideology; it has, in Althusser's strange phrase, a 'conditional necessity' (FM, 231). Althusser must resort to this term because if Marxism is more than a science, if it is a politics, and if politics is itself based on the assertion that human beings have certain rights, then Marxism must take something from the ideological sphere in order to accomplish something practically. The conjunction between ideology and science is a 'conditional necessity' required by action, but this *practical* conjunction does not abolish their *theoretical* break. As we can see, it is very difficult to comprehend that there may be something abolished theoretically but still existent in such a way that we must rely on it in order to act.

A second example in Althusser of a partial or regional ideology – the language is somewhat Husserlian – is the state. Here too Althusser introduces some important changes in Marxist theory. Althusser's main improvement is engendered by his linking ideology to its political function, that is, to the question of the reproduction of the system, the reproduction of the conditions of production. This problem has become quite popular among modern Marxists; their view is that Marx studied the conditions of production, but there must also be reflection on the conditions of the system's *re*production. Examination must be undertaken of all those institutions which have the function of reinforcing and reproducing the system's structure.

To make sense of this concept of reproduction, Althusser has to improve the rigid Marxist concept of the state, which originates in Lenin. In *State and Revolution* Lenin views the state as merely a structure of coercion. The function of the state is repression. Nothing is left from Hegel's idealized concept of the state as the integration of individuals who know themselves as citizens through the constitution. On the contrary, Lenin's view of the state is extremely pessimistic: the state is an instrument of repression, of coercion, for the benefit of the ruling class. The dictatorship of the proletariat will consist in the inversion of this coercive tool and its use against the enemies of this transformed state. Stalin effectively used this notion of inversion to enforce his own position, arguing that he was simply using the bourgeois structure of the state against its enemy. On the day these enemies disappear, he said, then there will no longer be a need for the state.

Althusser's contribution in *Lenin and Philosophy* is to say that we must in fact distinguish two aspects of state power. The first is the repressive and coercive state apparatuses: government, administration, police, courts, prisons, and so on. The second is the ideological state apparatuses: religion, education, the family, the political system, communications, culture, and so forth (LP, 136–37). The structure of the state is both repressive and ideological. To any who might object that introduction of ideology into the theory of the state involves inclusion of something private and not public, Althusser responds that this division between public and private is a bourgeois concept. If we deny the bourgeois concepts, which depend on the concept of private property, then we must consider the state as a system of apparatuses which extend far beyond administrative functions. Only for the bourgeois mentality are there private and public spheres. For Marxist theory these two spheres represent aspects of the same function.

We may connect the importance of the state's ideological apparatuses with the problem of the system's need to reproduce itself by understanding that this reproduction occurs through such ideological state apparatuses as education. I know many leftist educators in Europe – in Germany, Italy, France – who use this notion of reproduction to argue that the function of the school is to reproduce the system, not only by the teaching of technological skills but by the reproduction in students of the rules of the system. The system is maintained by the reproduction of its rule. (Once again there is an intersection with Freud; the ideological state apparatus has its counterpart in the superego.)

> The reproduction of labour power thus reveals as its *sine qua non* not only the reproduction of its 'skills' but also the reproduction of its subjection to the ruling ideology or of the 'practice' of that ideology, with the proviso that it is not enough to say 'not only but also', for it is clear that it is in the forms and under the forms of ideological subjection that provision is made for the reproduction of the skills of labour power (LP, 128).

A system of oppression survives and prevails thanks to this ideological apparatus which both places individuals in subjection and at the very same time maintains and reproduces the system. Reproduction of the system and ideological repression of the individual are one and the same. Althusser's analysis here is quite powerful. We have to join two ideas: a state functions not only by power but also by ideology, and it does so for the sake of its own reproduction.

There are parallels to this analysis outside Marxism. In Plato, for example, the role played by the sophists demonstrates that no master rules by pure force. The ruler must convince, must seduce; a certain distortion of language always accompanies the use of power. Naked power never works; in the use of political power an ideological mediation is unavoidably involved. My question, therefore, is not at all whether Althusser's description is a good one. [. . .] Instead, it is the concepts used which interest me, and in this context particularly the notion of apparatus. This concept belongs to the same anonymous language as superstructure and infrastructure. It is not by chance that Althusser's term is apparatus and not institution, because an apparatus is more mechanical. An apparatus is something which functions, and therefore it has more conceptual kinship with structures and reproduction, with structural language in general. All these functions are anonymous and can exist and go on by themselves. If, however, we raise the question: but how do these functions work, do we not need to introduce, once again, some element like persuasion and therefore a certain capturing of motivation? Once more the problem is one of legitimacy, of the claim to legitimacy and the process of justification, and I do not see how these issues work within the language of apparatus. My difficulty is with the conceptual framework of causality at a place where I think another – motivational – framework would be more helpful. The causal framework has been imposed at the beginning by the notion of the determinant factor in the last instance, and consequently all of the new and quite interesting changes Althusser introduces in Marxist theory have to be put within this imperative framework.

Let us set this point aside, though, and turn to the most interesting part of Althusser's analysis, his attempt to provide a definition of ideology in general. This attempt will be decisive for the rest of the lectures as a whole. Althusser's attempt allows us to move from what we might call a geography of ideologies to a theory of ideology. Althusser's discussion is located in two principal texts, pages 231–36 of *For Marx* and pages 149–70 of *Lenin and Philosophy*. The latter is the section of 'Ideology and Ideological State Apparatuses' entitled 'On Ideology' and is Althusser's most discussed text. I shall leave this text for the next lecture.

In *For Marx* Althusser puts forward three or four programmatic definitions of ideology, attempts to try, to test, and nothing more than that, since he thinks that this effort has not been undertaken in previous Marxist theory. As we shall see, Althusser's definitions may not be so easy to combine. Althusser's first definition is readily understood, though, because it is an application of the distinction between science and ideology.

> There can be no question of attempting a profound definition of ideology here. It will suffice to know very schematically that an ideology is a system (with its own logic and rigour) of representations (images, myths, ideas or concepts, depending on the case) endowed with a historical existence and role within a given society. Without embarking on the problem of the relations between a science and its (ideological) past, we can say that ideology, as a system of representations, is distinguished from science in that in it the practico-social function is more important than the theoretical function (function as knowledge) (FM, 231).

There are four or five important notions here. First, ideology is a system; this is consistent with what Althusser called a field – an anthropological field, for example – or a problematic. All these concepts overlap. Of what is ideology a system, though? A system of representation. This is its second trait. Althusser uses the vocabulary of the idealistic tradition; the vocabulary of idealism is preserved in the definition of ideology as *Vorstellung*, representation. Third trait, ideology has a historical role. Ideology is not a shadow, as it is in some Marxist texts, since it plays a role in the historical process. It is a part of the process of overdetermination. Thus, we must connect the notion of ideology's historical existence to its contribution to the overdetermination of events. All these traits are very coherent. What is more problematic is ideology's fourth trait, the relative import Althusser ascribes to ideology's practico-social function in contrast to its theoretical function. This trait is more difficult to accept because if, for example, we call humanism an ideology, surely it has some very theoretical claims. To take another case, what work is more theoretical than Hegel's? Althusser's point is quite difficult to comprehend, because nothing is more theoretical than idealism; Feuerbach and the young Marx in fact opposed Hegel's work precisely because it was theory and not *praxis*. Suddenly in Althusser, however, we discover that *praxis* is ideological and only science is theoretical. I do not see how Althusser's point here can be maintained.

Althusser's second definition of ideology is more within the framework of the opposition between the illusory and the real. As we recall from earlier lectures, this analysis has some grounds in the young Marx. This second definition of Althusser's will prevail in his later texts. Notice in the following quotation the use of the phrase 'lived relation,' *vécu*; this is the vocabulary of Husserl and of Merleau-Ponty, the language of existential phenomenology.

> So ideology is a matter of the lived relation between men and their world. This relation, that only appears as 'conscious' on condition that it is unconscious, in the same way only seems to be simple on condition that it is complex, that it is not a simple relation but a relation between relations, a second degree relation.

This is a torturous way of saying that ideology reflects in the form of an imaginary relation something which is already an existing relation, that is, the relation of human beings to their world. The lived relation is reflected as ideology. The more important part of the text follows:

> In ideology men do indeed express, not the relation between them and their conditions of existence, but the way they live the relation between them and their conditions of existence: this presupposes both a real relation and an 'imaginary', 'lived' relation. Ideology, then, is the expression of the relation between men and their 'world', that is, the (overdetermined) unity of the real relation and the imaginary relation between them and their real conditions of existence. In ideology the real relation is inevitably invested in the imaginary relation, a relation that expresses a will (conservative, conformist, reformist or revolutionary), a hope or a nostalgia, rather than describing a reality (FM, 233–34).

The vocabulary here is quite interesting, not only because we have the notion of the lived relation, but because this relation is lived in an imaginary mode. In an ideology the way of living this relation is imaginary. This definition introduces an important shift from the vocabulary of the young Marx, which it at first sight resembles. While in the young Marx the real and the imaginary are opposed, here the lived and the imaginary are coupled together. An ideology is both lived *and* imaginary, it is the lived *as* imaginary. Therefore, we have a real relation which is distorted in an imaginary relation. Anticipating our later discussion, we may note that it is difficult to adjust this definition to the rest of Althusser's work, since Althusser speaks here of the real relations of real individuals, even though real individuals do not belong to the basic phenomena. More generally, though, it seems that to give an account of ideology we must speak the language of ideology; we must speak of individuals constructing dreams instead of living their real life.

Althusser also introduces at this point the notion of overdetermination as applied no longer to the relation between instances – between elements of the superstructure and infrastructure – but to the relationship between the real and the imaginary. The concept of overdetermination is used in a context that is closer to Freud than to Marx; the mixture of the real and the imaginary is what Freud calls a compromise formation, and it is this notion that rules Althusser's analysis at this point. 'It is in this overdetermination of the real by the imaginary and of the imaginary by the real that ideology is active in principle . . .' (FM, 234). Thus, ideology is not something bad, it is not something that we attempt to put behind us; instead, it is something that pushes us, a system of motivation. Ideology is a system of motivation that proceeds from the lack of a clear distinction between the real and the unreal.

In his third definition of ideology, Althusser writes of ideology as expressed in the language of layers, of instances. Althusser needs this language to preserve ideology's reality, its real existence in history. As real, ideology must involve real instances, real layers, and not merely imaginary elements; the imaginary has a kind of inexistence. In his later article on 'Ideological Apparatuses', Althusser will try to adjust the definition of ideology to include both the terms of illusion and the terms of historical existence, arguing that ideology has its materiality in the famous ideological apparatus. The apparatus will give a certain material existence to these dreams. At the time of *For Marx*, however, Althusser had not yet solved this subtle discrepancy between his definitions. His third definition of ideology moves from the language of the lived to the language of instances.

> So ideology is as such an organic part of every social totality. It is as if human societies could not survive without these specific formations, these systems of representations (at various levels), their ideologies. Human societies secrete ideology as the very element and atmosphere indispensable to their historical respiration and life. Only an ideological world outlook could

> have imagined societies without ideology and accepted the utopian idea of a world in which ideology (not just one of its historical forms) would disappear without trace, to be replaced by science (FM, 232).

This text is quite positive toward ideology; it is a plea for recognition of ideology's indispensability. Althusser argues against the utopian view of those technocrats who believe that we are now beyond the age of ideologies, that we may now speak of the death of ideologies. In opposition to this theme, famous both in Europe and in this country, Althusser contends that there will always be ideology, because people have to make sense of their lives. This task is not the province of science, which cannot do everything, but rather the function of ideology. Althusser goes far in the direction of a positive appreciation of ideology. It is difficult, though, to think of ideology simultaneously as illusion (Althusser's second definition) and as a real instance essential to the historical life of societies. Perhaps the mediating point is the Nietzschean view that we need illusions to survive the hardness of life, that we would die if we saw the real truth of human existence. Also involved here may be the pessimistic view that people want ideologies because science does not give their lives meaning. Althusser is very antipositivist and again typifies as utopian the positivist view that science will one day replace ideology.

> [T]his utopia is the principle behind the idea that ethics, which is in its essence ideology, could be replaced by science or become scientific through and through; or that religion could be destroyed by science which would in some way take its place; that art could merge with knowledge or become 'everyday life', etc. (FM, 232).

Against those who maintain that ethics, religion, and art are 'survivals', lingering remnants of earlier non-scientific eras, Althusser tends to say that they are necessary ingredients of any society. Ideologies are indispensable; science cannot be everything.

For my part, I interpret this turn of Althusser's in the following way. If we raise the requirements of science so highly, then it is beyond our access. The higher in fact that we raise the concept of science, the broader becomes the field of ideology, because each is defined in relation to the other. If we reinforce the scientific requirement of a theory, then we lose its capacity for making sense of ordinary life. Therefore, the field of ideology is so wide because the field of science is so narrow. At least this is my interpretation of Althusser's discussion here. Althusser's differentiation between science and ideology explains his positive recognition of ideology as something in the indeterminate state of not being true but yet necessarily vital, a vital illusion. This perspective provides a way to interpret Marx's statement that in a class society ruling ideas have to take the form of universality. This necessity is not a lie, it is not a trick, for it is imposed by the unavoidable imaginary structure itself. No one can think without believing that what he or she thinks is in some basic sense true. The illusion is a necessary one.

The persistence of this illusion that is ideology extends even unto the hypothesized classless society. Whatever the classless society may mean – and again I do not discuss it at all in political terms but only according to its own condition of intelligibility – it has about it a quality of the eternal. (In Althusser's 'Ideological Apparatuses' article, the word 'eternal' returns and is compared to Freud's description of the atemporality of the unconscious.) Similarly, ideology is also atemporal. '[I]t is clear that ideology (as a system of mass representations) is indispensable in any society if men are to be formed, transformed and equipped to respond to the demands of their conditions of existence' (FM, 235). The suggestion is that in every society, even in one where by hypothesis class struggle no longer exists, there will always be a situation of inadequation between the demands of reality and our ability to cope. I am reminded of Freud's comments concerning death and the hardness of life, the fact that the price of reality is too high. The requirements of the conditions of reality are high, and our capacity to adjust to reality is limited.

> It is in ideology that the classless society lives the inadequacy/adequacy of the relation between it and the world, it is in it and by it that it transforms men's 'consciousness', that is, their attitudes and behaviour so as to raise them to the levels of their tasks and the conditions of their existence (FM, 235).

We have here nearly a fourth definition of ideology as the the system of means by which we try to adjust our capacity to change to the actual conditions of change in society in general. Therefore, ideology has a certain ethical function; it attempts to make sense of the accidents of life, the painful aspects of existence. We must introduce an existential language; when we speak of contradiction, it is not a logical contradiction, a conflict between structures, but a lived contradiction, a contradiction between our capacity to adjust and the demands of reality.

To my mind, Althusser's definitions of ideology in general raise the following questions. My broadest question is: if we assume the value of Althusser's analysis, are we any longer able to speak of ideology simply as non-science? Under this theme, several more specific questions follow, which I shall return to in later lectures. First, is not the quasi-ethical function of ideology just as valuable as science? Second, how can we understand the notion of the imaginary if the real is not already symbolically mediated? Third, is not the most primitive function of ideology – that which is said to emerge in classless society – not distortive but integrative? And finally, how do we know ideology if not because it belongs to a fundamental anthropology; is it not only within this philosophical anthropology that the vocabulary of Althusser's definitions – 'men', 'conditions of existence', 'demands', 'attitudes and behaviour' – makes sense? Is there not, therefore, a primitive connection between the lived and the imaginary that is more radical than any distortion?

The point about Althusser's expressions is that they belong to the vocabulary of humanism. To speak of ideology we must rejuvenate the vocabulary of humanism. Even in the concluding sentence of his discussion – a sentence perhaps, though, a concession to the reader – Althusser resorts to this vocabulary. 'In a classless society ideology is the relay whereby, and the element in which, the relation between men and their conditions of existence is lived to the profit of all men' (FM, 236). Who would say more than this, that we are all dreaming of the kind of society in which the relations between human beings and their conditions of existence are lived to the profit of all? But this is precisely the discourse of ideology. We must assume at least part of the discourse of ideology in order to speak of ideology. It seems as if we cannot speak of ideology in another language than its own. If we utilize the Althusserian language of science, then we can speak only of apparatuses, instances, structures, and superstructures and infrastructures, but not of 'conditions of existence', 'attitudes and behaviour', and so on. At least to a certain extent, therefore, only ideology may speak about ideology.

A few more points also need to be made about Althusser's contention that the 'disproportion of historical tasks to their conditions' (FM, 238) justifies the necessity of ideology. This relationship must be *lived* in order to become a contradiction and to be treated scientifically. The relation of disproportion also reinforces the prestige of the concept of alienation. Althusser maintains [. . .] that this concept can be done away with, but are we able to deny it theoretically and preserve it practically? Are not the lived contradictions the conditions for the so-called real relations? Althusser responds that if we return to the language of alienation, it is because we do not yet have a science of ideology. It is a provisory language in the absence of an adequate language. 'Within certain limits this recourse to ideology might indeed be envisaged as the substitute for a recourse to theory' (FM, 240) or as 'a substitute for an insufficient theory' (FM, 241). Althusser has accused all Marxist thinkers of theoretical weakness, but he assumes a certain theoretical weakness for himself in order to speak about ideology in positive terms. Because of the present weakness of our theory, he says, we need the language of ideology in order to speak of ideology; one day, however, our theory will be strong enough to cast aside this vocabulary. This argument is for me the most questionable of Althusser's claims. The question is whether this alleged confusion of ideology and scientific theory is not required by the problem itself. Does not this 'confusion' in fact express the impossibility of drawing the line between the lived contradiction and the real basis? In order to speak in a meaningful way of ideology, do we not have to speak of the motives of people, of individuals in certain circumstances, of the adequate or inadequate relation between human behaviour and its conditions? We cannot eliminate as a problem the status of a philosophical anthropology if we want to speak about these issues.

[. . .]

Althusser's most advanced attempt to provide an inclusive concept of ideology appears in the *Lenin and Philosophy* essay titled 'Ideology and Ideological State Apparatuses'. The purpose of this essay, we should recall, is to argue that the fundamental function of ideology is reproduction of the system, training of individuals in the rules governing the system. To the problem of production raised by Marx we must add the problem of *re*production. On the basis of this reconceptualization, we must then reformulate the Leninist concept of the state – defined only in terms of coercion – by adding the notion of what Althusser calls ideological state apparatuses. Ideology is institutionalized and so appears as a dimension of the state. There is a dimension of the state which is not merely administrative or political but specifically ideological. The superstructure is related to reproduction through specific institutional apparatuses, and the problem of a general theory of ideology is proposed in conjunction with this reformulation.

In this text, Althusser goes so far as to ascribe to ideology all positive functions which are not science. At the same time, he emphasizes more strongly than ever the illusory character of imagination. Here Althusser borrows from Spinoza the theme that the first kind of knowledge is merely a distorted conception of our relation to the world. He also and more importantly borrows from the distinction made by the French psychoanalyst Jacques Lacan between the imaginary and the symbolic. Significantly, Althusser drops the notion of the symbolic to retain the notion of the imaginary understood on the model of the mirror relationship. The imaginary is a mirror relation at a narcissistic stage, an image of oneself that one has in a physical mirror and also in all the situations of life in which one's image is reflected by others.

In turning to the text, we shall focus particularly on the section of Althusser's essay called 'On Ideology'. Althusser begins by contrasting his position to that of Marx in *The German Ideology*. Here, Althusser claims, Marx did not take seriously the paradox of a reality of the imaginary.

> In *The German Ideology* . . . [i]deology is conceived as a pure illusion, a pure dream, i.e. as nothingness. All its reality is external to it. Ideology is thus thought as an imaginary construction whose status is exactly like the theoretical status of the dream among writers before Freud. For these writers, the dream was the purely imaginary, i.e. null, result of 'day's residues',

> presented in an arbitrary arrangement and order, sometimes even 'inverted', in other words, in 'disorder'. For them the dream was the imaginary, it was empty, null and arbitrarily 'stuck together' (*bricolé*) (LP, 150–51).

Against this purely negative text Althusser maintains that ideology has a reality of its own: the reality of the illusory. This statement seems to challenge another assertion of *The German Ideology*, that ideology has no history. (The argument, we remember, was that only economic history really exists. This became the framework for all orthodox Marxist approaches to history.) Althusser in fact agrees that ideology is non-historical but in a very different sense than that argued by *The German Ideology*. Ideology is non-historical not, as the orthodox approach would have it, because its history is external to it but because it is omni-historical, just like Freud's unconscious. Once more the influence of Freud is strongly reinforced. In his essay, 'The Unconscious', Freud said that the unconscious is timeless (*zeitlos*), not in the sense that it is supernatural but because it is prior to any temporal order or connections, being prior to the level of language, of culture, and so on. (An earlier, similar assertion appeared in the seventh chapter of Freud's *The Interpretation of Dreams*.) Althusser's explicit parallel between ideology and the unconscious draws on this basis and takes a step further by rendering timelessness as the eternal: 'ideology is eternal, exactly like the unconscious' (LP, 152). Althusser suggests that in the same way that Freud attempted to provide a theory of the unconscious in general – as the underlying structure of all the cultural figures of the unconscious, which appear at the level of symptoms – similarly, he himself proposes a theory of ideology in general that would underlie the particular ideologies.

On this basis the imaginary features of ideology must be qualified and improved. Here I raise two points. First, what is distorted is not reality as such, not the real conditions of existence, but our relation to these conditions of existence. We are not far from a concept of being-in-the-world; it is our relation to reality which is distorted. 'Now I can return to a thesis which I have already advanced: it is not their real conditions of existence, their real world, that "men" "represent to themselves" in ideology, but above all it is their relation to those conditions of existence which is represented to them there' (LP, 154). This leads to a most important insight, because what is a relation to the conditions of existence if not already an interpretation, something symbolically mediated. To speak of our relation to the world requires a symbolic structure. My main argument, therefore, is that if we do not have from the start a symbolic structure to our existence, then nothing can be distorted. As Althusser himself observes: 'it is the imaginary nature of this relation which underlies all the imaginary distortion that we can observe . . . in all ideology' (LP, 154–55). We are not far from a complete reversal in our approach to the problem of the imaginary. We could not understand that there are distorted images if there were not first a primary imaginary structure of our being in the world underlying even the distortions. The imaginary appears not only in the distorted forms of existence, because it is already present in the relation which is distorted. The imaginary is constitutive of our relation to the world. One of my main questions, then is whether this does not imply before the distorting function of imagination a constitutive function of imagination. Or, to use the language of Lacan, is there not a symbolic role of imagination distinct from the narcissistic component of imagination, that is to say, distinct from the imaginary taken in the sense of the mirror relationship?

My second remark is that this relation to our conditions of existence no longer falls very easily within the framework of causality. This relation is not causal or naturalistic but rather an interplay between motives, between symbols; it is a relation of belonging to the whole of our experience and of being related to it in a motivational way. Althusser himself hints that this relationship destroys the general framework of superstructure and infrastructure expressed in terms of causation; he says that here we need 'to leave aside the language of causality' (154).

Thus, we must introduce two levels of imagination, one which is the distorting, and another which is the distorted and therefore the primary.

> [A]ll ideology represents in its necessarily imaginary distortion not the existing relationships of production (and the other relationships that derive from them), but above all the (imaginary) relationship of individuals to the relations of production and the relations that derive from them. What is represented in ideology is therefore not the system of the real relations which govern the existence of individuals, but the imaginary relation of those individuals to the real relations in which they live (LP, 155).

Expressed more simply, this means that in fact we are never related directly to what are called the conditions of existence, classes and so on. These conditions must be represented in one way or another; they must have their imprint in the motivational field, in our system of images, and so in our representation of the world. The so-called real causes never appear as such in human existence but always under a symbolic mode. It is this symbolic mode which is secondarily distorted. Therefore, the notion of a primitive and basic distortion becomes questionable and perhaps completely incomprehensible. If everything were distorted, that is the same as if nothing were distorted. We must dig in under the notion of distortion. In so doing, we rediscover a layer not far finally from what *The German Ideology* described as real life or real individuals placed under certain circumstances. Althusser denies this anthropological approach, however, claiming that it is itself ideological. As a result, this discourse remains *en l'air*, floating without a basis, because we must use the so-called language of ideology, the anthropological language, in order to speak of this primitive, ineluctably symbolically mediated relation to our conditions of existence.

Perhaps anticipating this difficulty, the text suddenly takes a quite different approach. Althusser relinquishes the language of representation and substitutes for it that of apparatus. He turns away from the questions he has just raised to consider the material criteria of ideology. Althusser's thesis here is that ideology has a material existence. The claim is that while no Marxist can say anything that is not ideological concerning the roots of distortion in some more imaginary layer, he or she may still speak scientifically of the ideological apparatus within which the distortion works. The only Marxist language about the imaginary bears not upon its ontological, anthropological rooting but upon its incorporation in the state apparatus, in an institution. Therefore, we have a theory about imagination as institutionalized but not about imagination as a symbolic structure.

> While discussing the ideological State apparatuses and their practices, I said that each of them was the realization of an ideology. . . . I now return to this thesis: an ideology always exists in an apparatus, and its practice, or practices. This existence is material (LP, 156).

The materialist approach asks, in which apparatus does ideology work? And not, how is it possible according to the fundamental structure of human being? The latter question belongs to an ideological language. Questions about the underlying imaginary – the non-distorted or predistorted imaginary – must be cancelled for the sake of questions about the apparatus. The apparatus is a public entity and so no longer implies a reference to individuals. Althusser talks about individual beliefs as belonging to an 'ideological "conceptual" device (*dispositif*)' (157). In French *dispositif* expresses the idea of something which functions by itself, something which shapes behaviour.

It is difficult, though, to speak of the practice of a believer, for example, merely in terms of an apparatus unless the apparatus is reflected in the rules governing the behaviour. The ideological device which shapes the behaviour of the believer – the example is Althusser's (LP, 157) – must be such that it speaks to the attitudes and therefore to the motives of the individual involved. We must link the apparatus with what is meaningful for the individual. The apparatus is an anonymous and external entity, however, so it is difficult to connect and to have intersect the notion of apparatus with the notion of a practice, which is always the practice of someone. It is always some individual who is bowing, praying, doing what is supposed to be induced in him or her by the apparatus.

In order not to speak the language of ideology about ideology, Althusser must put the notion of practice itself into a behaviourist framework, the latter being something more appropriately connected with the Marxist concept of apparatus. The language of ideology, says Althusser, 'talks of actions: I shall talk of action inserted into practices. And I shall point out that these practices are governed by the rituals in which these practices are inscribed, within the material existence of an ideological apparatus...' (LP, 158). For Althusser the concept of action is too anthropological; practice is the more objective term. Finally, it is only the material existence of an ideological apparatus which makes sense of practice. The apparatus is a material framework, within which people do some specific things.

The behaviourist overtone in Althusser is evident in the following quotation:

> I shall therefore say that, where only a single subject... is concerned, the existence of the ideas of his belief is material in that his ideas are his material actions inserted into material practices governed by material rituals which are themselves defined by the material ideological apparatus from which derive the ideas of that subject (LP, 158).

The word 'material' is used in four ways: material actions, kneeling, for example; material practices, kneeling as religious behaviour; material rituals, kneeling as part of a service of worship; and the material ideological apparatus, the church as an institution. Just as Aristotle said that 'being' has several meanings, so Althusser gives several meanings to matter, a comparison he explicitly acknowledges with some humour (LP, 156). While admitting that the four inscriptions of the word 'material' are affected by different modalities, though, Althusser provides no rule for their differentiation. 'I shall leave on one side,' he says, 'the problem of a theory of the differences between the modalities of materiality' (LP, 159). In fact, then, we must qualify our concept of what is material in order to apply it properly to something that is not material in the way, for instance, that a chair is. We must rely on a polysemy of the word 'matter' to make sense of these differences, and this is hardly forbidden, because in ordinary language we use the word in so many divergent contexts. We rely on a common sense concept of matter or on the rules of everyday language, in the Wittgensteinian sense, to extend and stretch the notion of materiality in order that it covers the notion of practice.

The remaining part of Althusser's essay is devoted to the functioning of the category of the subject in ideology. Althusser says that the function of ideology and of the subject is for each to give content to the other.

> I say: the category of the subject is constitutive of all ideology, but at the same time and immediately I add that the category of the subject is only

> constitutive of all ideology insofar as all ideology has the function (which defines it) of 'constituting' concrete individuals as subjects (LP, 160).

Althusser puts 'constituting' within quotation marks because this is the language of Husserl. The phenomenology of the ego falls under the concept of ideology to the extent that it defines ideology; ideology is humanism, humanism relies on the concept of the subject, and it is ideology which constitutes the subject. Ideology and the subject are mutually constitutive. Whereas someone like Erik Erikson argues that ideology is a factor of identity and so maintains that the relationship between ideology and the subject should be taken in a positive sense, the language of Althusser is much more negative. We are forced to put on the side of ideology what in a sense is the most interesting philosophical problem: how do we become subjects? It is a bold attempt to give so much to ideology in order to deny it so much also. This is why I have said that if we give too much to science, we have to give still more to ideology. It becomes more and more difficult to treat ideology merely as a world of illusions, of superstructures, because it becomes so constitutive of what we are that what we might be when separated from ideology is completely unknown; we are what we are precisely thanks to ideology. The burden of ideology is to make subjects of us. It is a strange philosophical situation, since all our concrete existence is put on the side of ideology.

Althusser's interesting analysis of what he calls 'interpellation' demonstrates more specifically the relationship between ideology and the subject. 'As a first formulation, I shall say: all ideology hails or interpellates concrete individuals as concrete subjects, by the functioning of the category of the subject' (LP, 162). We are constituted as subjects through a process of recognition. The use of the term 'interpellation' is an allusion to the theological concept of call, of being called by God. In its ability to interpellate subjects, ideology also constitutes them. To be hailed is to become a subject. 'The existence of ideology and the hailing or interpellation of individuals as subjects are one and the same thing' (LP, 163). The idea is that ideology is eternal and so does not belong to the history of classes and so on, and it acts to constitute and be constituted by the category of the subject. The theory of ideology in general rebuilds the framework of a complete anthropology, but it does so with a negative cast. This anthropology is the world of illusion.

Althusser's claim about the illusory nature of what constitutes us as subjects is based on the Lacanian notion of the mirror-structure of the imagination. 'We observe that the structure of all ideology, interpellating individuals as subjects in the name of a Unique and Absolute Subject is speculary, i.e. has a mirror-structure, and doubly speculary: this mirror duplication is constitutive of ideology and ensures its functioning' (LP, 168). When emphasis is placed on the primacy of illusion in the symbolic process, all ideology must be illusory. Here there is a complete merging of the concept of the mirror – the narcissistic structure – with ideology. Ideology is established at the level of narcissism, the subject looking at itself indefinitely. Althusser takes as an illustrative example religious ideology. He says that the function of Christian theology is to reduplicate the subject by an absolute subject; they are in a mirror relation. 'The dogma of the Trinity is precisely the theory of the duplication of the Subject (the Father) into a subject (the Son) and of their mirror-connexion (the Holy Spirit)' (LP, 168 *n.*). Althusser's treatment here is not a good piece of work; I do not think it makes much sense. It is expeditive; Althusser summarizes Trinitarian theology in a footnote. We perhaps could say that the mirror relation would be more interesting as an expression of a neurotic way of life. If we took, for example, the Schreber case analyzed by Freud, and in particular what Freud called Schreber's theology, we would see this reduplicative process, there being in fact no god to worship but only a projection and retrojection indefinitely of oneself, a projection and assimilation of one's own image.

It is most difficult, therefore, to construct the whole concept of the subject on the narrow basis of the narcissistic relation of mirroring. We can more easily understand this relation as distortive, the distortion of a constitution, but it is difficult to understand it as constitutive itself. The only way to maintain that this relation is constitutive – and this is Althusser's stance – is to argue the radical position that the constitution is the distortion, that all constitution of a subject is a distortion. If ideology is eternal, though, if there are always already interpellated individuals as subjects, if the formal structure of ideology is continuingly the same, then what happens to the epistemological break? The problem of the epistemological break has to be removed from the sphere of particular ideologies to that of ideology in general. The break with religious ideology, with humanism, and so on is nothing compared to the break with this mutual constitution of primary ideology and subjectivity. I would agree that a break must occur, but not where Althusser places it. Instead, we may break and we have to break with the 'miscognition' (*méconnaissance*) that adheres to recognition (*reconnaissance*). What point would there be in a critique of miscognition if it were not for the sake of a more faithful recognition? We must make sense of true recognition in a way that does not reduce it to ideology, in the narrow and pejorative sense of that term. Althusser, however, rejects this possibility. He talks of 'the reality which is necessarily ignored (*méconnue*) [so 'miscognized', not ignored] in the very forms of recognition . . .' (LP, 170). All recognition is miscognition; it is a very pessimistic assertion. If ideology must have no value in itself, then it must be the world of miscognition, *méconnaissance*. The whole dialectic of recognition is broken by Althusser's ideological reduction of the problematic of the subject.

Instead of there being a relation of recognition, Althusser correlates the mirror relation with a relation of subsumption. 'There are no subjects except by and for their subjection' (LP, 169), he says. Althusser uses the play on words to indicate that the subject means both subjectivity and subjection. The two meanings are in fact reduced to one: to be a subject means to be submitted to. Yet is there not a history of the individual's growth beyond the 'speculary' stage? What about the dialectic of the speculary and the symbolic within imagination itself? For Althusser, however, to be a subject means to be subjected, to be submitted to an apparatus, the ideological apparatus of the state. To my mind, if ideology must be tied to the mirror stage of the imagination, to the submitted subject, I do not see how it would ever be possible to have as citizens authentic subjects who could resist the apparatus of the state. I do not see from where we could borrow the forces to resist the apparatus if not from the depths of a subject having claims that are not infected by this supposed submissive constitution. How else will someone produce a break in the seemingly closed shell of ideology?

The task, then, is to disentangle recognition (*reconnaissance*) from miscognition (*méconnaissance*). I shall later connect my analysis of Habermas precisely at this point. The problematic for Habermas is the need to start from a project of recognition. Ideology is troublesome because it makes impossible the true recognition of one human being by another. Further, if this situation is placed entirely on the side of ideology, then no weapons exist against ideology, because the weapons themselves are ideological. Therefore, we need a concept of recognition, what Habermas' more recent work speaks of as a concept of communication. We need a utopia of total recognition, of total communication, communication without boundaries or obstacles. This supposes that we have an interest in communication which is not, we might say, ideology-stricken from the beginning. In order to connect, as does Habermas, the critique of ideology to an interest in liberation, we must have a concept of recognition, a concept of the mutual task of communication, that is not ideological in the distortive sense of that word.

Before we reach our examination of Habermas, however, we shall spend some time discussing Mannheim and Weber, and we have some final questions of Althusser as well. To prepare for the transit from Althusser, I would like to present a general framework of the questions arising from our readings of his work. I shall consider five main problems. First is the question of the scientific claim of Marxism: in what sense is it a science? While Althusser speaks in some more recent writings of the discovery of a continent, the continent of history, even here the subject-matter is to be raised to the level of a systematic science. The focus of this history is not empirical historiography but the systematic concatenation of stages in the development of economic relationships (from primitive communism to feudalism to capitalism and so forth). If we speak of science in a positivist sense, then a theory must be submitted to verification and therefore to the whole community of, we might say, intellectual workers. It is hard, though, to identify this science with the science of a class. To put the notion of scientific verification within the framework of class struggle introduces a practical concept within the theoretical framework. My question, then, is in what sense can Marxism be a science if it is not verifiable or falsifiable in the Popperian sense? Perhaps it can be scientific in another fashion, that of a critique. But what motivates a critique if not an interest, an interest in emancipation, an interest in liberation, something which pulls a critique necessarily into the ideological sphere? It is quite difficult to think of a non-positivist science that is not supported by a human interest, a practical interest. It is also difficult to think of a science that is not understandable for all, even for members of other classes. As we shall discover, the problem of Mannheim's paradox in fact starts from the generalization of the concept of ideology at the point where ideological analysis is raised to the level of a science, that of the sociology of knowledge.

Our second problem, a corollary of the first, concerns the notion of the epistemological break. Is a complete break understandable without some kind of intellectual miracle, a sense of someone emerging from the dark? In Althusser's more recent *Essays in Self-Criticism*, even while subjecting himself to reproach (saying that he has been too theoretical and needs to return to the class struggle in a more militant way), he still reinforces his concept of the epistemological break. He says that it is an unprecedented event. Althusser even speaks of Marx as a son without a father, a kind of absolute orphan. He argues that it is the idealists who are always seeking continuity. Possibly a certain providentialism does imply continuity, but I do not know why historical continuity alone should be considered necessarily ideological and, perhaps, even theological. The concept of discontinuity gives rise to difficulty itself. It does so principally if we consider, once more, the motivation of this break. The epistemological break appears to be motivated, and if we want to connect this break to the emergence of a certain interest, then we have to borrow this motivation from the ideological sphere. The motivation belongs to the anthropological sphere, to the interest in being more fully human. We cannot completely separate the idea of the break from a certain human project which is to be improved, possibly even disclosed, by this science.

For my part Althusser's representation of the epistemological break does great damage not only to the theory of ideology but to the reading of Marx. It causes us to overlook an important break in Marx; it causes us to place the break at a different point from where it should be. Though I am not a Marxist scholar, my reading of Marx reinforces a conviction that the more important change at the philosophical level comes not after *The German Ideology* but between the *Manuscripts of 1844* and *The*

German Ideology, that is to say, in the emergence of the concept of the real human being, real *praxis*, individuals acting in certain given conditions. Seen in this light, the destiny of anthropology is not sealed by that of idealism. The great damage done to Marx by Althusser is that he forces us to put under one heading – anthropological ideology – two different notions. The first is an ideology of consciousness, with which Marx and Freud have rightly broken. The second, though, is the ideology of real, concrete, human being, a being composed of drives, labour, and so on. This latter notion, I believe, can be expressed in non-idealist terms. Ideology and idealism, therefore, are not identified in such a way that no place any longer exists for an anthropology. For me, a non-idealistic anthropology is the only way to make sense of all the other problems that we shall consider during the rest of the lectures. Marx's breakthrough must make sense at the level of this deep-rooted interest in the plenitude of indvidual existence.

The issues here lead us to a third question arising from our reading of Althusser, the problem of his conceptual framework. The conceptual framework of infrastructure and superstructure is a metaphor of a base with stories, an edifice with a base. This metaphor is quite seductive at first sight, but it becomes very dangerous when taken literally to mean something prior to something secondary or derived. One of the signs that this metaphor is misleading when frozen and taken literally is the difficulty of reconnecting the action of the base and the reaction back on the base by the superstructure. We are caught in a scholasticism of determinant factors and real but non-determinant factors. This scholasticism, I believe, leads nowhere, but the metaphor is harmful for even more important reasons. It is not that the metaphor creates paradoxes, for all doctrines in fact proceed by solving their own paradoxes. Rather, the conceptual framework here prevents us from making sense of some very interesting contributions of Althusser himself to Marxist doctrine. In particular I think of the concept of overdetermination, that is, recognition of the simultaneous action of infrastructure and superstructure, the fact that in history the base never acts alone but is always intertwined with actions, specific historical events, and so on. I wonder whether we could not make more sense of the concept of overdetermination if we placed it in another conceptual framework than that of infrastructure and superstructure. This might cause us, in fact, to reconsider what finally is really the base.

If we raise this radical question about what is basic for human beings, we may come to realize that a great deal of what is placed in the superstructure is basic from another point of view. Take into consideration any culture, and we find that its symbolic framework – its main assumptions, the way in which it considers itself and projects its identity through symbols and myths – is basic. It seems that we can call basic exactly what is usually called the superstructure. The possibility of this juxtaposition is always present with a metaphor. We must destroy a metaphor by the use of a contrary metaphor; we therefore proceed from metaphor to metaphor. The opposing metaphor here is the notion of what is basic for human beings: what is basic for human beings is not necessarily what is the base in Marxist structure. Indeed, I wonder whether the notion of overdetermination does not imply that we must in fact give up the distinction between infrastructure and superstructure.

This point is made even more evident when we realize that the very action of the superstructure implies some intermediary concepts which break the infrastructure/superstructure framework. Once again let me refer to the concept of authority. A system of authority never works only by force, by sheer violence; instead, as we have discussed, it works through ideology, through some meaningful procedures. These procedures call for the comprehension of individuals. Althusser's schema of 'effectivity' must be improved or perhaps completely recast in order to make room for the claim to legitimacy, which is characteristic of a ruling authority whether a group or class. I shall later turn to Max Weber to deal with this problem further, because his fundamental problem was how a system of authority works. For Weber the problem of domination implied a system of motives wherein the claims to legitimacy of an authority attempt to meet the capacity of belief in this legitimacy. We are forced to deal, therefore, with beliefs and claims, and it is difficult to put these psychological factors within a framework of infrastructure and superstructure.

Another reason we should question this conceptual framework is if we want to make sense of another of Althusser's claims, that ideologies have a reality of their own. I think that Althusser is right to assert the relative autonomy and self-consistency of ideologies; in this he opposes the classical Marxists, with the possible exception of the Italians, Gramsci above all. The relative autonomy of the superstructure, though, requires that ideologies have a content of their own. In turn, this requires before an understanding of these ideologies' use a phenomenology of their specific mode. We cannot define these ideologies' structure only by their role in the reproduction of the system. We must make sense of their meaning before considering their use. The assumption that ideologies' content is exhausted by their use is without justification; their use does not exhaust their meaning. We can take as an example the problem raised by Habermas, that in modern societies – and particularly in the military-industrial structure of the capitalist world – science and technology function ideologically. This does not mean that they are constitutively ideological but rather that they are being used ideologically. The present capture of science and technology by a certain interest – in Habermas' terms, an interest in control – is not constitutive of the inner meaning of their field. We must distinguish between the inner constitution of a given ideological field (granting, for the moment, that we still want to call it an ideology) and its function. The problem of distortion does not exhaust the constitution of a certain sociological force or structure.

As an example here, we may return to Lenin's definition of the state. In determining that the state is defined only by its coercive function, Lenin neglected its many other functions; he did not see that the coercive function is a distortion of these other functions. Lenin's approach, however, typifies the orthodox Marxist model. Religion is said to have no other constitution than its distorting function, and some now say the same of science and technology. Again I wonder, though, is not the only way to give meaning to the relative autonomy of the superstructural spheres to distinguish between the rules of their constitution and the distortive modes of their use? If we cannot make this distinction, then we have to say that the procedure of unmasking is constitutive of its object. The content of an ideology becomes uniquely what we have unmasked and nothing more than that, a very reductive procedure.

The failure to recognize the specificity of each superstructural sphere – the juridical, political, religious, cultural – has not only dangerous theoretical consequences but dangerous practical and political consequences also. Once it is assumed that these spheres have no autonomy, then the Stalinist state is possible. The argument is that since the economic base is sound and since all the other spheres are merely reflexes, shadows, or echoes, then we are allowed to manipulate the latter spheres in order to improve the economic base. There is no respect for the autonomy of the juridical, the political, or the religious, because they are said to have no existence in themselves.

Do we not want, then, a quite different theoretical framework in which the process of distortion would have as its condition of possibility a constitution which would not be defined by the distorting function? This would entail that the juridical sphere, for example, retain a certain constitutive specificity even though it may be true that it has been captured by the bourgeoisie for the latter's benefit. If we take the relation between work and capital expressed in the notion of the wage, the wage is presented as a contract, and the contract is represented as a juridical act. The juridical form of the exchange suggests no one is a slave, since people hire out their work and receive a wage in return. This is clearly a grave distortion, because the juridical concept of contract is applied to a situation of domination. Here the real situation of exploitation is concealed in an exchange of work and salary that is only apparently reciprocal. My claim is that while the juridical function is greatly harmed by the way this juridical framework in the capitalist system serves to conceal the real structure of exploitation, it is not exhausted, as the orthodox Marxists maintain, by this distortive function. I insist on the possibility of disconnecting and reconnecting the distortive and constitutive functions; this presupposes, once again, a motivational framework.

The fourth problem arising from our reading is that of particular ideologies. We may start here from the previous problem and ask what makes these particular ideologies specific. Let us take the example of humanism. In the United States the argument for humanism may be too easy, because humanism is a positive term, which is not always the case in Europe. We must reconsider the concept of humanism in order to disentangle what about it is ideological in the bad sense of that word, that is, a mere way to cover up real situations. We must look for a strong concept of humanism, which would not be ideological in a pejorative sense. Here I think that a theory of the system of interests, like Habermas', could help to show that there exists a hierarchy of interests that is not reducible to the mere interest in domination or control. This would imply construction of a complete anthropology and not a mere assertion of humanism, the latter being merely a claim if not a pretence. This strong concept of humanism must be linked to three or four other concepts within the same conceptual framework. First is the concept of the real individual under definite conditions, which has been elaborated in *The German Ideology*. This notion provides a strong philosophical basis for a humanism that would not be merely a claim. A strong concept of humanism is implied, second, in the entire problematics of legitimacy, because of the individual's relation to a system of order and domination. Perhaps here is the individual's major fight to achieve his or her identity over against a structure of authority. We need to stress, then, the important dialectic between individual and authority within the polarity between belief and claim. Third, I would say that the epistemological break relies on the emergence of this humanistic interest. We can make no sense of the sudden outburst of truth in the midst of obscurity and darkness if it is not the emergence of something which was distorted in ideology but now finds its truth. In a sense, the break must be also at the same time a recovery of what was covered up by ideology. I wonder whether a notion of radical break can be thought.

The fifth and final problem to arise from our reading is that of ideology in general. This raises that most radical question: what is distorted if not *praxis* as something symbolically mediated? The discourse on distortion is itself neither ideological nor scientific but anthropological. This is in agreement with all the previous suggestions concerning a philosophical anthropology that includes motives and symbols. The parallelism between the discourse on ideology in general and Freud's discourse on the unconscious in general reinforces the argument. Thus, we must have a theory of symbolic action. Recourse to the material existence of ideology does not suffice, for how can an imaginary relation be an apparatus? The functioning of the category of the subject in ideology becomes a warrant for ideology. We cannot speak of miscognition (*méconnaissance*) without the background of recognition (*reconnaissance*), a background that is not ideological but anthropological. [. . .]

NOTES

1 *For Marx*, Allen Lane, London, 1969, p. 89. Further references to this work will be indicated in the text in parentheses by the abbreviation FM, followed by a page number.

2 *Lenin and Philosophy and Other Essays*, New Left Books, London, 1971, p. 150. Further references to this article will be indicated in the text in parentheses by the abbreviation LP, followed by a page number.

4

HISTORY AND INTERACTION: ON THE STRUCTURALIST INTERPRETATION OF HISTORICAL MATERIALISM

Axel Honneth
(Translated by Gordon Finlayson)

The group of Marxist theorists which has gathered around Louis Althusser since the 1960s has been working on a new reading of Marxist theory that has both theoretical and political ramifications. The cogency of Althusser's reading of Marx depends upon its dual trajectory. It attempts to make the elucidation of strategic questions which concern the labour movement dependent upon the resolution of the central problems of Marxian theory. Althusser thus remains true to the goals of a philosophically informed tradition of oppositional Marxism – namely, to deal with actual political problems by means of a reinterpretation of Marxist theory. The theoretical component of the Althusserian programme consists in a critique of traditional Marxism. However, the critique is pitched at such a fundamental level that even manifestly opposed and discrepant interpretations of Marxism are elucidated on the basis of identical theoretical premises. Althusser contends that Stalinist Marxism and the philosophical critique of Stalinism share the same erroneous assumption, one that was already part and parcel of both the social-democratic revisionism of the Second International and the Hegelian-Marxist critique of this position. In short, the critical claims of Althusser's reading of Marx are far-reaching and powerful. Between his structuralist reading of Marx and his theoretical project proper, Althusser practically endorses only Lenin's brand of Marxism, whilst all intermediary positions (including legitimation theory and oppositional theory) are consigned wholesale to the same history of error. In its own self-understanding the Marxism offered by the Althusserian circle is therefore an epochal reading, countering traditional Marxist theory. The programme of structural Marxism is advanced in place of the common assumption of economistic

Marxism and the *praxis*-philosophical critique, which the Althusser group repudiates.

Marxism's theoretical relocation is then supposed to provide the only legitimate access to the history of the labour movement. The political component of Althusser's programme is to indicate the political and strategic consequences of the theoretical failures of Marxism, and thereby indirectly to make them pertinent to contemporary discussions of strategy. Althusser is convinced that the central theoretical errors of the history of Marxism were always linked to the strategic and organizational mistakes of the labour movement. Thus he judges the interpretations of Marxism which he deems erroneous to be direct indications of political failures. Just as today the abortive theoretical critique of Stalinism points to as yet unresolved strategic problems of the Communist Parties, so Hegelian Marxism's abortive critique of economism betrays a strategically reckless form of politics – namely, one based upon spontaneity.[1] Consequently, the Althusserians, in line with their political self-understanding, attempt to forge a link with orthodox Leninist party politics, one which identifies with neither the right nor the left wings of the labour movement – i.e., one that lies between the political conceptions of social democracy, on the one hand, and soviet democracy, on the other.

Because the political self-conception of the Althusserians is bound up with the critique of the systematic misinterpretation of Marxist theory, it is dependent on the presuppositions of their interpretation of Marxism. In this light I shall confine myself to the theoretical aspect of their self-conception. My interest lies chiefly in the systematic development of the theory of history in *Reading Capital*, within which the Althusser school wants to identify and execute the programme of a structural Marxism on the basis of a structuralist reinterpretation of historical materialism. The theory of history forms the theoretical core, because it provides the reasons for the Althusserian school's bilateral move, distancing itself from traditional Marxism, whilst simultaneously elaborating its new interpretation. My critique pursues the logical argument in the construction of this theory up to the point at which it manifests its latent political function.

I

The extraordinary significance of Althusser's structural reinterpretation of the west European discussion of Marxism principally derives from its main aim, which is to solve the core problems of Marxist theory with the aid of structuralist models of thought. The interpretation of Marxism offered by the Althusser group merges two avenues of thought: an expansion of the domain of structuralist theory and a self-reflection on the part of the tradition of Marxist thought. Notwithstanding frequent attempts to distance structural Marxism from social-scientific structuralism,[2] the two approaches share a basic methodological stance, which stems from the model of structural linguistics. The object-domain of the social sciences is investigated as a system, in terms of deep structures which constitute the relations between empirical manifestations or events. These relations then provide the theoretical focus of interest. Just as the structuralist analysis of language takes its methodological reference points from the distinction between actual linguistic utterances (*parole*) and the linguistic rule system (*langue*), so the structuralism of the social sciences is based on the distinction between the empirical context of events and the deep structure which determines that context.[3] The structural Marxism founded by Althusser, though, gives a bold new gloss to this established notion of method. When he put the structuralist method to the test, Lévi-Strauss was still able to presuppose a collective mind with an invariant structure, and thus managed to reconstruct the rule-systems of archaic kinship relations and mythical world-views. In Foucault the same procedure assumes the form of a retrospective reconstruction of the fundamental rules of epochal forms of knowledge. But Althusser extends the object-domain of structuralism beyond the domain of cultural symbolic media of human sociality (i.e., linguistically structured manifestations); he now imputes the forms of organization of social systems themselves to deep structures.

The second characteristic which structural Marxism shares with social-scientific structuralism is the 'decentering of the subject'. Accordingly, the object domain of the social sciences, whether construed as symbolic forms of knowledge, or material forms of domination, can no longer be understood as the constitutive achievement of an individual transcendental or species-subject. The object domain is now understood to be the rule-system which first constitutes the particular form of subjectivity. The aporias of 'anthropological dogmatism' (Foucault), which would refer the social context to a human centre of action, are to be resolved from the standpoint of a structuralist theory, which conceives the social context as a centreless system of order. This basic theoretical position was originally mobilized in France against the theoretical hubris of the epistemological subject.[4] The original intention was to criticize the phenomenological attempt to treat the whole social nexus as an objectivation, into which the subjectivity of a transcendental consciousness had externalized itself. However, the trenchancy of the structuralist critique is in inverse proportion to its self-confidence. By his critique of Marxist theories of the subject Althusser himself problematically weakens the intention of social-scientific structuralism – namely, to impute the constitution of social formations to centreless structures rather than to a transcendental subject. The 'decentering of the subject' in structural Marxism is levelled not only against Marxist attempts to adapt phenomenological transcendentalism to its own purposes, but is also invoked willy nilly against existential, anthropological and *praxis*-philosophical versions of Marxism. Thus, Althusser reformulates the central questions of Marxism at a deep level, below the threshold at which social processes can still be described as complexes of intentional action.

Finally, structural Marxism adopts the concept of history from social-scientific structuralism, a concept which is supposed to result necessarily from the 'decentering of the subject'. Since structuralism reduces the historical sequence of symbolic forms or hegemonic structures to the sequence of invariant rule-systems, the historical context of which can no longer be guaranteed by the unifying achievements of a subject, the category of history itself must now be understood as the discontinuous, but integrally structured, rule-systems, which merely follow one another. Lévi-Strauss and Godelier have utilized just such a concept of history, purged of all remnants of continuity, to great effect in the field of ethnology, as has Foucault in the field of the history of science. However, in the Marxism of the Althusser school the structuralist concept of history assumes a very particular function.[5] This is due to the claim that the programme of a structuralist interpretation of historical materialism can be made plausible via the critique of all non-structuralist conceptions of history in traditional Marxism. According to its inner foundations, structural Marxism is to be vindicated by criticizing the classical interpretations of Marx, in such a way that the theoretical suggestions offered by the tacitly endorsed structuralist theory of history are made explicitly convincing.

With this project in mind Althusser takes up the dualistic model into which Soviet Marxism had pressed Marx's theory. However, structuralist Marxism does not construct an ontological duality from the distinction between historical and dialectical materialism, unlike Soviet Marxism, which envisages a separate ontological discipline, grounding the materialist theory of history. In the early works of the Althusser school a distinction is made between epistemology, construed as a 'theory of theoretical practice', and a theory of history. Today, the same dichotomy of disciplines is used to distinguish between a philosophy which politically vindicates the basic assumptions of Marxism and the theory of history; the theory of theoretical practice is now conceived as a specific component of the broader discipline of historical materialism.[6] By subscribing to this dichotomy of Marxian theory Althusser and his collaborators seek to overcome weaknesses in the foundations of the traditional concept of historical materialism, with the help of the structuralist concept of history. In their critique of 'historicism' they undertake to demonstrate the convergence of discrepant interpretations of Marxism in a false conception of history.

The category of historicism, which is to play such a decisive role in the structuralist interpretation of historical materialism, is achieved by thinking the structuralist 'decentering of the subject' together with its consequences for the concept of history. The structuralist approach calls into question the use of the concept of continuous history, which requires the presupposition of a unifying subject. In 'historicism . . . the different levels of the totality of a social structure, their relation to one another and their principle of cognition are grounded in an account of their genetic constitution both by a creative subject of society and a linear principle of history, pertaining to the self-development of this subject.'[7] However, as a characterization of the different traditions of Marxism, identified by structuralism, the category of 'historicism' is still unclear. If structural Marxism is to prove itself capable of grasping the specific ideological content of those versions of Marxism it rejects, then it must first provide a clearer conceptual definition of either the notion of 'history', or the notion of 'the subject' which historicism contains. Making this very objection, Poulantzas has emphasized the variety of senses which can be given to the concept of the 'subject' within 'historicism'. 'In the course of the development of Marxist thought the place of the subject has been occupied by the social class *qua* the subject of history, the concrete individual as the species-being of history, and also social labour.'[8] Similarly, the concept of history which 'historicism' employs displays a whole gamut of meanings, from evolutionary models of history, on the one hand, to teleological philosophies of history, on the other.[9]

The flexibility of the concept of 'historicism' seems to be its virtue. By exploiting the variety of its possible meanings, structural Marxism has expanded 'historicism' into a system of ideology-critical sub-predicates. Together these designate interpretations of Marxism which share the historicist prejudice, but differ in their respective conceptions of the subject and of history. Two of the most prominent types of traditional Marxism which Althusser constructs in this way, are 'humanism' and 'economism'. 'Humanism' uses the model of historicism to ground an interpretation of Marxism in which the concept of history is guided in a variety of ways by the idea of human self-creation. Althusser's worries pertain to the obsessive way in which humanist thought conceives history as a continuous self-objectivation of the human species. This crude caricature, into which Althusser presses such divergent theories as phenomenological and Hegelian Marxism, has been formed not so much from the original versions of these interpretations of Marxism, but rather from their existentialist or anthropological reconstructions. In each case, it is drawn from the critique of Stalinism which prevailed in France, and which focused entirely on the early works of Marx.[10] By 'economism' Althusser understands both the Marxism of the Second International and that of Stalinism. In these theories the means of production are conceived of as the central unity through which the forces of production advance the course of history.[11] 'Economism' and 'humanism' – or, to use Althusser's pointedly political formulation, Stalinism and the critique of Stalinism – have a common denominator. They share the theoretical ambition of reducing the complexity of the historical process to either an instrumental or an anthropological centre, so as to interpret the different domains of reality as 'expressions' of this centre. In Stalinism this concept of history legitimates political power as an instrumentally coerced expression of the economic system. In the humanist critique of Stalinism the same concept of history takes the form of an ethically oriented anthropology, which still only understands power relations globally as a manifestation of alienation. Althusser concludes that in both these conceptions of Marxism the specific social form of a transitional socialist society remains unclear.[12]

Now we are in a better position to understand how structural Marxism attempts to educe its own theoretical programme from the critique of historicism. Rather than a centre of history being imputed to historical materialism, there is the structure of a mode of production, within which the (relatively autonomous) social sub-systems assume a rule-governed relation to each other, the rules of which stem from an ultimately determinant economic sub-system. Instead of a temporal continuum of history there are mutually independent temporalities, which in each case are fixed by the particular mode of functioning of the social sub-systems that support them.

Before examining what ensues from these basic assumptions of materialism, I would like briefly to reconstruct the tacit presuppositions of Althusser's conception of 'historicism'.

II

The concept of 'historicism' plays a constitutive role in the vindication of structural Marxism. In the writings of the Althusser school it comes to designate all theoretical positions which recalcitrantly hinder a correct reconstruction of Marxist theory. In his own works Althusser so extends the concept of 'historicism' that it eventually covers the whole tradition of philosophies of history. The label of 'Marxist historicism' is then affixed to all versions of Marxism which, whatever their divergent political and theoretical aims, nonetheless proceed from the assumption, inherited from the philosophy of history, of a self-developing centre of history. The arguments with which the Althusser school tends to substantiate its global suspicions of Marxist historicism are to some extent congruent with West German debates about the crisis in the foundations of the historical sciences. Here, the philosophy of history which is presupposed by the modern concept of history has recently been reconstructed, in order to counter the social-scientific naivety of historicism, by redefining the methodological presuppositions of a theoretically oriented science of history. In this context two theoretically distinct challenges have been made to the categorial implications of the modern conception of history – implications whose

Marxist credentials have likewise been challenged by Althusser. The first challenge comes in the wake of Reinhart Koselleck's conceptual history, which seeks out the socio-historical presuppositions of the category of 'history' in the singular. The second comes from the analytic philosophy of history (Danto), and consists in an epistemological investigation of the way in which continuity is imputed to the modern understanding of history. Arguments of both kinds can also be found in Althusser.

In a series of articles Koselleck has undertaken the task of tracing the modern conception of history back to the experiences in which, during the French Revolution, the historical context of events crystallized into an object of theory. The plural form of the word *Geschichte* (stories/histories) which, up until the outbreak of the French Revolution, referred to historical events as an aggregate of individual histories, is replaced by the collective singular form of the noun *Geschichte* (story/history) in the modern experience of history, because in the course of the revolutionary years the potential for progress and the uniqueness of history became palpable. The category of 'history' which integrates historical events into the context of a process which is in principle alterable, suppresses the category of many 'histories' in which historical events are thought together as self-contained episodes. 'Behind this finding of linguistic history our specifically modern experience begins to make itself heard: movement, alterability, acceleration, openness to the future, revolutionary trends and their astonishing uniqueness, modernity ceaselessly renewing itself – the sum of these temporal experiences of our modern age is covered by the collective singular form of history and the concept thereof.'[13]

This terminological mutation ushers in the theoretical fiction of a substantial unity of action, which guarantees the relations between historical events within a process of history. The basic assumption of bourgeois philosophy of history, which arises with this conceptual alteration, is the adoption of a historical macro-subject (the people, the state, or the species). History can then be understood as the process of the self-development of this macro-subject. Odo Marquard, drawing on Koselleck's conceptual history and on the work of Karl Löwith, has taken issue with this tendency of the philosophy of history, by attacking the various versions of the fictional subject of history.[14] Jürgen Habermas traces the same conceptual alteration analyzed by Koselleck back to the socio-economic constellations in which the modern experience of history is originally rooted. Accordingly, it is not so much the abstract experience of the historical process [*historischer Prozessualität*] that provides the backdrop in front of which history can be philosophically represented as progress, as the capitalist system of production which aims for a perpetual increase in productivity. The experience of progress in the philosophy of history is accompanied by the experience of crisis, induced by the social context of capitalism, in such a way that progress and crisis are the conjoint central categories from which the philosophy of history emerges in the eighteenth century. The world-historical subject then becomes the theoretical quantum by means of which the crisis-ridden flux of history and the progressive autonomy of action can be thought together in a process of emancipation which encompasses all parochial and social indeterminacies.[15] H. J. Sandkühler sees the fiction of the species-subject, by dint of which historical events can be assigned to a common history, as the pressure for legitimation which arises when the bourgeoisie insists that its particular class interests, as opposed to the feudal claim to domination, are the universal interests of the human species. 'The consciousness of "history" in the singular is not, in the final analysis, a result of the dispute between the revolutionary bourgeoisie and the feudal ideology of legitimation, for it is not simply mankind, but rather mankind as the bearer of the mandate of divine rule, which is empowered to make history.'[16]

The Althusser school implicitly endorses considerations of this kind when it tries to show that historicist versions of Marxism rely on patterns of thought which are invariably congruent with the philosophy of history. In his dispute with John Lewis Althusser explains the theoretical presuppositions of the bourgeois philosophy of history as the bourgeoisie's interest in self-legitimation. He claims that in the assumption of a macro-subject in control of history the revolutionary bourgeoisie recasts its own role as that of the rational subject of action. The concomitant concept of history only made sense insofar as 'the revolutionary bourgeoisie was struggling against the feudal regime which was then dominant. To proclaim *at that time*, as the great bourgeois Humanists did, that it is *man* who makes history, was to struggle, *from the bourgeois point of view* (which was then revolutionary), against the religious Thesis of feudal ideology: it is *God* who makes history.'[17] Althusser concludes that, with the break-up of the political constellations of the bourgeois revolution, the theoretical grounds of its conception of history also vanish: namely, the assumption of a universal centre of action, which reduces the complexity of history to a linear temporal development. The unification of history in the positing of an historical macro-subject seems to Althusser to be a legitimate theoretical move, only insofar as the politically progressive (but still partial) interests of the bourgeoisie require the cloak of universalism against the feudal claim to power. From this point of view the historical-materialist versions of the modern concept of history, which presuppose the macro-subject either *qua* class-consciousness (in the philosophy of consciousness), or substantially *qua* the forces of production, can only be regarded as bourgeois relics in the tradition of Marxism. In fact these versions of Marxism share with bourgeois philosophies of history not only the same conception of history, but also the same interest in legitimation.

Althusser attempts to show that 'economism' and 'humanism' share the ideological ambition to locate the politically authoritative unity of action in the centre which they each assign to history. What Althusser means by the 'economism' of the Second International, or of Stalinism, is conceptions of Marxism which try, in a self-legitimizing gambit, to reduce the domain of political action to the progress of the system, which is autonomous with respect to theory and merely instrumental in character. In the 'humanism' of Hegelian Marxism or existentialism Althusser is pointing to conceptions which philosophically mask their political impotence vis-à-vis the organization of the labour movement, with the concept of a class or species-subject in control of history. Althusser contends that 'humanist historicism may, for example, serve as a theoretical warning to intellectuals of bourgeois or petty-bourgeois origin, who ask themselves, sometimes in genuinely tragic terms, whether they really have a right to be members of a history, which is made, as they know or fear, outside them.'[18] Thus far these lines of argument have been pursued no further in structural Marxism. Althusser himself has only briefly sketched his own thoughts on the matter.

H. M. Baumgartner's work can help us to demonstrate the second area in which West German theoretical discussions complement the Althusserian reflections on historicism.[19] Drawing on the work of A. C. Danto, Baumgartner has produced a philosophical reconstruction of the notion of continuity in the philosophy of history. He undertakes an epistemological inspection of the various conceptions of a unified history, in order to make clear the outline of a new historicism. His criticism is levelled at those versions of critical theories of history which seek to overcome the ontological conceptions of continuity in metaphysical history, by exposing them as reifications. He sets out to prove that even the post-Hegelian attempts to think the continuity of history as the unifying achievement of a cognitive subject are tied to the ontological presupposition that history provides an objective context of meaning. Baumgartner argues that it is impossible to construct a systematically representative relation between the multiplicity of historical events and the notion of historical continuity, since the historical language of the object fails in principle to reproduce the whole 'factical' course of history. Therefore the expressions employed by the critical theory of history ought not to be associated with any ontological notions of continuity. However, Baumgartner finds just such associations in concepts like life, development and formation (*Bildungsprozess*) which are used in the tradition of the epistemological philosophy of history.

Baumgartner draws some radical conclusions from his analysis: 'If the continuity of history is neither the tranquil certainty of continual change, nor the task of creating a nexus of events, to be accomplished by intellect, action or self-reflection, then history in general is not to be understood as a process, but only as a phenomenon of consciousness, namely man's mastery of the past with respect to its possible interpretation now and in the future.'[20] Baumgartner no longer values continuity as a feature of the historical object domain itself, but as the mere formal principle of every historical proposition. The unification of historic events to historical continuity according to interests now necessarily belongs to the transcendental structure of narrative formation, within which alone we may experience historical events as 'history'. There is no longer a straight path from this result of Baumgartner's investigations to the critique of historicism in the Althusserian school. However, from his critique of the ontological notion of continuity we can begin to show what theoretical path must be taken by structural Marxism, if it is to redeem its promise to reject objective notions of historical continuity, and at the same time to avoid Baumgartner's transcendental philosophical solution.[21]

Like Baumgartner Althusser criticizes concepts of history which harbour the notion of historical continuity as an ontological presupposition. In some places he traces the historicist versions of Marxism back to the Hegelian conception according to which historical time can be thought as a homogeneous continuum of history. History can be read as the process in which spirit comes to itself in a dialectical self-identification.[22] Althusser rightly sees a characteristic weakness of traditional Marxism in this trope, an insight which holds independently of the material content of his critique of Hegel. The question of the conditions of the theoretical unification of history – a question posed by the disintegration of the idealistic philosophy of history – is dogmatically prejudged by the very fact that history is represented as a process of self-realization. If history can be thought as a process of the internal development of a supra-individual systematic unity or unity of action, to which all historical events may be ascribed, then the self-realizing macro-subject must already be presupposed. This relic of the metaphysics of history has assumed the form of a dehistoricization of the concept of the proletariat in the Hegelian-Marxist tradition. Lukács has taken the category of the proletariat so far beyond any historical and empirical determination that he ultimately depicts the emancipation of the proletariat as the formation (*Bildungsprozess*) of the subject of history. For Lukács the actuality of history in historical materialism can only come to self-knowledge because the proletariat recognizes this actuality as its own creation. The idea of self-knowledge then contains the notion of historical continuity, since it grasps all historic events as objectivations of a single identical subject.[23] In the tradition of the Second International the relic of the metaphysics of history assumes the form of an economistic ideology of history. Here the dialectic between the forces and the relations of production has been so narrowly circumscribed to the role of the instruments of production that historical changes have to be interpreted as causal consequences of the development of production. History is understood in sum as an autonomous progression, the locomotive of which is the unfolding of the techniques of production.[24] The development of productive forces which has shrunk to a mere vector thus purports to provide the meaning of all historical events.

In the cases of Hegelian Marxism and the Marxism of the Second International alike the unity of history is vouchsafed by the process of development of a self-creating subject. Structural Marxism opposes this theoretical presupposition. However, whereas Baumgartner reads the continuity of history merely as a methodological trope, Althusser replaces it himself ontologically with the notion of discontinuity. Althusser goes beyond the structural model of the *Annales* School, which starts from the assumption of objectively overlapping layers of continuity with varying temporal rhythms, by conceiving history as the discontinuous succession of modes of production each with their own time. Althusser even assumes that there are different social strata, each with its own internal temporality, within the confines of these modes of production. History then becomes plural: a complex series of complete, yet internally differentiated, temporalities. 'We can and must say: for each mode of production there is a peculiar time and history, punctuated in a specific way by the development of the productive forces. The relations of production have their peculiar time and history, punctuated in a specific way; the political superstructure has its own history . . . scientific formations have their own time and history, etc. Each of these peculiar histories is punctuated with peculiar rhythms and can only be known on condition that we have defined the concept of the specificity of its historical temporality and its punctuations (continuous development, revolutions, breaks etc.).'[25] The quotation demonstrates how radically structural Marxism departs from the notion of continuity in the philosophy of history. Continuity becomes a possible form of historical time; with respect to the discontinuity of historical development, however, it is secondary. Whilst Baumgartner draws the transcendental philosophical conclusion that continuity is merely the formal principle of historical cognition, the Althusserian school make discontinuity into the objective form of the course of history. Whilst for Baumgartner the collective singular form of history dissolves into a multiplicity of histories, to which we assign historical events from the standpoint of prevailing interests, in structural Marxism the unity of history splits into different histories, composed of their own respective modes of production and sub-systems. Both conceptions are obviously rooted in a single premise: namely, they rule out the possibility that the idea of historical continuity could be vindicated internally to the historical process. Neither Baumgartner's transcendental grounding of historicism, nor the structuralist conception of historical materialism, take into consideration that not one but two histories have to be unified: the history that is only construed as a nexus of continuity by thought, and the history that creates from itself a real nexus of continuity. The continuity of history need not always be presupposed as an ontological nexus of all historical events, but can still be grounded objectively in the social contexts of action, in which historical events are always interpretatively embedded in an historical continuum.

If we start from this theoretical possibility, then the conceptual presuppositions of Baumgartner and Althusser become problematic. The theory of history would then have to contend with an inter-subjectively already constituted object-domain. The process of history would then be neither the chaotic field of events which, according to Baumgartner, is only unified by the construction of narratives, nor the discontinuous succession of rule-systems which, according to Althusser, completely excludes notions of continuity, but rather a binding process that is only disclosed by interaction. Theoretical representations of historical continuity are then materially embedded in the context of a life-world, within which history is collectively appropriated and bequeathed. The representations would refer to communicatively generated interpretations of history, in which social groups and classes have already unified historical events prior to any scientific theories.[26] The idea of a real nexus of world history can then be thought materialistically, insofar as the process of capitalist internationalization amalgamates the space of unifying actions into an equally real global unity. Under these conditions the concept of the subject of history no longer becomes a merely ontological posit, but a normative projection, in which the historically possible integration of all socially and regionally varying unities of action would be thematized in terms of a self-conscious humanity. The 'subject' of historical materialism is not to be understood as a presupposed theoretical quantum, the self-realization of which constitutes history as a whole, but rather as a global unity of action, which results from the process of its self-formation.

This construction cannot be accomplished in structural Marxism, where the concept of the subject of history can only be seen as a necessary result of the philosophy of history, whilst the notion of historical continuity is deemed a mere metaphysical self-delusion. Hence the limitations of 'historicism' are also the limitations of structural Marxism. Whilst it is true that the concept of 'historicism' remains bound up with relics of the Marxist tradition of the philosophy of history, not all conceptions of history can be tarred with the same brush, for certain among them could still provide a new material basis for the old notions of the philosophy of history. According to the assumptions from which the critique of historicism proceeds, it is impossible to distinguish the philosophical idea of the historical macro-subject from the materialist notion of an interactively constituted world society. In both cases Althusser would see only historicism, as if there were no difference between them. The systematic reason for this logical impasse lies in the structural version of historical materialism. Here the object domain of history is conceived along structuralist lines as a deep structure that categorially occludes the inter-subjective process of interpretation in which historical continuity could be anchored. This short-circuit in the critique of historicism is at the same time the index of a conceptually over-simplified reconstruction of historical materialism.

III

Marx understood the unification of many different histories into a single world-history as itself an historical event. In *The German Ideology* world-history is held to be the result of a process whereby local productive communities gear into each other, by dint of their increasing market dependency, and are finally united in the world market as a real complex of relations. 'However far, in the course of this development, the individual circles that act upon each other expand, however much the original self-contained natures of the single nationalities are broken down by the development of the modes of production, circulation and thus the naturally cultivated division of labour between different nations, to this extent history becomes world-history . . . It follows that this metamorphosis of history into world-history is not an abstract accomplishment of self-consciousness, world-spirit or some such metaphysical spectre, but rather a wholly material, empirically demonstrable event, an event the proof of which lies in every individual, in its walking, talking, eating, drinking and even its way of dressing.'[27] The unity of history to which we now refer in the collective singular form is not assumed to be an historical macro-subject, whose development yields the process of history, but is rather a result of the historical concatenation of individual histories. The continuity of the process of history becoming world-history is, strictly speaking, only conceivable in theory if it can find support in a comprehensive historical experience which underlies all particular interpretations of history. Only from this perspective can a notion of history be produced, which would sublate all preceding interpretative systems in the unity of world-historical continuity. With the concept of the proletariat Marx wanted to grasp this universal experience of history, in which the manifold of historical events forms itself into an action-orientated continuity. Unfortunately, he was unable consistently to avoid over-taxing the concept of the proletariat from the standpoint of the philosophy of history. However, Althusser is not even able to pursue this line of Marx's thought, which returns in the mature works, owing to the theoretical presuppositions of his own critique of historicism, wherein the idea of a world-historical continuity can only be understood as a metaphysical fiction of history.

Althusser is forced into dividing the Marxian oeuvre into a pre-scientific phase, which he finds problematic, and a scientifically mature theory. Although constantly revising the dating, Althusser had to distinguish an historicist from a post-historicist stage of Marxian theory. However, historicism is relevant here only in its humanist form. In Althusser's eyes the historicist elements of Marx's argumentation are those which refer the spheres of political and socio-economic phenomena back to an anthropological substrate (either species or labour), in order then to treat them as an alienation of the human essence. Initially, Althusser levelled the objection against this trope of the philosophy of history only with reference to the early works influenced by Feuerbach – in particular, the *Economic and Philosophical Manuscripts*. However, later in his systematic critique of Hegelianism, Althusser pursues Marx's historicism even in the minutiae of the arguments in the mature works.[28] Nonetheless the works of the Althusser school are sustained by the systematic supposition that the idea of a non-historicist theory of history can be derived from the theoretical structure of Marx's *Capital*.

In *Reading Capital* Althusser takes issue with the concept of totality in the tradition of Hegelian Marxism. Whilst in this intellectual tradition all social appearances can be shown to relate concentrically to an historical substrate, structural Marxism thinks the social totality as a decentred unity. If Hegelian Marxism is organized on the model of an 'expressive totality' which orders the different social domains around a centre, understood as essence, so Althusser attempts to derive from Marx's *Capital* a model of social totality which sets out the social sectors in a centreless, yet hierarchically structured, system of relations. In the concept of the 'structural totality' society is conceived as a whole, within which social sub-systems are interrelated in a manner determined by the economic base-system. 'We know that the Marxist whole cannot possibly be confused with the Hegelian whole; it is a whole whose unity, far from being the expressive or "spiritual" unity of Leibniz' or Hegel's whole, is constituted by a certain type of complexity, the unity of a *structured whole* containing what can be called levels or instances which are distinct and "relatively autonomous", and co-exist within this complex structural unity, articulated with one another according to specific determinations, fixed in the last instance by the level or instance of the economy.'[29]

The notion of 'structure' is supposed to supersede the historicist conceptions of historical materialism harboured by the philosophy of history, because it posits the social nexus as a unity, whose elements are not concentric to a middle point, but rather are determined by their mutual positions. From this notion of a 'structural totality' Althusser hopes to derive a Marxist theory of history which presupposes its object to be neither a continuous, nor a subject-centred, nexus of events. According to Althusser, historical materialism is a theory of history which penetrates the course of historical occurrences to the relevant structural totalities beneath – totalities which determine the 'epiphenomena' of which we have only empirical analysis. Hence the attempts in the tradition of Hegelian Marxism to conceive historical materialism as a theoretical system for making sense of anti-capitalist social experience is unsound, precisely because they take theory, in historicist fashion, to be an expression of the historical centre of reality.[30]

By contrast, Althusser wants to understand historical materialism as a theory of structural totalities, which applies throughout history. He finds the basic form of such a structural totality in Marx's category of the 'mode of production'. This notion is the connection between Althusser's reading of *Capital* and a theory of history denuded of any remnant of the philosophy of history. He starts out from the large assumption that in *Capital* Marx had already worked out the deep structures of capitalist systems from a politico-economic point of view, and that the Marxist theory of history can only analyze historical phases of development in general by widening the scope of its social theory. Althusser's version of historical materialism attempts sociologically to enrich and historically to generalize a concept which Marx had already developed in the critique of political economy. 'The object of history as a science has the same kind of theoretical existence and occupies the same theoretical level as the object of political economy of which *Capital* is an example, and the theory of history as a science lies in the fact that the theory of political economy considers one relatively autonomous component of the social totality whereas the theory of history in principle takes the complex totality as such for its object. Other than this difference there can be no distinction between the science of political economy and the science of history, from a theoretical view-point.'[31]

The Marxist critique of political economy provides the model, complete with categories and method, according to which Althusser construes a whole Marxist theory of history. The work of the Althusserian school largely amounts to the attempt to extrapolate a general theory of history from the conceptual framework and the methodological articulation of *Capital*.

In Althusser's estimation the category of practice is the key term with which the concept of the 'mode of production', developed by Marx from his analysis of capitalism, is to be transposed into a concept applicable to history in general. Even in his early essays he takes the category of practice as the basis of historical materialism, by understanding social systems as a relational nexus of practices. Each social sub-system can be thought as a socially stabilized form of practice, such that under the general rubric of 'social practice' Althusser distinguishes between economic, political, ideological and theoretical types of practice. In a social system it is, in the last analysis, always the economic instance – i.e., the institutionally reproduced structure of economic practice – which determines the relevant hegemonic factor. The concept of 'structural causality' maintains the methodological aim not to conceive the influence of the economic base on the superstructure in the manner of historicism, where the latter is directly dependent on the former, but in structuralist fashion, so that the economic base merely delimits the functions of the superstructure. In structural Marxism social systems are taken as hierarchical matrices of relations based on an economic sub-system, within which the non-economic sub-divisions are only determined in terms of the scope of their influence, and not in terms of their internal modes of functioning. The category of 'practice', however, which is to some extent supposed to characterize the substrate of this kind of social system, is no longer used by Althusser in its Marxian sense, as the purposive or goal-oriented activity of one or more acting subjects, but is itself used in a structuralist way to designate an intrinsically subjectless relation of elements in action. On the model of instrumental action all forms of practice should be conceived as structures, in which the agent, the technique and the object of action functionally interlock. 'By practice in general I shall mean any process of *transformation* of a determinate given raw material into a determinate *product*, a transformation effected by a determinate human labour, using determinate means ("of production"). In any practice thus conceived, the *determinant* moment (or element) is neither the raw material nor the product, but the practice in the narrow sense: the moment of the *labour of transformation* itself, which sets to work, in a specific structure, men, means and a technical method of utilising the means. This general definition of practice covers the possibility of particularity: there are different practices which are really distinct, even though they belong organically to the same complex totality.'[32]

Societies should be unstintingly broken down into forms of practice, and 'transformational labour' is the model which globally represents the inner functional nexus of these practice forms. Individual types of practice are not seen as processes of action which are to a certain degree supra-subjective, yet still intentionally articulated; rather, they are read as self-contained systems of rules, which are independent of the subject, and in which a corresponding 'material' is reworked with the help of systematic techniques. Althusser can then grasp the social instances, of which social systems are composed, as sub-systems in which the relevant, historically formed structures of such objective practices are stabilized. Along with the four forms of practice he therefore also distinguishes four social instances: the economic system, the state as hegemonic apparatus, ideology-forming institutions, and the instance of theoretical practice.

Althusser pluralizes the concept of practice in yet another prophylaxis against the historicist concept of history. He distinguishes between several independent forms of practice in order not to have to reduce history to labour, in the sense of a world-constituting life practice. Another singularity of Althusser's concept of practice – namely, its quasi-cybernetic constitution – results from a similar consideration. In order not to have to anchor the social substrate of action in an intentionally acting subject, Althusser grasps social practice *per se* as instrumental action – that is, as the systematic activity of working on an object. However, Althusser only eludes historicism on this point at the cost of an even crasser reduction; if, in historicism, social development can only be thought as the self-objectivation of the species through labour, for Althusser all social dimensions of action are conceived in terms which are tailored to instrumental-objective actions.

Balibar too presupposes this instrumentalist reading of the category of practice, which Althusser explicitly bases upon the notion of labour in *Capital*, when he tries to establish what is in fact the central proof of structural Marxism. In 'The Basic Concepts of Historical Materialism' Balibar argues that the concept of mode of production, which Marx developed in the critique of political economy, already contains the basic conceptual equipment by means of which history as a whole can be reconstructed as a discontinuous succession of social totalities. Balibar claims more explicitly than Althusser that modes of production cannot be completely reduced to the relevant structures of technical actions, but must be seen as the social forms of organization of the labour process: with the category of 'modes of production' Marx reads the economic structure of society as the unity of productive forces and relations of production.

To make this insight into capitalist societies capable of forming the basis of an historically universal theory, Balibar breaks down 'modes of production' into their components. The constitutive elements of all historically conceivable modes of production are: (a) direct producers (labour-power); (b) means of production (objects and instruments of labour); (c) non-labourers (appropriators of surplus labour). Furthermore, Balibar draws a distinction between two systems of relations, in which these three systematic elements are always inter-connected. In the relation of appropriation direct producers, means of production and non-labourers are connected in the transformation of nature; in the property relation the same three instances are connected in the distribution of hegemony. In this way modes of production are differentiated by virtue of the relation that crystallizes in each case between the relevant structure of the forces of production (appropriation relation) and that of the relations of production (property relation). 'By varying the combination of these elements according to the two connexions which are part of the structure of every mode of production, we can therefore reconstitute the various modes of production, i.e. we can set out the presuppositions for theoretical knowledge of them, which are quite simply the concepts of the conditions of their historical existence.'[33]

In order to arrive at a concept of social totality from this concept of the mode of production, as prescribed by the programme of a general theory of history, Balibar begins by construing all other instances of practice according to the same model of the combination of invariant elements. The social sub-systems, like the economic system that Marx encapsulates in the concept of the 'mode of production', are composed of elementary components the function of which is ordered in historically changing structures. '. . . [A]ll levels of social structure . . . are themselves presented in the form of specific complex *combinations* (*Verbindungen*). They therefore imply specific *social relations*, which are no more patterns of the intersubjectivity of the agents, than are the social relations of production, but depend on functions of the process concerned: in this sense I shall be rigorous in speaking of political social relations or *ideological* social relations.'[34] However, these social sub-systems only become integrated in the logical context of a structural social totality if the mode of production is not simply one instance of practice amongst others, but is the socially determinant instance. Then the structures within which the non-economic levels of practice are socially stabilized, are once again subordinate to the economic structure. Althusser deploys the term 'matrix' to refer to this role of the mode of production as the structure of structures; the economic system is thereby represented as the all-encompassing social structure, containing the remaining social instances as its own components. From this point of view the mode of production is no longer merely the self-contained economic system of relations, but the deep structure which regulates all other structures of practice. A displacement in the structure of one mode of production sets in train displacement in the structure of its other instances of practice. In this way we can construct a picture of a social system as an hierarchically constituted system of dependencies, which does not have to treat the dependent sub-systems of a society as mere epiphenomena.

Balibar wants to illustrate this with the example of the history of science. From the perspective of the structural theory of history scientific labour is only of interest insofar as it emerges in the relational network of instances of practice, established by the economic structure. The system of science, which Balibar deems intrinsically autonomous, only becomes theoretically relevant in the function that it assumes, in the confines of a mode of production, for another sub-system. According to Balibar, Marx worked out 'that intellectual production is a branch of production in the economic sense of the term. But it does mean that intellectual production intervenes in the history of the mode of production (in the strict sense) *through its products*, which are susceptible to importation (knowledges). And the analysis of the displacement of elements within the mode of production, which I have reproduced above, alone enables us to explain why and in what form this intervention takes place. This analysis cancels out all the questions that have been posed as to the technological "routine" of the ancient world and the middle ages, since the application of science to production is not determined by the "possibilities" of that science, but by the transformation of the labour process which is an organic part of the combination of a determinate mode of production.'[35] According to this picture, the relation between economic mode of production and social instance of practice can be elucidated in the following general manner. The economic system is taken as the structural template which establishes the functional nexus in which the social instances of practice are co-ordinated. Because the notion of a mode of production not only describes the structure of an economic instance or practice, but also has a say in the functional composition of a social totality, Marx managed to lay the foundations of a Marxist theory of history in *Capital*.

Thus all further basic concepts of historical materialism, which (to begin with) were supposed to grasp the historically unspecific deep structure of history, can be installed as sub-structures or functional quanta in terms of the central category of the 'mode of production'. In this manner Balibar derives both the concept of social 'reproduction' and of 'transition' between modes of production. 'Reproduction' is a reference system that consists of historically invariant elements such as the subsistence level of labour, and the division of production into means of production and means of consumption. The historically specific structure of this reference system is always established by the relevant mode of production, and guarantees the permanence of the social framework of practice in structurally determinate ways. By 'transitional' form between two modes of production Balibar understands a particular type of mode of production in which the economic axis of the productive forces is differently structured from the relations of production. In the fully differentiated capitalist mode of production both the process of production and the system of property divide the labourer from the means of production (Marx terms this 'real subsumption'). However, in the pre-capitalist transitional stage the manufacturing labour process still conjoins the labourer and the means of production, although they are already separated in the manufacturing system of property ('formal subsumption'). Balibar generalizes this scenario into the assumption that in the modes of production of historically transitional stages the structures of production relations and productive forces are always distinctly or 'non-homologously' organized. The disjunction between the structure of production and the structure of property, which arises with the dual determination through former and future modes of production, here puts an end to the capacity of a society to reproduce itself (a capacity which is part and parcel of its structural constitution), and instead frees the individual instances of practice from their dependence on the economic base structure. Only the advent of newly stabilized modes of production will cause the instances of practice to be once more articulated hierarchically with the functional constitution of an economic structure.[36]

By way of this kind of conceptual explanation structural Marxism inflates the categories of Marx's *Capital* into a theory of history, which eventually even conceives individual human beings as functional elements of a mode of production. Rather as Marx, in the notion of the 'character mask', sees acting subjects as mere personifications of economic relations, individuals in the theory of history are supposed to be treated in general as links in supra-subjective chains of practice. Not acting subjects but forms of individuality are now the focus of theoretical interest. Beyond the politico-economic viewpoint of *Capital* these forms of individuality can be distinguished from each other by instances of practice which determine their respective functions. 'We can now say that these "men", in their theoretical status, are not the *concrete men*, the men of whom we are told in famous quotations, no more than that they "make history". For each practice and for each transformation of that practice, they are the different forms of individuality which can be defined on the basis of its combination structure. . . . Men do not appear in the theory except in the form of supports for immanent structural relations and the forms of their individuality only appear as determinate effects of the structure.'[37] As in functionalist role-theory, structural Marxism only ever regards that portion of individual actions which is already subordinated to the claims of social functions. Processes of socialization, which in the structural-functionalism of Parsons are still conceived as mediating processes between the drives and energies of individuals, on the one hand, and the cultural system of norms, on the other, go by the board, in order to avoid the danger of any anthropocentric argumentation entering through the back door of socialization theory. This means, however, that the social integration of the acting subjects into functional supports in this theory becomes simply one system-immanent mechanism amongst others. The structure of society is not reproduced by means of individual personality structures. On the contrary, it subordinates individuals, as structural elements, to the functional hierarchy. The agencies of socialization do not mediate between the claims of the functioning of society and the needs of individuals, but rather reflect the norms of class hegemony straight onto the *tabulae rasae* of personality structures.

Althusser's concept of practice fosters this reductionism, in which acting subjects become deindividualized systemic units, in order that social integration can be treated as systemic integration. Because he deems social contexts of action merely to be systemic labour processes, he can only explain the functioning of the ideological instances of practice – i.e., of the socialization agencies – with the aid of instrumental notions. The agencies of socialization 'work upon' individuals 'by means of ideologies'. With this picture, redolent of theories of manipulation, in his essay 'Ideology and Ideological State Apparatuses' Althusser wants to establish those areas of social reproduction within which individuals are moulded into politically conformist and functionally competent members of the system. The concept of ideological practice here is simply the complement, in social theory, to the idea of the functional 'support' or 'bearer'. In conjunction both notions are supposed to explain the process by which individual actions become functionalized into socially determined forms of behaviour, which Balibar and Althusser term 'forms of individuality'. Even in the notion of an ideological labour of the state individuals are tacitly presupposed as merely passive objects of practice, that can be influenced willy nilly, which is precisely what is meant by the concept of 'functional support'. Both categories underplay the structural-functionalist notion of the 'role', by bracketing out of their analysis the motivational and affective dimensions of personality by means of which hegemonic norms first become socially binding; Parsons, by contrast, acknowledges these dimensions as categories of basic socialization.

Structural Marxism is forced into this conceptual position because it wants to make not only the categorial framework, but also the methodological articulation, of *Capital* into the prototype of a general theory of history. According to Althusser's reading of the scientific structure of Marx's analysis of capital, this prototype of the theory of history requires theoretical abstraction from all individual contexts of action. In their stead the theory of history reconstructs, like the analysis of capital, the non-intentional mechanism of its object, before systematically examining the historical forms of its realization. Just as Marx worked analytically through the historical reality of capitalism to the internal structure of the economic system, so the theory of history aims to capture the 'fundamental forms of historical existence' – that is, the structural totalities specific to the modes of production. From here the theory draws inferences regarding the reality of history:

> It is true that the theory of political economy is worked out and developed by the investigation of a raw material provided in the last resort by the practices of real concrete history; it is true that it can and must be realized in what are called 'concrete' economic analyses, relating to some given conjuncture or given period of a given social formation; and these truths are exactly mirrored in the fact that the theory of history, too, is worked out and developed out by the investigation of raw material, provided by real concrete history and that it too is realized in the 'concrete analysis' of 'concrete situations'.[38]

In order to make the methodological parallel between Marx's analysis of capital and Marx's theory of history clear, Althusser evidently makes use of the Marxist distinction between order of investigation (*Forschung*) and order of exposition (*Darstellung*). With these two categories Marx wanted to distinguish between the processes of scientific investigation and scientific exposition, which would be useful in the formation of the theory of political economy. The concept of the 'order of investigation' is intended to cover the broad procedures of data creation and data evaluation. In Marx's own case these included the treatment of economic statistics, the testing of classical economic theories, and the evaluation of everyday experience. By the concept of 'order of exposition', however, Marx wants to designate the particular form in which scientific presentation does not pursue chronological development, but rather the 'internal logic' of capitalist relations. *Capital* reconstructs the capitalist social totality not by historical stages of the process of capitalization, but by the logically necessary steps of the creation and accumulation of capital.

Now, Althusser's theory of history takes as its methodological prototype precisely the same pattern of reflection with which Marx, in the course of his material social research, infers the 'concrete totality' of capitalism from the relation of capital which is fundamental to society. As with Marx's critique of political economy, Althusser's theory of history is methodologically grounded in material historical investigation and concerned with historiography. The structural theory of history elaborates the historically fundamental modes of production from the material under investigation – modes of production which can be conceptually reproduced according to the 'logic' operative in the articulation of their instances. From this 'logical' plane of analysis the theory rises to the level of historical reality, by gradually encapsulating the historical context of events in the increasingly comprehensive categorial network of social-structural totalities. In this process, however, historical periods can never be completely grasped in theory by reference to the structural totality of a mode of production. Rather, they must be brought into the framework of mutually overlapping modes of production (or social formations). Historical events are only adequately explained when, as Karsz succinctly puts it, their 'social historical functional mechanism' is established.[39]

Over and above the methodological vagueness in which this concept of historical explanation is shrouded, it also reveals a singular consequence of Althusser's argument. If sections of historical reality – in Althusser's terms, 'concrete situations' – can only be grasped in the structuralist theory of history when integrated into the logical context of a social-structural totality, then only the already systemically organized parts of these 'concrete situations' can be grasped by thought at all. This is because in the theoretical reference system of 'modes of production' socio-historical phenomena only ever occur *qua* structural elements or functional quanta. An historical complex of events can only be partially derived by analyzing the scale of its functional mechanisms – namely, as an objective domain of events; however, the historical and factual exploitation of leeway in the system takes place within interactive contexts of action, which Althusser's theory must ignore. Because, with the analytic framework of the structurally unified theory of history, the historical process takes as its model only the reproduction of a social-structural totality, this theory of history is not able to thematize the communicative process of interpretation through which the system-process becomes relevant to action and thereby creates situations in the first instance. Due to this conceptual shortcoming, the historical reality which Althusser's theory of history is in a position to grasp remains an impoverished reality; in this theory historical reality exists only as a functionally hierarchized history of a system, not also as a collectively experienced history of actions.

Althusser and his students seem not to be aware of this analytic obstacle to their theory of history. They begin from the assumption that the categorial framework of the universal theory of history already contains all the concepts needed to describe the real process of history in Marxist fashion, as a nexus of events. Under this presupposition a materialist version of history is a mere application of the structural theory of history. Althusser's reference to the 'concrete analysis of concrete situations' towards which the theory of history is supposed to be heading, bespeaks the same methodological self-understanding. Clearer still are Althusser's claims to be able to infer seamlessly from the level of abstraction of the general theory of social-structural totalities to the empirical history of events. These are made explicit in a demand that Althusser makes upon his own version of Marxism. 'Marxism cannot claim to be the theory of history, unless, *even in its theory*, it can think the conditions of its penetration into history, into all strata of society, even into men's everyday lives.'[40] This sentence reproduces a classical claim of Marxist theory. Historical materialism must be able to determine the social-structural presuppositions and historical domains of action within which it has a good chance of being translated into a politically effective programme of action. Only when theory has been informed as to the emancipatory content of collective repositories of needs and orientations of interests can it hope to deduce orientations of practice adequate to the situations of social groups.

However, Althusser seems not to notice that his own structural theory of history, in its dispute with historicism, conceives historical development merely as a structural displacement of functional mechanisms, and therefore expressly abstracts from situations of communicative action. But how is the theory of history supposed to be able to inform itself about social learning processes, from which it could draw political strength, when dealing with specific historical situations, when it has already decided that it has to abstain from this historical context of interaction? The structural theory of history has purified its basic concepts so thoroughly of determinations of social action that not even retrospectively – *qua* historiography – can it understand individual historical occurrences in the interactive network of social struggle and collective processes of agreement. Hence in the ambit of its own analytic framework the structurally re-interpreted historical materialism is indeed able, with increasing precision, to confine the historical domain of events to the functional limitations of social sub-sectors. In other words, it can describe an historical period as an epoch of structurally enabled possibilities of action. However, the social realization (or rather non-realization) of the objective logic of reproduction is not theoretically accessible.

Pierre Vilar has difficulties such as this in mind when he questions the theory of history advocated by the Althusserian school as to its potential for practical investigation. For how can a materialist historiography which concentrates on '*this* country, *this* time, *or this* conflict' be theoretically focused by means of basic structural concepts, when these basic concepts cannot be transposed onto an historical context of events?[41] Urs Jaeggi reaches a similar conclusion: he attacks the categorial exclusion of the 'class struggle' in structural Marxism's theory of history.[42] In the opinion of these two authors the structuralist reformulation of historical materialism reaches its limits where a materialist analysis of a particular historical reality begins. Both authors nonetheless still hold the structural theory of history to be superior to alternative approaches and think that it would be relatively easy to extricate it from the difficulties that seem to beset its analysis, by simply extending its categories. For this reason the systematic limitations of Althusser's reading of Marxism remain hidden in their appraisal of his theory. In contrast I hope to show, by way of conclusion, that structural Marxism only succeeds in reinterpreting historical materialism by means of the methodologically unsound move of making Marx's analysis of capital into the prototype of a general theory of history.

IV

Althusser and his students have taken the critique of historicism to the point at which their programme of structurally re-interpreting historical materialism comes clearly into focus. The structural concept of history is supposed to suppress the received ideas that have been so influential within the history of Marxism, and which imply that historical reality is the result of a collective human or technological progress of creation. Whilst these historical conceptions depend upon the assumption of a history-constituting subject, Althusser seeks to gain access to the historical totality in a wholly different way, not via the philosophy of history. To this end his structuralist premises play the role of fundamental assumptions with which historical processes can be understood as supra-individual acts of reproduction. If 'modes of production', which Marx investigates with the example of capitalism, can be understood structurally, as systems of rules, then every historical process of development can be conceived as a succession of internally regulated processes of reproduction. In this manner Althusser can convert the whole of history into an object of theory, which does not have to make the complementary presuppositions of an historical macro-subject and the continuity of all historical occurrences. In this theory history is only accessible in the various histories in which operative modes of production structurally reproduce themselves. However, the limits of this programme of the theory of history are only really visible against the backdrop of Althusser's theoretical self-understanding. Both the critique of historicism and the carefully constructed theory of history promise more than they deliver.

The critique of historicism blurs the difference between a continuity of history which is simply presupposed as an appendage of the philosophy of history, and a continuity which has been reconstructed from material history, by imputing to both the same basic notion of the subject. Althusser makes no distinction between a Marxism which only speaks of a unified history with respect to the real historical unification of all particular readings of history, and a Marxism which already presupposes this unity in the guise of a unified centre of all historical occurrences. In both cases Althusser attacks the notion that all historical processes are centred around a macro-subject, although it is only in the latter case that the unification can be imputed either to a collective subject of action or to a technological substrate of history; whilst the former conception of history orientates itself around the historical relations of inter-subjectivity. But then, in the former case, the critique of historicism is useless, for history is no longer thought as the product of a history-constituting macro-subject, in analogy to a world-constituting epistemological subject. Althusser makes no effort to distinguish between a conception of the subject that is over-burdened by the philosophy of history and a conception of historical inter-subjectivity; he is therefore forced to leap from the critique of a Marxism which is grounded in the philosophy of history to the concept of a supra-individual systemic history, without even becoming aware of the function of interactive contexts of action in realizing history. However, he pays the price for the false critique of historicism in his exposition of the theory of history.

The structural theory of history attempts to explain an historically concrete nexus of events simply by reconstructing the functional logic of the social-structural totality. It is interested solely in the supra-individual systemic nexus so as to avoid completely the danger of dissolving the social process of reproduction into inter-personal actions. Furthermore, it is interested only in the structure of this systemic nexus in order to exclude theoretically the historical centering of history in a history-constituting subject. However, Althusser can only identify the actual course of history by its structural possibilities and cannot provide a concrete material explanation of events as historical realities. Althusser's theory of history fails to consider that the structurally construed functional tendencies of social systems are only translated into real historical occurrences through the interactive historical practices of subjects of action, which is precisely what his approach categorically excludes. The social framework of instances does not isolate individual actions *per se*, but only in the form of their social interpretation, in order that the historical 'surface of events' can then be composed from these actions. For by methodologically isolating social functions from the interactive relations in which they are realized as situations, the structuralist theory of history encounters similar analytical limitations to structuralist linguistics, with its division of linguistic rule-systems from the practical context of spoken language.

Since the systematic conception of the structural theory of history cannot be derived solely from the critique of historicism, Althusser is forced to call upon the scientific model of Marx's analysis of capital in order to make it intelligible. The general theory of history is scientifically established insofar as it is a fruitful generalization of the methodological and categorial framework of *Capital*. Only this prior structuralist reading of the critique of political economy enables Althusser to transpose the basic tenets of structuralism onto a Marxist theory of history. This is because in Althusser's view the analytic framework of the analysis of capital is tailored wholly to the supra-individual functional mechanism of the capitalist process of reproduction, and by virtue of this narrowness of analytic focus the theory of history manages to mesh with the structuralist conception of the event-constituting system of rules. Moreover, it is only because, in Althusser's view, the categorial framework of Marx's analysis of capital is tailored to the elementary components of the capitalist process of reproduction, that the theory of history is supposed to be able to confine itself categorially to the structural elements of the mode of production. The vindication of the structuralist unification of historical materialism then hangs on a very tenuous thread of argument. Althusser makes the theoretical claims of his theory of history depend solely on the contention that Marx, in the critique of political economy, also worked out the general framework from which a theory of historical totality could be extrapolated. In this contention, though, Althusser and his collaborators subscribe to a crass misunderstanding of Marx's own claims for his analysis in *Capital*. One does not need a highly nuanced critique of the structuralist reading of *Capital*, but only the most cursory glance at the fundamental structure of the analysis of capital, to show that Marx made his conception of method and the categorial formation of his theory depend unequivocally on the historically specific structure of the capital relation. *Capital* is so closely interwoven with the socio-historical presuppositions of its object of enquiry, that it can only be made into a general theory of history by over-simplifying its analysis.

Recently, several different attempts to clear up the method of the analysis of *Capital* have been able to throw light upon the historical content of Marxian theory.[43] In direct confrontation with Althusser's reading of *Capital* these works focus their interest on the theoretical presuppositions under which Marx harnesses the structure of Hegel's *Logic* for a systematic critique of capitalism. They follow a line of questioning which has been well known since Lenin's reference to the exemplary status of Hegel's *Logic*, but has never been given a detailed and explicit treatment. I shall make do at this juncture with a brief sketch of the results of these interpretations, insofar as the different accounts find points of agreement. They concur in the contention that, although Marx distances himself from Hegel in his early works, with his critique of idealism, he nonetheless gravitates back towards

Hegel's systematic form of reflection in the economic theory of the late work.

The Marx of the *Economic and Philosophical Manuscripts* thinks Hegel's *Phenomenology* as an anthropological and epistemological insight into the universal-historical significance of human labour. Against Hegel Marx emphasizes the left-Hegelian motif of the facticity of human subjectivity, which evaporates under the presuppositions of identity philosophy to a moment of the self-developing spirit. At this stage Marx holds the theory of capitalism to be a theory of the self-alienation of labour through private property. The Marx of *Capital*, however, seeks a quite different methodological access to the critique of capitalism. He no longer describes capitalist social relations from the immediate standpoint of human subjectivity as a relation of alienation, but rather immanently follows the capitalist suppression of subjectivity. Marx takes the real historical autonomy of the capitalist process of valorization as the point of departure for the analysis of capital, by making the self-valorization of value into the subject of theory. Because Marx sees the 'structural identity' (*Reichelt*) of capital through the lens of Hegelian 'Spirit', he is able to make systematic use of the structure of argument in the *Logic*. The process of the unfolding of capital can be expounded in the dialectical figures of thought of the self-knowing Spirit. Marx thus abstracts, along with Hegel, from all human subjectivity in order to be able to harness the latter's dialectical logic as a model method for the analysis of capital, suited to the real abstraction of capitalism. However, as a critique of capitalism this method remains embedded in the anthropologically grounded theories of the early work, from which perspective the subject of capital can be shown to be an illusory subject that is grounded in human labour.

These sketches alone suffice to demonstrate the consequences of such interpretation for Althusser's theory of history; for if the critique of political economy systematically grasps only the process in which capital subsumes living social relations, then the historical reality which is investigated in this critique can also only be the social nexus which has been oppressed and deformed by capitalism. The price of the form of exposition borrowed from Hegel's *Logic* is an attenuated picture of reality. 'The fully fledged critique of political economy does not aim to expound the historical phenomenon of capitalism, but first and foremost the "general concept of capital". Thereby history, insofar as it amounts to more than the documentation of social struggles, can only be thematized from standpoints covered by this concept. History steps into the purview of theory exclusively as the ground upon which the general concept of capital is realized.'[44] Structural Marxism ignores precisely this methodological limitation of historical reality in *Capital*: instead it blithely generalizes the methodological and categorial basis of the analysis of capital into a theory of history, whereas Marx took it exclusively as a scientific attempt at the exposition of capitalism.

In the critique of political economy Marx abstracts from social relations of interaction, because he wishes theoretically to expound only those domains of reality which have already been subsumed by the capitalist process of valorization. He denotes acting subjects with the category of 'character masks' because, in terms of the methodological analysis of the framework of capital, he is only interested in the functions of individuals which are relevant to valorization. Moreover, he largely reduces the social context of action to instrumental or instrumentalized social relations, because in the process of capital accumulation only these reduced forms of action could be relevant. However, this conceptual move only makes sense owing to the methodological presupposition of the analysis of capital and does not suffice for either an explanation of the reality of history under capitalism, or an analysis of other social formations. Marx is fully aware of this; his historical and political works, and his remarks about pre-capitalist societies, change their basic conceptual framework according to their theoretical perspective. By contrast, Althusser believes that he can transpose the analysis of capital back onto the theory of history, without taking this deliberate methodological reduction into consideration, through a categorial consideration of communicative processes of action. Only in this way can he generalize from the concept of the 'character mask' to that of the 'form of individuality', and from the concept of 'abstract labour' to that of the 'form of practice', in order that modes of production as a whole can be conceived as functional logical systemic unities.

Because Althusser and his collaborators wrench the analysis of capital apart from the unique historical context in which it is theoretically located, they can only perceive the whole of historical reality as a process of reproduction, independent of the relations of interaction. Although Marx describes historical reality in the same terms, for him this is only a description of social relations under conditions of capitalism. The tacit transformation of the restricted historical perspective of the critique of political economy into the whole truth of a Marxist concept of history allows the Althusserian school to reconstruct historical materialism on the basis of structuralist theory. For only on the assumption that the historical reality which is theoretically conceived in *Capital*, is in fact coextensive with the whole of scientifically accessible history, can the historical object of investigation be so utterly divorced from relations of interaction that it can ultimately be understood on the structuralist model as a theory of social rules of determination. Such a theory has to occlude the communicative dimensions of action, which constitute a social framework of relations as historical reality in the first place, because it mistakes Marx's abstraction from the history-forming context of action as an historically neutral theoretical strategy.

Such a crass misunderstanding ultimately entails practical-political consequences. The theory of history which the Althusserian school develops by the methodological dehistoricization of Marx's analysis of capital attenuates the concept of socialist *praxis* along with the concept of historical reality. Because Althusser's historical materialism conceives the capitalist process of history only as a reproduction of the social-structural formation, not as the experiential process of social groups and classes, it cannot even forge a political link with the self-interpretation of social revolutionary movements. This is why Althusser is politically tied to Lenin's conception of the party. In place of a theoretical relation to the consciousness and interests of of the class movement steps the party, as a surrogate for class consciousness. The political acts of the party with respect to social movements are instrumental, just like Althusser's representation of systematic practice in general.

NOTES

I would like to thank my friends Hans Joas and Rainer Paris for their advice and comments.

1 Of course, this picture of the history of Marxism is challenged by the attempt of the early Lukács to combine the Hegelian critique of the objectivism of the Second International with the philosophical legitimation of Leninist politics.
2 Cf., in particular, Louis Althusser, 'Elements of Self-Criticism', in his *Essays in Self-Criticism*, New Left Books, London, 1976, chapter 3, and Saül Karsz, *Théorie et politique: Louis Althusser*, Fayard, Paris, 1974, chapter 6.
3 See Jean Piaget, *Structuralism*, Routledge and Kegan Paul, London, 1971 and François Wahl, ed., *Qu'est-ce que le structuralisme*?, Editions du Seuil, Paris, 1968.
4 Georges Canguilhem, 'Mort de l'homme ou épuisement du cogito?', *Critique* 242, 1967. Pierre Bourdieu and Jean-Claude Passeron have expounded the theoretical development of the French social sciences since 1945 as a dispute with subject-centred tropes of thought: 'Sociology and Philosophy in France since 1945: Death and Resurrection of a Philosophy without a Subject', *Social Research* 34, 1967.
5 Compare Claude Lévi-Strauss, *The Savage Mind*, Weidenfeld and Nicolson, London, 1972, chapter 9 ('History and Dialectic'); Maurice Godelier, 'Le concept de tribu. Crise d'un concept ou crise des fondements empiriques de l'anthropologie', in his *Horizon, trajets marxistes en anthropologie*, vol. I, François Maspero, Paris, 1977; Michel Foucault, Introduction to *Archaeology of Knowledge*, Tavistock, London, 1972; Louis Althusser and Etienne Balibar, *Reading Capital*, New Left Books, London, 1970, pp. 119–44.
6 For the early conception of the difference between historical and dialectical materialism in Althusser, see 'On the Materialist Dialectic' in his *For Marx*, Allen Lane, London, 1969, p. 161, and *Reading Capital*, p. 182. On the new conception of the difference, see 'Elements of Self-Criticism', chapter 2.
7 Nicos Poulantzas, 'Theorie und Geschichte. Kurze Bemerkung über den Gegenstand des "Kapitals" ', in W. Euchner and A. Schmidt, eds, *Kritik der*

politischen Ökonomie heute. 100 Jahre 'Kapital', Frankfurt/M., 1968, pp. 58–59.

8 Ibid., p. 60.

9 Here structural Marxism remains very vague in its categories; for the most part the differences between a social-scientific concept of evolution and the concept of 'teleology' in the philosophy of history are blurred; see *Reading Capital*, p. 120.

10 See the very early review article by I. Fetscher, 'Der Marxismus im Spiegel der franzöischen Philosophie', in *Marxismus Studien*, Tübingen, 1954. And cf. Mark Poster, *Existential Marxism in Postwar France: From Sartre to Althusser*, Princeton University Press, Princeton, 1975. On Althusser's concept of 'humanism', see 'Marxism and Humanism', in *For Marx; Reading Capital*, pp. 119ff.; 'Reply to John Lewis', in *Essays in Self-Criticism*; and 'Marx's Relation to Hegel', in Althusser, *Politics and History: Montesquieu, Rousseau, Hegel and Marx*, New Left Books, London, 1972.

11 On the economism of the Second International see Lucio Colletti, 'Bernstein and the Marxism of the Second International', in his *From Rousseau to Lenin*, New Left Books, London, 1972. For Althusser's concept of 'economism', see *Reading Capital*, pp. 138ff., and 'Note on "The Critique of the Personality Cult" ', in *Essays in Self-Criticism*.

12 'Note on "The Critique of the Personality Cult"', *passim*. For a critique of this conception, which completely divorces Stalinism, theoretically and politically, from Leninism, see Valentino Gerratana, 'Althusser and Stalinism', *New Left Review* 101/102, January/April 1977.

13 Reinhart Koselleck, 'Wozu noch Historie?', in H. M. Baumgartner and J. Rüsen, *Seminar: Geschichte und Theorie*, Frankfurt/M., 1976, pp. 17, 23. See the same author's 'Historia Magistra Vitae', in *Natur und Geschichte: Festschrift für Karl Löwith*, Stuttgart, 1969.

14 See O. Marquard, *Schwierigkeiten mit der Geschichtsphilosophie*, Frankfurt/M., 1973, especially pp. 66ff.; Karl Löwith, *Weltgeschichte und Heilsgeschehen*, Stuttgart, 1953.

15 Jürgen Habermas, 'Über das Subjekt der Geschichte', in his *Kultur und Kritik*, Frankfurt/M., 1973.

16 H. J. Sandkühler, 'Zur Spezifik des Geschichtsbewusstseins in der bürgerlichen Gesellschaft', in R. Koselleck and W. Stempel, eds, *Geschichte: Ereignis und Erzählung*, München, 1973.

17 'Reply to John Lewis', p. 46 n. 9.

18 *Reading Capital*, p. 142.

19 H. M. Baumgartner, *Kontinuität und Geschichte*, Frankfurt/M., 1972.

20 Ibid., p. 253.

21 However, Althusser's early works were so epistemologically vague that some of his finest critics thought they had discovered arguments stemming from Kant: see André Glucksmann, 'A Ventriloquist Structuralism', *New Left Review* 72, March/April 1972. Since then Althusser has clarified his epistemology in such a way as to dispel such worries (cf. 'Is it Simple to be a Marxist in Philosophy?', in *Essays in Self-Criticism*).

22 *Reading Capital*, pp. 93–95.

23 Georg Lukács, 'Reification and the Consciousness of the Proletariat', in his *History and Class Consciousness*, Merlin, London, 1971.
24 Cf. Nikolai Bukharin, *Historical Materialism* (1922), Ann Arbor Press, Michigan, 1969.
25 *Reading Capital*, p. 99.
26 See Habermas' objections to Baumgartner's transcendental narrativism in 'Geschichte und Evolution', in his *Zur Rekonstruktion des Historischen Materialismus*, Frankfurt/M., 1976.
27 Marx and Engels, *Werke*, volume 3, p. 45.
28 On the distinction between the 'humanist' and 'scientific' parts of Marxian theory, see Jacques Rancière, 'The Concept of "Critique" and the "Critique of Political Economy"' (1965), in Ali Rattansi, ed., *Ideology, Method and Marx*, Routledge, London, 1989. On the dating and re-dating of the 'epistemological break' in Marx's oeuvre, see Althusser, 'Preface to *Capital* Volume One', in his *Lenin and Philosophy and Other Essays*, New Left Books, London, 1971.
29 *Reading Capital*, p. 97.
30 See Alex Callinicos' Althusser-oriented critique of Hegelian Marxism in *Althusser's Marxism*, Pluto Press, London, 1976, pp. 10ff.
31 *Reading Capital*, p. 109.
32 *For Marx*, p. 166.
33 *Reading Capital*, p. 216.
34 Ibid., p. 220.
35 Ibid., p. 250.
36 Ibid., pp. 309ff.
37 Ibid., p. 300; see also pp. 112ff.
38 Ibid., pp. 109–10.
39 *Théorie et politique*, p. 171.
40 *Reading Capital*, p. 128.
41 Pierre Vilar, 'Marxist History, A History in the Making', reprinted as chapter 2 of this volume (here p. 39).
42 See Urs Jaeggi, *Theoretische Praxis: Probleme ines strukturalen Marxismus*, Frankfurt/M., 1976, pp. 93ff.
43 I am referring especially to the works of H. Reichelt, *Zur logischen Struktur des Kapitalbegriffs bei Karl Marx*, Frankfurt/M., 1970; M. Theunissen, 'Krise de Macht: Thesen zur Theorie des dialektischen Widerspruchs', in W. R. Beyer, ed., *Hegel-Jahrbuch 1974*, Köln, 1975; and R. Bubner, 'Logik und Kapital. Zur Methode einer "Kritik der politischen Ökonomie"', in his *Dialektik und Wissenschaft*, Frankfurt/M., 1973. All these works are inspired by the seminal essay of H. J. Krahl, 'Zur Wesenslogik der Marxschen Warenanalyse', in his *Konstitution und Klassenkampf*, Frankfurt/M., 1971.
44 Theunissen, 'Krise der Macht', p. 325.

5

ALTHUSSER, STRUCTURALISM, AND THE FRENCH EPISTEMOLOGICAL TRADITION

Peter Dews

The central theme of philosophical debate in France in the immediate post-war period – the problem of the relation between the individual subject and the overarching structures of history – may be seen as the product of conflicting moral and theoretical imperatives. Both Sartre and Merleau-Ponty, deeply influenced by the general interpretation of history offered by Marxism, became dissatisfied with the unconditional status accorded to consciousness in the phenomenological tradition, and increasingly attempted to account for the embeddedness of consciousness in a social and historical world with its own immanent laws. Yet neither thinker could entirely abandon the starting-point of the perceiving and acting subject inherited from phenomenology, for within their frame of reference, to do so could only mean surrender to the objectivism and determinism represented by the codified Marxism of the French Communist Party. Sartre's solution, exhaustively developed in the *Critique of Dialectical Reason*, was to place the individual subject – no longer primarily a subject of thought and perception, but of *praxis* – within the complex and perpetually shifting structures of group, party and class, in an attempt to show how the original freedom and lucidity of *praxis* could be transformed into the inexorability and opacity of the social and historical world. Yet, despite the ingenuity of its elaboration, Sartre's position remained open to the objection, first voiced by Merleau-Ponty in *The Adventures of the Dialectic*, that history cannot be seen as neatly divided between the transparency of wills and the opacity of things, but is rather composed of an 'interworld' of significations which are neither entirely subjective nor entirely objective. More broadly, Sartre shows a remarkable innocence in his use of a vocabulary of dualities – subject and object, interiority and exteriority, necessity and freedom – inherited from the western metaphysical tradition. By contrast, Merleau-

Ponty's last work is reticent, tentative, oriented towards a domain in which subjectivity is so bound up with an inherited world of meaning – of which the pre-eminent bearer is language – that any strict separation between the two becomes impossible. The very categories of the philosophical tradition are to be revealed in their inadequacy when confronted with the primary experience of what Merleau-Ponty terms *l'être vertical* or *l'être sauvage*.

At the start of the 1960s, however, these lines of enquiry were temporarily to be cut short. Sartre's concern with the process in which 'Structures are created by an activity which has no structure, but suffers its results as a structure',[1] with the way in which an original freedom can turn against itself and become its own prison, was to remain neglected until over a decade later, when Deleuze and Guattari's *Anti-Oedipus* would revive the same paradoxes in the new vocabulary of 'desire'. And Merleau-Ponty's attempts to circumvent the illusions generated by the very language of philosophy would not find their continuation until the emergence of Jacques Derrida's project of deconstruction. For a time the centre of the philosophical stage remained unoccupied, as attention was displaced towards the 'human sciences' – particularly the anthropology of Lévi-Strauss – and the renaissance which they appeared to be enjoying under the impact of methods imported from the field of structural linguistics. Lévi-Strauss himself tended towards the view that philosophy can only be a premature and speculative attempt to deal with problems whose real solution must depend upon an extension of the domain of science, and this was a view which gained credence in some quarters. Certainly there was a widespread feeling that the field of philosophical thought was undergoing a fragmentation, and that the totalizing ambitions of 'metaphysics' (a term implicitly equated with 'Sartrianism') now stood in the way of a scientific knowledge of human beings and their social practices. The evident incompatibility between the premises of Lévi-Strauss' apparently rigorous and successful explanations – an abstraction from all considerations of genesis and development, and a view of human activity as entirely determined by social structure – and the central concerns of the philosophy of the 1950s reinforced the plausibility of this assumption. The advent of structuralism was experienced both as a 'crisis of the subject' and as a 'crisis of history'.[2]

However, this crisis cannot simply be attributed to a temporary enthusiasm for a particular blend of positivism and rationalism among sections of the French intelligentsia. The Hegelian and existentialist assumptions which had been central to French philosophy since Kojève's influential lectures in the 1930s were long overdue for reconsideration, and Lévi-Strauss' characteristic amalgam of sound argument and sophistry – particularly as exemplified by the set-piece battle with Sartre which concludes *The Savage Mind* – successfully identified the vulnerable points in the philosophical architecture of the *Critique*. For Sartre the fundamental narrative of human history is defined by the notion of a loss and recovery of freedom. Despite their apparent hopelessness, the 'counterfinalities and infernal circularities' which characterize the field of the practico-inert represent the only means by which humankind can advance towards a new, non-antagonistic form of reciprocity, the attainment of which will mark the end of historicity as we understand it. History thus recounts the consequences of a fall from a state of original innocence – free individual *praxis* – which can only be recovered on a collective level at the 'end of time'. However, since for Sartre 'scarcity' is present at the beginning of history and constitutes one of its preconditions (although it is not a sufficient condition), and since human history is 'born and developed within the permanent framework of a field of tension produced by scarcity',[3] the original freedom of *praxis* can only be mythical: it cannot be equated with the stasis of actually existing 'primitive' societies. Such societies do in fact have a history behind them, but have reached a state in which scarcity is no longer a source of destabilization and development, but is lived as an equilibrium, as a 'practical project of keeping institutions and physical corporate development at the same level'.[4] Yet the members of such societies do not thereby evade the miseries of the historical process, rather they are condemned 'to work from dawn till dusk with *these* (primitive) technical means, on a thankless, threatening earth'.[5] Since, for Sartre, it is only within history that the true potential of humanity can be realized, what he terms 'societies of repetition' must remain trapped in an endless cycle of deprivation, abandoned on the margins of time.

Lévi-Strauss finds this vision of history, and of humankind's status within it, scientifically unacceptable and morally abhorrent. Above all, his objections are centred on the vision of history as a process of convergence towards a single universal ideal, for such a vision reduces past societies and cultures to a series of hierarchically ordered stepping-stones on the path to a true humanity. Against this Lévi-Strauss argues that past and 'primitive' societies cannot be seen as forms of alienation in which human capacities are confined and distorted: 'Man does not realize his nature in an abstract humanity, but in traditional cultures whose most revolutionary changes still retain whole sections and are themselves explained as a function of a situation strictly defined in time and space.'[6] In part Lévi-Strauss' resistance to any evolutionary ranking of humanity is based on the standard philosophical argument that any criterion for the comparative evaluation of cultures must itself be the product of a particular culture. But in relation to this question, as to a number of others, it is possible to detect in Lévi-Strauss' work a tendency to substitute for explicit philosophical argument the statement of an ostensibly 'scientific' position. Thus Lévi-Strauss' relativism at the level of culture can be seen as dependent on his theory of the relation between mind and society, which is itself rooted in a materialist ontology. For if all social and cultural forms are simply permutations and projections of certain innate characteristics of the human mind (perhaps even of a pattern of binary oppositions physically coded in the brain), then all must be seen as equal – and by implication equally valuable – 'realizations' of human potential. Correspondingly, the transition from one social or cultural form to another cannot itself be seen as an expression of human capacities in this sense. Historical change must be consigned to a region where, as Lévi-Strauss' metaphors – the throw of the dice, the turning of a kaleidoscope – emphasize, contingency and accident reign. Thus Lévi-Strauss' view dispossesses human *praxis* of what is for Sartre its defining characteristic: an ability to realize a communal project in transcending a pre-given situation. Since, for Lévi-Strauss, human action is uniquely determined by social structure, it cannot be the source of the transition from one structure to another. Time ceases to be the privileged dimension of human self-realization, and Sartre's Hegelian-Marxist myth of history is exposed as 'the last refuge of a transcendental humanism'.[7]

This critique of the Sartrian vision of history is clearly premissed on an account of the status of social-scientific knowledge which differs radically from that of Sartre. The *Critique of Dialectical Reason* must be placed within the post-Kantian hermeneutic tradition, a tradition which affirms that the kind of systematic knowledge appropriate to human action must be based on a form of 'understanding', rather than the kind of causal explanations employed in the natural sciences. This is because, unlike events in nature, actions cannot even be correctly identified without taking account of the intentions and interpretations of agents. In the classic form elaborated by Dilthey, understanding involves a 're-experiencing' (*Nacherlebnis*) in which the thought-processes of the agent are imaginatively recreated; the capacity of the historian to interpret the traces of the past is directly attributable to his or her own breadth of experience and receptivity. In Sartre's version of this principle the participatory aspect of understanding is pushed to an extreme in which it is the individual who 'makes' history who is also the ideal interpreter of history. '*Comprehension*', states Sartre, 'is simply the translucidity of *praxis* to itself, whether it produces its own elucidation in constituting itself, or recognizes itself in the *praxis* of the other.'[8] The assumption of the *Critique* is that an implicit interpretation of the entirety of history can be gathered up into the immediacy of the moment of free action.

For Lévi-Strauss, however, any philosophy which attempts to found knowledge in the immediate experience of *praxis* is condemned to remain within a circle of illusion. The experience of *praxis* cannot be considered as common to all human beings in all times, and therefore as the initial bridgehead of understanding, since such experience is determined by 'unconscious' categorial structures which are specific to a particular culture. Thus Lévi-Strauss' remark that 'Descartes believes that he proceeds directly from a man's interiority to the exteriority of the world, without seeing that societies, civilizations – in other words worlds of men – place themselves between these two extremes',[9] equally expresses his attitude to Sartre. The fundamental error of the phenomenological approach to human action is that it reads experience within a particular society as universal human experience; it strives to attain a 'general interiority', whereas there are only the 'interiorities' of specific cultures. For Lévi-Strauss 'understanding' must consist in total participation – in which case the social scientist ceases to be an 'interpreter' – or it cannot take place at all. In contrast to Sartre's view of the original lucidity of *praxis*, he considers that 'a conscious being aware of itself as such poses a problem to which it provides no soultion.'[10] However, there does exist a solution, which consists in considering human action as governed by an unconscious system of social rules comparable to the rules of a grammar. To isolate this system of rules requires a deliberate break both with the immediate experience of the members of the society under investigation, and with the assumptions which the enquirer brings from his or her own culture. Thus, although Lévi-Strauss rejects the possibility of a 'general interiority', he does accept what could be termed a 'general exteriority', which he equates with the domain of a structuralist social science.

In the early and middle 1960s the spread of procedures originating in structural linguistics to other areas – mythology, literature, cinema, in fact all symbolic social practices – and their apparent success in isolating certain formal principles of organization, seemed to vindicate entirely Lévi-Strauss' stand against an all-embracing Dialectical Reason. Voices as diverse as those of Lucien Goldmann, Paul Ricoeur, and Henri Lefebvre were raised against the new intellectual fashion, but were inevitably isolated cases of resistance to what was in effect a massive shift of sensibility: for a time to raise objections to structuralism could only mean preferring some form of metaphysic to 'science'. In some quarters it was acknowledged that the status and explanation of historical change had now become problematic. But in general it was either asserted that structuralist procedures could already deal with the diachronic dimension, or that the question of 'diachronic structures', although posing more difficulties than that of synchronic structures, could eventually be resolved by structural analysis. Certainly Lévi-Strauss staunchly defended himself against the charge of having rendered historiography epistemologically disreputable. His only aim, he suggested, was to challenge the privileged position which had been accorded to historical knowledge by post-war phenomenology.[11]

Yet a closer look at the arguments contained in the final chapter of *The Savage Mind* makes clear that, although Lévi-Strauss begins with a refutation of the particular vision of history represented by the *Critique*, he concludes by disqualifying history – understood as the temporal succession of events in human societies – as an object of rigorous knowledge. Contemporary accounts of Lévi-Strauss sought to minimize this implication, pointing to the passages in his writings where he pays tribute to the work of historians and suggests a complementarity between the perspectives of history and of anthropology. Yet in fact this apparent complementarity is the thin disguise of a crude subordination: history exists as a reservoir of fact to be absorbed and ordered by synchronic analysis. This is not a temporary aberration on Lévi-Strauss' part, but a view which has remained constant throughout his career. In an article on 'History and Anthropology' first published in 1949 Lévi-Strauss writes: 'By showing institutions in the process of transformation, history alone makes it possible to abstract the structure which underlies many manifestations and remains permanent throughout a succession of events.'[12] While in his polemic against the *Critique* he remarks: 'History consists wholly in its method, which experience proves to be indispensable for cataloguing the elements of any structure whatever, human or non-human, in its entirety.'[13] Insofar as only certain of the potential variants of a structure are concretely realized, anthropology must 'begin by bowing before the power and the inanity of the event'.[14] Once the underlying structure has been identified, however, it can be instated as the true object of science, while its empirical realizations must be abandoned to the domain of an untheorizable contingency.

In one respect Lévi-Strauss agrees with the phenomenologists: since a narration of all past events, even if it were possible, would amount to no more than a meaningless chaos of data, the writing of history requires a principle of selection which will be dependent on the interests and ethical-political commitments of a particular individual or group. History, he argues, is always 'history-for'. But whereas for Sartre, as for other hermeneutic thinkers, this distinction supplies the knowledge of history with a special human relevance and epistemological dignity (in the natural sciences, Sartre suggests with evident distaste, Reason must transform itself into 'a system of inertia'),[15] for Lévi-Strauss this 'subjective' factor in the codification of events renders historiography unfit for inclusion amongst what he calls the 'hard' sciences. Yet this critique of the subjective element in historical knowledge inevitably raises questions about the epistemological assumptions on which Lévi-Strauss' own work is based. For, at first glance, it is difficult to appreciate why anthropology should differ from history in its need for a selection and organization of material, which will be based on certain preferences and interests. Either these preferences must be seen as not ultimately affecting the results of an enquiry whose aim is objective explanation (but then why cannot history aim for such explanation?), or the objections which Lévi-Strauss raises to the codification of historical events can also be raised about the codification of anthropological data.

Lévi-Strauss' only answer to this difficulty relies on the bare affirmation that structural anthropology is 'objective' because it isolates and describes objectively existing structures, while history is condemned to remain marred by subjectivity since it consists of 'a method with no distinct object corresponding to it'.[16] Significantly, Lévi-Strauss is also scornful of what he considers to be the dilettantish use of structuralist procedures in literary analysis, precisely because, here also, structure is a product of the method and not a property of the object.[17] Viewed in this light, Lévi-Strauss' repeated affirmations that the importation of the methodological tools of structural linguistics has enabled the social sciences to cross a major epistemological threshold, and that they can now aspire to equality with the sciences of nature, cannot be viewed as occasional lapses into positivism. They are an integral part of an epistemological position which affirms that 'structural hypotheses . . . can be compared with independent, well-defined systems, each in its own right enjoying a certain degree of objectivity, which test the validity of the theoretical constructs.'[18] In Lévi-Strauss this tendency is reinforced by an assumption that 'objective' must ultimately mean 'material'. Like Freud, Lévi-Strauss cannot resist taking out the 'insurance policy' of supposing that statements about the 'human mind' should ultimately be reducible to statements about the physical structure of the brain. He affirms that the human sciences are merely a 'shadow theatre', the direction of which has been temporarily entrusted to them by the sciences of nature.[19]

This objectivist and reductionist conception of the status of the human sciences produces a number of curious discrepancies in Lévi-Strauss' work. As we have seen, Lévi-Strauss has a strong affective commitment to the cognitive and cultural parity of all societies – 'Those societies we call primitive', he affirms, 'are no less rich in Pasteurs and Palissys than the others.'[20] Yet his own methods of analysis are a vivid indication of the cognitive asymmetry of cultures, since they rely on the assumption that the anthropologist may be able to provide an account of social practices which is unavailable to members of a society. In addition, Lévi-Strauss' view of the natural sciences as a model to be emulated by the human sciences clearly requires him occasionally to admit what he terms the 'absolute superiority of Western science'.[21] Thus Lévi-Strauss' fundamental affirmation that 'man thinks the world in accordance with certain mental constraints, and the way in which he thinks the world determines very largely the way he acts upon it',[22] is never allowed to impugn the status of knowledge in the culture to which he himself belongs. Similarly, Lévi-Strauss' rationalist argument that the method of structural anthropology demands a sharp break with the evidences of experience is never reconciled with his repeated use of analogies based on a highly experimentalist view of the natural sciences. It is one of the paradoxes of Lévi-Strauss' work that it repeatedly and powerfully raises the question of the cultural relativity of knowledge, only to dismiss this question as a 'philosophical' diversion from the explanatory tasks of science.

Set against these incoherences of Lévi-Strauss' position, certain aspects of the early project of Althusser and his collaborators, which emerged more or less simultaneously with the vogue for structuralism, spring into clearer relief. Althusser is concerned, like Lévi-Strauss, with the critique of Hegelian accounts of history and of phenomenological theories of knowledge. Indeed, he wishes to make this critique the foundation of a renovated Marxism. But he also wishes to avoid the structuralist relegation of the historical to the status of a contingent and untheorizable residue, and its concomitant, a naively positivist view of social science. However, in approaching this task, Althusser does not reject the assumption that only objects governed by certain immanent laws of structure can be rigorously known, or reassign to temporality a status superior to that of the synchronic. Rather, he argues simultaneously on two fronts: against the phenomenological assumption that history possesses a distinctive dialectical form of intelligibility, and against the Lévi-Straussian assumption that structural intelligibility is not characteristic of history. Thus Althusser's task is both to show that there exists a set of concepts in accordance with which it is possible to organize the historical past as an object of scientific knowledge; and to justify these concepts not by a bare affirmation of their correspondence with their object, or by illusory analogies with the experimentalism of the natural sciences, but by a theoretical reflection on the historical process of formation of scientific concepts, and on the particular formation of the concepts of Marxist theory. It is precisely these two tasks which Althusser sees as the central, though as yet unconsolidated achievements of the work of Marx himself: 'Marx could not possibly have become Marx except by founding a theory of history and a philosophy of the historical distinction between ideology and science.'[23]

In many of its fundamental assumptions Althusser's conception of the 'science of history', which he takes to have been founded by Marx, closely resembles Lévi-Strauss' conception of a structural anthropology. For Lévi-Strauss social structures are 'entities independent of men's consciousness of them (although they in fact govern men's existence), and thus as different from the image which men form of them as physical reality is different from our sensory perceptions of it and our hypotheses about it.'[24] The cognitive, affective and practical capacities of the individual are determined by systems of relations between categories which are unconsciously shared by all members of a given community. In Lévi-Strauss' account a society is formed by an ensemble of such 'symbolic systems', of which language, marriage rules, economic relations, art, science and religion are amongst the most prominent, and between which it is possible to detect relations of correspondence, transformation and reversal.

Although Lévi-Strauss affirms strongly that it is structural linguistics which provides the model for the analysis of these diverse systems, he is far more ambivalent about specifying any order of determination between them. At one point in *The Savage Mind* he argues that 'Men's conception of the relations between nature and culture is a function of modifications of their own social relations.'[25] Yet in the same work he also suggests that it is always the 'conceptual scheme which mediates between *praxis* (understood as the general human capacity for action) and individual practices'.[26] In fact, if an ultimately determinant factor is to be isolated in Lévi-Strauss' work, this factor is not of a social character at all, but is rather the 'objective structure of the psyche and brain': culture must in the last resort be reducible to nature. By contrast, Althusser's theory remains resolutely at the level of social structure, and follows the traditional priorities of Marxism in attributing ultimate determination to the economic level of society. In common with Lévi-Strauss, however, Althusser sees the social formation as a 'structure of structures' whose functioning escapes the consciousness of its members. Human individuals are nothing more than the supports or bearers of various kinds of social relations – economic, ideological, political – whose forms cannot be dissolved back into an original intersubjectivity. For both Althusser and Lévi-Strauss all effects are effects of structure.

Despite these convergences, Althusser is highly critical of the implications of Lévi-Strauss' conception of structure for the epistemological status of history. He perceives clearly that, in Lévi-Strauss' scheme, 'Diachrony is reduced to the sequence of events and to the effects of this sequence of events on the structure of the synchronic: the historical then becomes the unexpected, the accidental, the factually unique rising or falling in the empty continuum of time for purely contingent reasons' (RC, 118). In addition, Lévi-Strauss sees societies as constituted by a complex pattern of mirrorings and correspondences; the various symbolic systems 'aim to express certain aspects of physical and social reality, and to an even greater extent, the relations which these two types of reality maintain with each other and which the symbolic systems themselves maintain with each other'.[27] In this respect, argues Althusser, the intelligibility of symbolic systems does not greatly differ from that of the Hegelian 'expressive totality', each part of which serves to summarize all the others: in both cases essence is revealed by a synchronic section which erases the real diversity of practices. In Althusser's account the converse error is committed by certain historians associated with the *Annales* school. Although the notion of diverse 'historical times' introduced by authors such as Braudel, Labrousse and Febvre represents an advance over the expressive totalities of Hegelian historiography, the *Annales* authors tend merely to affirm the existence of different temporal strata and rhythms – the political, the economic, the geographical – without attempting to establish any systematic links between them. Faced with these two opposing tendencies, Althusser's task is to elaborate a theory of history which will avoid the spurious homogeneity of the Hegelian conception, without allowing the historical past to become fragmented into a plurality of unrelated diachronies.

The Althusserian solution to this problem depends on a return to one of the fundamental principles of Marxist theory: a periodization of the history of human societies in terms of modes of production. Étienne Balibar, Althusser's collaborator in *Reading Capital*, goes so far as to suggest that 'Marx's construction of the central concept of the "mode of production" has the function of an epistemological break with respect to the whole tradition of the philosophy of history' (RC, 210). The argument behind this affirmation, revealed by Althusser in the course of an analysis of Hegel (RC, 93–97), is that there exists a close relation between conceptions of the social formation and conceptions of historical time: in Hegel's case the expressive totality of any given moment is complemented by the teleological continuity of history as the development of Spirit. If this is correct, then the as-yet-unconstructed Marxist concept of historical time will depend upon the elucidation of Marx's theory of social formations as governed by their modes of production, which is implicit in the analysis of the capitalist mode of production to be found in *Capital*. In this way a Marxist theory of history can be recovered from the work of Marx's scientific maturity, avoiding a reliance on earlier texts in which Marx himself appears to equivocate over the relation between structure and agency.

According to Althusser, the distinguishing feature of the Marxist conception of the social whole is its refusal to reduce real complexity to some underlying principle of unity, whether this principle be envisaged as spiritual or material. He suggests that two forms of such a reduction, which he refers to by the generic title of 'historicism', have been active in the Marxist tradition itself. One of these, originating in the Marxism of the Second International, envisages an automatic progress of civilization based on the dialectic of forces and relations of production, and tends politically towards reformism. The other, associated with the Hegelian Marxism of the young Lukács, identifies Marxist philosophy with the self-consciousness of the proletariat, which it sees as being potentially the universal subject-object of history, and implies an ultra-leftism. Both these forms achieve an all-too-literal inversion of the Hegelian vision of history as the progressive unfolding of Spirit, while failing to displace the core of Hegel's philosophy: the very notion of a subject of history. By contrast, Althusser affirms that a social formation must be viewed as a 'decentred totality' in which each instance – the economic, the political and the ideological being the initial three which Althusser distinguishes – possesses its own autonomy and effectivity. This conception implies that each instance or practice is determined not simply by the economic level, as in reductionist Marxism, but is 'overdetermined' by the totality of other practices, which it also in part reciprocally determines. However, Althusser is careful not to allow this conception of the social formation to result in an equality of interaction between all instances. He affirms that in each social formation there is one instance which is dominant. This need not necessarily be the economic – under feudalism, for example, it is politics which is in command. But it is the mode of production which ultimately *determines* which level is to be *dominant*. Thus the traditional Marxist affirmation of the causal primacy of the forces and relations of production should be taken to mean that it is the economic 'base' which distributes effectivity between the instances of a social formation.

Undoubtedly, in the years immediately following the publication of *For Marx* and *Reading Capital*, Althusser's reformulation of the central concepts of Marxist theory, although portrayed by its opponents as dogmatic and mechanistic, was primarily experienced as a liberalization and a liberation. The introduction of the concept of 'relative autonomy' meant that it was no longer necessary to trace the form and function of each superstructural instance back to its determination by the economy. Art, politics, science, ideology: each had its own particular immanent structure and temporal rhythm which merited an independent and untrammelled investigation. Significantly, conservative critics of Althusser within the French Communist Party accused him of having weakened the explanatory basis of Marxism by lapsing into an incoherent pluralism. Both those for and against Althusser, however, tended to overlook that Althusser's liberalization' was accompanied by a highly inflexible and aprioristic conception of adequate historical explanation. In Althusser's view the causal and narrative sequences of traditional historiography have no scientific validity: a historical event has not been truly 'explained' until it has been identified as an overdetermined effect of the complex structure of a social formation. In this area the concept of 'determination in the last instance' has a vital role to play, since it is only this concept which 'makes it possible to escape the arbitrary relativism of observable displacements by giving these displacements the necessity of a function' (RC, 98). But since the notion of 'structural causality' on which this necessity relies has yet to be elaborated, judged by Althusser's criterion no historiography so far produced can be considered to have crossed the threshold of scientificity. Althusser places himself in a position no less absurd than that of those English-speaking philosophers who have insisted that historical explanation should conform to the 'covering-law' model appropriate to an inductivist conception of the natural sciences, despite the fact that the practice of historians shows no tendency whatever to approximate to this model.[28] Althusser's similar attempt in *Reading Capital* to force all scientific knowledge of history into a preconceived mould leads to a number of equally perverse conclusions. He suggests, for example, that the apparently 'historical' pages of *Capital* dealing with 'primitive accumulation', the struggle for the reduction of the working day, the transition from manufacture to industry, are merely raw materials for a history, since these events are not subsumed under formal laws of structure. On the other hand, the theoretical sections of *Capital* are more truly 'historical' since they construct the theory of one region of the science of history. Indeed, Althusser argues that 'The only difference that can be established between the theory of political economy and the theory of history lies in the fact that economics considers only one instance of the social totality, whereas history considers the totality as a whole' (RC, 109).

It will be clear that Althusser's attempt to rescue historical knowledge from its complicity with phenomenology, while avoiding its demotion at the hands of structuralism, concedes far too many structuralist assumptions. Perhaps the most crucial of these is the assumption that the elements of a social whole exist in a relation of mutual support, and therefore form an autonomous and self-perpetuating system, for it is this which underlies Althusser's decision to take modes of production as the fundamental forms of historical being. In *Structural Anthropology* Lévi-Strauss argues that kinship systems could not be 'the arbitrary product of a convergence of several heterogeneous institutions . . . , yet nevertheless function with some sort of regularity and effectiveness'.[29] Accordingly, kinship practices should not each be traced back to a disparate source, but rather integrated within a synchronic system. Similarly, Althusser argues in *Reading Capital* that knowledge of a society must be 'obtained exclusively from the theory of the "body", i.e., of the *contemporary structure of society*, without its genesis intervening in any way whatsoever' (RC, 65). In neither case is any attempt made to justify the belief that all the components of a social system must be necessary and functional elements of that system. Althusser simply affirms that 'when we speak of the "existing conditions" of the whole, we are speaking of its "conditions of existence" ',[30] thereby eliminating the possibility of variations *within* a structure. Indeed, Althusser's concept of 'structural causality', of the structure as only being 'present in its effects', implies that – correctly read – these variations simply *are* the structure.

By introducing this concept of 'structural causality', Althusser hopes to distance his theory both from the position of Levi-Strauss, in which the social system is seen as a contingent realization of a set of necessary relations, and from the position of Engels – criticized in *For Marx* – in which the necessity of historical events is the product of an interaction of microscopic contingencies. Althusser considers that if a science of history is to be possible, its object must be governed by a strict necessity at all levels of its theorization. Yet, in thinking this necessity, Althusser does not take the usual view that each particular historical configuration must be seen as determined by a preceding configuration, and so on in an open-ended sequence. Rather, both Althusser and Balibar tend in *Reading Capital* towards a Spinozist view of science – although this is never made fully explicit – according to which all knowledge of necessity must be logico-deductive in form. 'All theory is synchronic', suggests Balibar, 'in so far as it expounds a systematic set of conceptual determinations' (RC, 298). The Spinozist distinction between the random sequence of ideas produced in the mind by the impact of external bodies, and the 'concatenation of ideas which takes place according to the order of the intellect and enables the mind to perceive things through their first causes',[31] becomes the Althusserian distinction between the realm of ideology and the empirical, and the rigour of a Marxist science in which all the characteristics of a social formation can be *deduced* from a 'theoretical object', the concept of its mode of production. Similarly, the Althusserian concept of 'structural causality' is modelled on the relation which Spinoza envisages between God and the finite modifications of his attributes. That the hopelessness of this rationalism was not more frequently appreciated at the time may be attributed to the fact that Althusser tacitly adopts the Spinozist assumption of the metaphysical identity of logical and causal relations. He can therefore speak indifferently either of the deterministic mechanism of the social formation itself, or of the logical implications of the 'theoretical object' which corresponds to it: 'we are confronted with a system which, in its most concrete determinations, is governed by the regularity of its "mechanism", the specifications of its concept'.[32] It is for the same reason that Althusser never appears unduly concerned about the relation, which many commentators have found highly problematic, between the 'real object', which remains in its self-identity outside thought, and the theoretical object of Marxist science.

One of the intentions behind Althusser's decision to view the autonomy and necessity which he considers to be essential to any object of science as characteristics of a structure, is to allay any lingering suspicion that Marxism conceives of history as an inelectable progress towards a preordained goal. If historical events are only truly 'explained' by being deduced from the structure of a social formation, if there is 'no history in general, but specific structures of historicity, based in the last resort on the specific structures of the different modes of production' (RC, 109), then the totalizing ambitions of a Sartre are vain. Most importantly, no social formation can be seen as automatically giving birth to its successor, for if it is axiomatic that a mode of production is a self-reproducing structure, then the dissolution of that structure must a be process of a 'completely different kind' (RC, 274). Yet this critique of teleology overshoots the mark. For if modes of production are the fundamental forms of historicity, there can be no 'historical time' in which the transition from one mode of production to another takes place. In *Reading Capital* Balibar attempts a solution to this problem by introducing what he terms 'forms of transition': 'manufacture', for example, may be considered as a form of transition between feudalism and capitalism. Yet since these forms are themselves considered by Balibar to be 'temporary' modes of production, this 'solution' leads only to an infinite regress. Thus one of the ironies of Althusser's theory of history is that it ends by reproducing that division between a synchronic necessity and an untheorizable contingency which he had originally criticized in Lévi-Strauss.

In traditional empiricist theories of knowledge, objectivity is ultimately guaranteed by the possibility of a – more or less complex – reduction of theoretical statements to statements about the experience of a perceiving subject, which are considered to form a secure epistemic base-line. However, Althusser follows the structuralist lead in affirming the socially relative and symbolically determined status of 'immediate' experience. He argues that 'Without a critique of the immediate concepts in which every epoch thinks the history it lives, we shall remain on the threshold of a true knowledge of history, and a prisoner of the illusions it produces in the men who live it.'[33] As a result he is obliged to follow the Lévi-Straussian dictum that 'in order to attain the real, one must first repudiate lived experience.'[34] Yet, unlike Lévi-Strauss, he is aware that the affirmation of this principle raises many epistemological problems of its own; in particular, that an alternative account of the objectivity of scientific knowledge is required.

One of the major resources to which Althusser turns in order to solve this problem is the work of the French school of historical epistemology, most eminently represented by Gaston Bachelard, a philosopher principally concerned with the physical sciences and with the theory of the imagination, and by Georges Canguilhem, an historian and philosopher of the life sciences who owes certain fundamental assumptions to Bachelard. This recourse was entirely in accord with the temper of the 1960s, for in Bachelard's work, produced at a time when phenomenology and existentialism were the dominant currents within French philosophy, and the prestige of the natural sciences at a low ebb, it is possible to find a highly developed critique of empiricist and phenomenological theories of knowledge. Unlike its structuralist successors, however, Bachelard's critique of phenomenology is ultimately based on a philosophy of the human mind, which he sees as marked by a fundamental duality, divided between a 'nocturnal' facet which constantly inclines towards reverie and the archetypes of the unconscious, and a 'diurnal' facet which strives towards increasing abstraction and the rational application of concepts. In Bachelard's view our everyday experience (*l'expérience commune, l'expérience vulgaire*) is inevitably imbued with affective colourings, and haunted by the values and libidinal investments of the unconscious. More generally, the mind shows a spontaneous tendency towards both exaggerated particularity and facile generalization which form an obstacle to the development of a scientific knowledge of phenomena. In consequence, such knowledge can only be initiated by an 'epistemological break' (*rupture épistémologique*) with the assumptions and givens of the everyday world, and a purging of the sensuous – and even animistic – overtones which cling to the concepts of pre-scientific theory. For Bachelard this break is not simply a regrettably necessary preliminary to the real process of development of scientific knowledge, but is an essential moment of its constitution. No statement which appears 'flatly and evidently true' can claim the name of science:

self-evidence should rather be a cause for suspicion. For it is only in correcting a previous error that knowledge identifies itself as such. 'The essence of reflection', states Bachelard, 'is to understand that one had not understood.'[35]

Accordingly, the gravamen of Bachelard's critique is that phenomenology rests complacently within the orbit of immediate experience, attached to the misleading axiom that 'the primitive is always the fundamental.' In doing so, it remains prey to precisely that play of imaginary investments which it is the task of science to recognize and suppress. Furthermore, phenomenology encloses itself within an outmoded cognitive individualism. It fails to take account of the fact that the elaboration of knowledge can only be a collective process, that the experience of the individual cannot be considered as unimpeachable, but must be laid open to the testing of the 'labourers of the proof', the community of scientists engaged in enquiry. Free of this collective constraint, the phenomenologists can simply indulge 'the facile convictions of a soul illuminated only by its intimate experience'.[36] In a striking anticipation of Lévi-Strauss, Bachelard suggests that the phenomenologist must 'end by describing a personal vision of the world as if he had naïvely discovered the meaning of the whole universe'.[37] Unlike Lévi-Strauss, however, Bachelard does not consider the domain of science to be automatically protected from such dangers. Even here a constant guard must be mounted to prevent the purified rationality of the concept from sliding back towards the reverie of the image. The 'psychoanalysis of objective knowledge' which Bachelard began to develop as a result of his investigations into the imaginary explanations of pre-science, is intended to aid the detection and neutralization of unconscious intrusions into the field of scientific rationality.

These views lead Bachelard towards a distinctive account of the object of scientific knowledge and the nature of scientific truth. Since he denies that scientific knowledge can be seen as an extension or inductive generalization of 'common sense' or everyday experience, Bachelard is obliged to argue that the object of science is not discovered, but is rather 'constructed' by a system of concepts, whose reference to sense-experience becomes increasingly tenuous. At the same time, since he tends to identify immediate experience with the 'real', Bachelard does not assume that such a system of concepts corresponds to some deeper reality underlying appearances.[38] Already in his doctoral thesis of 1928 he had dismissed as an 'epistemological monstrosity' the 'idea of a coincidence between thought and reality, of an adequation between theory and experience'.[39] Rather, the truth of science is embodied only in the constant susceptibility of scientific theories to rectification and adjustment in the light of further evidence, and in the increasing coherence and comprehensiveness of their fundamental concepts which this brings about. This process is not simply one of minor correction within a broad accumulation of knowledge. For major scientific advances can provoke shock-waves which reach down to the very foundations of scientific method. Thus, even after the initial break with the lived world, the history of science continues to reveal significant epistemological discontinuities.

In his discussions of Marx's theoretical development, Althusser makes crucial use of the Bachelardian concept of an 'epistemological break', for it is this concept which allows him to discredit Hegelian and existentialist readings of Marx, by arguing that the central texts on which these readings are based – above all the *Economic and Philosophical Manuscripts* of 1844 – must be seen as belonging to a 'pre-scientific' phase of Marx's work. Marx's early texts are dominated by Hegelian and Feuerbachian modes of thought, in which human beings are seen as the unconscious, and therefore 'alienated', creators and movers of their own social world, and as such they precede the discoveries through which Marx establishes his own distinctive theoretical terrain. Althusser argues that the epistemological break in Marx's work takes place around 1845, and is most evident in *The German Ideology* and the *Theses on Feuerbach*. It is in these works that Marx begins to abandon his early 'anthropological' assumptions, and to think the history of human societies in terms of an entirely new system of concepts: mode of production, relations of production, ruling class/oppressed class, ideology. This new system of concepts no longer leaves any room for human agents as the 'makers' of history: Marx decisively abandons the 'obviousness' of the belief of bourgeois humanism that 'the actors of history are the authors of its text, the subjects of its production'. By using the term 'epistemological break' to describe this process, Althusser stresses that the later 'scientific' Marx cannot be seen as a development or – in Hegelian terms – as the 'truth' of the young Marx. The concepts of 'alienation', 'species-being', '*praxis*', cannot be simply amalgamated with the theoretical system of a work such as *Capital*: they belong to a different 'problematic'.

It is this last term which Althusser employs to describe the solidarity of the fundamental concepts of a theory, and their priority over its supposedly empirical engagements. The term is rarely used in Bachelard, but in principle is clearly present throughout his work. In *The Philosophy of No*, for example, he argues that the results of experiment and observation in the physical sciences can have no significance unless they are placed within a specific theoretical framework, since it is only a structure of attitudes and expectations which can cause the scientist to *look* and *examine*, rather than simply see. In *Reading Capital* Althusser develops this argument into a general critique of theories of knowledge, founded on the metaphor of vision, which assume the possibility of an unfettered encounter between subject and object. He points to 'a fact peculiar to the very existence of a science: it can only pose problems on the terrain and within the horizon of a definite theoretical structure, its problematic, which constitutes its absolute and definite condition of possibility' (RC, 24). The failure to note certain facts within a particular scientific theory is not the result of a fortuitous oversight, for within any problematic there is 'an organic link binding the invisible to the visible' (RC, 24). Within this general parallelism, however, there is one major difference between Althusser and Bachelard. For Bachelard a problematic, as an organization of pertinent questions, is a sign of the maturity of a science, of a capacity to narrow and direct attention, to be contrasted with the vague spontaneity of the untutored mind. Furthermore, there cannot be a *theory* of this mind, of the native imagination: 'the image', claims Bachelard, 'can only be studied by means of the image, in dreaming images such as they assemble in reverie. It is nonsense to claim to study the imagination objectively.'[40] For Althusser, to abopt these assumptions would be to remain tributary to the humanism which Marx has theoretically discredited. He argues that the epistemological break does not consist in a leap from the spontaneous to the organized, from nature to culture, but rather in a shift from one system of concepts to another: from an 'ideological problematic' to the problematic of a science. This is not primarily a passage from incoherence to coherence, for an ideology may offer a highly systematic view of the world. The central distinction between ideology and science is that the problematic of the former is prescribed by practical and social determinations of which it cannot be conscious, while the problematic of a science makes possible an autonomous development in accordance with an immanent criterion of truth. In the case of Marxism there is an additional distinction, however. The epistemological break not only reveals the pre-history of a science as erroneous, it makes possible an explanatory account of that error: precisely a 'theory of ideology'.

On the basis of this account, Althusser is able to launch a further attack on that broad current within the Marxist tradition to which he gives the title 'historicism'. As we have already seen, historicism tends to reduce the structured complexity of the social formation to some simple unifying principle. But it can now be perceived that, in the particular domain of epistemology, the characteristic fault of historicism is to possess no rigorous conception of the break between science and ideology. In its central Hegelian form – to be found in Lukács or Gramsci – historicism affirms that the cognitive validity of theory cannot be assessed independently of its role in expressing the world-view of certain social forces at a particular epoch. Marxism tends to be viewed as simply the most recent and the most universal of a series of philosophies which have structured human thought and action throughout history. Thus historicism places knowledge in dependency upon a form of historical reality which is considered to be more fundamental, thereby impugning its autonomy and (by implication) its authority. Precisely because he places such emphasis on the independence of Marxist theory, Althusser considers the status attributed to scientific and philosophical knowledge to be the 'symptomatic point' (RC, 132) at which the reduction of levels characteristic of historicism reveals itself. Far from viewing Marxism as a theorization of the experience of anti-capitalist struggle, Althusser considers that the only possible relation between theory and politics – already indicated in his early essay on Montesquieu – is 'the correction of errant consciousness by well-founded science'.[41]

In his discussions of the theory of science and of the general theory of history in *Reading Capital*, there is one corpus of historical research to which Althusser refers with unwavering approval. This is the work of Michel Foucault. The innovatory studies produced by Foucault of the transformation of medical and psychiatric discourses in the west – of the historicity of our conceptions of mind and body – are taken by Althusser to be exemplary in their dismantling of continuist accounts of the history of science, and their investigation of the 'paradoxical logic of the conditions of production of knowledges' (RC, 45). Foucault shows how the 'self-evidence' of the gaze of clinical medicine, or of the perception of madness as a malady of the mind, is the result of a complex overlapping of medical, legal, religious, ethical and political practices, which are themselves determined by the economic, political and ideological structures of a particular epoch. In this respect Foucault's work not only offers a model for that 'theory of the history of the production of knowledges' which the earlier Althusser takes to be the task of Marxist philosophy; it teaches a general lesson concerning the structure of a historical time which cannot be reduced to the 'ideological' categories of expressive simultaneity or teleological succession.

Althusser was not mistaken in identifying a convergence between his own interests and those of his former pupil during the 1960s. For the historical analyses of scientific discourse, or 'archaeologies', which Foucault produced at that period are clearly indebted to the tradition of historical epistemology which is also central to Althusser's work. Indeed, from the point of view of Althusserianism, Foucault tended to be seen as simply the inheritor and developer of this tradition. As late as 1971 Dominique Lecourt, a follower of Althusser who has specialized in epistemology, could suggest that Bachelard, Canguilhem and Foucault belonged to a common current of 'anti-positivism' (understood as the rejection of any general theory of scientific method) and 'anti-evolutionism' (understood as the denial of any unilinear growth of knowledge) in the philosophy of science.[42] Foucault and the Althusserians diverged, however, with regard to their predominant allegiances within this tradition. Althusser's central interest was in the theory of epistemological discontinuity developed by Bachelard, a theory which could be used to re-periodize Marx's work and to re-establish the scientificity of Marxism. Although, during the 1960s, Foucault placed an equal – if not stronger – emphasis on discontinuities in the development of knowledge, his work is much closer to the studies in the history of the life sciences produced by Georges Canguilhem, in which the concerns of historiography tend to predominate over those of pure epistemology. Furthermore, whereas Bachelard tends to define the matrix from which science *emerges* in terms of an atemporal psychology of the unconscious, Canguilhem is far more interested in the social relativity and normative foundations of certain basic biological concepts, and even allows that the life sciences may be permanently dependent on certain figurative modes of expression, often of a political or ideological origin. Placed in this lineage, Foucault can be seen as once more shifting the focus of attention, this time from the 'life' to the 'human sciences', and as extending the consideration of ideological factors to include the social and institutional frameworks within which these sciences have emerged.

The keystone of this tradition as a whole is the assumption that knowledge can only be adequately understood if studied in its historical development, rather than considered as the product of an encounter between empirical reality and certain immutable faculties of the mind. Ultimately, the influence of this assumption in France must be traced back to Comte, who – in the first lesson of the *Cours de philosophie positive* – debunks the 'psychological method' ('the so-called study of the mind by the mind is a pure illusion') and argues that the task of positive philosophy is to trace 'the course actually followed by the human mind in action, through the examination of the methods really employed to obtain the exact knowledge that it has already acquired'.[43] Comte's determination to take history seriously also entails an appreciation of the fact that 'in order to devote itself to observation the mind needs some kind of theory',[44] an insight which will remain central to the tradition as renewed by Bachelard and transmitted to the epistemology of the 1960s. However, the way in which this priority of theory over experience is presented by Althusser and Foucault differs widely. In Althusser's work the critique of empiricist theories of knowledge takes the form of a theoretical debate, centred on the concept of a scientific problematic. In Foucault's writings, by contrast, one rarely discovers explicit philosophical argument; rather, his philosophical positions emerge from a skein of narrative whose ostensible concern may be more with political and social transformations than with the theory of the sciences. This is a technique which Foucault derives from Nietzsche, with whom he shares a profound suspicion of the traditional discourse of philosophy. Like Nietzsche, he is in search of a novel mode of expression which will evade absorption by 'the interiority of our philosophical reflexion', without lapsing into 'the positivity of our knowledge'.[45]

The Birth of the Clinic, the first of Foucault's works to be written in the shadow of structuralism, offers a clear example of this oblique procedure. Apparently, Foucault is concerned to analyse certain transformations which took place in medical discourse at the end of the eighteenth and the beginning of the nineteenth centuries, and their relation to the social and political upheavals of the French Revolution. But *The Birth of the Clinic* may also be read as a critique of phenomenological accounts of knowledge. In his later work Merleau-Ponty had attempted to outline what he referred to as a 'genealogy of truth': he wished to show how discursive knowledge must, at some ultimate point, be anchored in a revelation of being which is prior even to the division between subject and object. Down to the very headings of its chapters (*voir, savoir, l'invisible visible*), *The Birth of the Clinic* offers a subtly inverted echo of Merleau-Ponty's positions. In place of a 'genealogy of truth', Foucault proposes an 'archaeology of the gaze' which will show how 'immediate perception' must be seen as a complex end-product rather than as a point of departure. His historical analysis shows that the supposedly pristine look with which clinical medicine contemplates the body of the diseased patient is in fact the result of the congelation of a complex set of procedures of observation and registration, institutional rules and forms of conceptualization; while his description of the faith of the initiators of clinical medicine – 'The gaze will be fulfilled in its own truth and will have access to the truth of things if it rests on them in silence, if everything keeps silent around what it sees'[46] – offers a sly allusion to the naïveté of phenomenology, its belief in the possibility of access to a pure, pre-linguistic level of experience. Thus, despite striking differences in mode of presentation, the positions of Foucault and Althusser in the early 1960s appear to be parallel. In both cases a critique of the traditional metaphor of knowledge as a form of vision leads to a conception of the relations between the perceived and the unperceived as linguistically determined. Althusser's 'problematic' seems to reappear in what Foucault terms 'the original distribution of the visible and invisible insofar as it is linked with the division between what is stated and what remains unsaid'.[47]

In both Althusser and Foucault, however, this argument goes a crucial step beyond anything to be found in Bachelard, or in Canguilhem. There can be no contesting that Bachelard's philosophy stresses the primacy of theory over experience: he often refers to his position as a 'rationalism' – although an 'open rationalism' – in which the increasing conceptual coherence and mathematization of theory, rather than an accumulation of empirical detail, is seen as the true mark of scientific advance, and he tirelessly criticizes philosophies which view scientific knowledge as 'the pleonasm of experience'.[48] Yet Bachelard never suggests that theories uniquely determine the facts to which they are applied, or that experience and experiment play no role in the construction of theory. And while he criticizes the abstract opposition between subject and object which he sees as characteristic of traditional metaphysics, this is not to reduce both subject and object to 'effects' of the determinism of conceptual systems, but in order to explore a more subtle dialectic between 'theory' and 'experiment' as it is manifested in the actual practice of the sciences. For

Bachelard the task of an adequate philosophy of science is to steer a delicate course between realism and rationalism, rather than clinging blindly to one or other of these alternatives. Indeed, his conception of an 'open rationalism' consists precisely in the readiness of the scientist to revise his theories in the light of new evidence. 'When it is experimentation which brings the first message of a new phenomenon', states Bachelard, 'the theoretician ceaselessly modifies the reigning theory, to enable it to assimilate the new fact.'[49] Nor is this adjustment limited to the superficial and *ad hoc* elements of theory, major transformations being attributed purely to conceptual innovation. In the concluding chapters of *The Philosophy of No* Bachelard suggests that no theoretical principle, not even fundamental logical principles such as the law of identity, can be considered as immune to revision in the light of novel experimental evidence.

In Althusser's work, however, the possibility of a 'feedback' from experience to theory is entirely excluded. This becomes apparent in a number of contexts. Firstly, from *For Marx* onward, Althusser adopts the metaphor of scientific activity as a 'theoretical practice', a process of production in which the concepts of a theory (which he terms 'Generality II') operate on a 'raw material' which consists of ideological concepts, scientific 'facts', and already elaborated scientific concepts (Generality I), in order to produce new knowledge (Generality III). This metaphor of production implies that experience, which Althusser globally equates with 'ideology', can only be a passive primary material which the concepts of a science must shape and elaborate: Althusser speaks of 'the priority of Generality II (which works) over Generality I (which is worked on)' (FM, 191). Secondly, in his discussion of the concept of a 'problematic' in *Reading Capital*, Althusser describes the problematic as constituting 'the absolute determination of the forms in which all problems must be posed at any given moment in the science' (RC, 25). If this determination is absolute, however, there can be no possibility of a modification of the problematic being provoked by an empirical discovery; indeed, the distinction between the empirical and the theoretical becomes meaningless. Lastly, Althusser's neglect of the role of empirical evidence is reinforced by his Spinozism. In *Reading Capital* he argues that once sciences have been 'truly constituted and developed they have no need for verification from external practices to declare the knowledges they produce to be "true", i.e., to be knowledges' (RC, 59). This is because, as we have already seen, Althusser envisages a science which has successfully constituted its 'theoretical object' as operating in a purely logico-deductive manner. On this basis Althusser is led to argue that the experiments of the physical sciences are in some way internal to their 'theoretical practice', thereby rendering incomprehensible the role and significance of prediction, which necessarily assumes a theory-independent reality. In general, any attempt to identify correlations and distinctions between theory and experience is condemned by Althusser as a lapse into 'pragmatism'.

In Foucault the relation between theory and experience is similarly presented as one of unidirectional determination, although in his case the reasons for this conception are considerably wider. Althusser's argument is specifically concerned with the 'theory-laden' status of scientific facts; he only touches on the question of a general priority of language over experience in his implicit recourse to the Lacanian concept of the Symbolic as the basis for a theory of ideology. In Foucault, however, the argument is presented from the start in terms of a primacy of the discursive over the 'lived', of the kind broadly asserted by structuralism. Thus Foucault's denial of 'the heaven which glitters through the grid of all astronomies'[50] is less an expression of his adherence to Bachelardian epistemology, than to the kind of viewpoint suggested by Lévi-Strauss' argument that: 'there are no natural phenomena in the raw. These do not exist for man except as conceptualisations, seemingly filtered by logical and affective norms dependent on culture.'[51] In *The Birth of the Clinic*, for example, when Foucault argues that – at the level of his analysis – there exists 'no distinction between theory and experience, methods and results; one had to read the deep structures of visibility in which field and gaze are bound together by *codes of knowledge*',[52] these codes tend to be seen as merely particular embodiments of the general codes of a culture. At the close of the book Foucault suggests that both the emergence of clinical medicine and the lyrical poetry of a Hölderlin can be seen as symptoms of a new consciousness of mortality, of an 'irruption of finitude', which characterizes one phase of nineteenth-century thought. In his following book, *The Order of Things*, Foucault greatly expands this conception, arguing that all the discourses of a particular epoch must be seen as determined by an underlying structure which he refers to as the *episteme*. This structure, which Foucault terms an 'historical a priori', constitutes the fundamental ordering principles of a culture, thereby providing an implicit ontology in which all its concrete modes of knowledge are rooted. As a result, there can be no possibility of any particular empirical discovery disturbing this ontology: change can only come with the global shift from one *episteme* to its successor. In Foucault's account, the history of western culture since the Renaissance is divided into three immense and disconnected blocks.

In *The Archaeology of Knowledge*, the retrospective discourse on method which was the last of his books of the 1960s, Foucault greatly modifies this conception, under the guise of a correction of misinterpretations of his earlier work. He now denies that the *episteme* should be viewed as 'a form of knowledge or type of rationality which, crossing the boundaries of the most varied sciences, manifests the sovereign unity of a subject, a spirit or a period'.[53] If the term *episteme* is still to be used, it should be taken to denote a fluid system of disparate yet interlocking 'discursive practices'. However, this lessening of the rigidity of the *episteme* does not extend to an admission of a possible interaction between empirical discovery and the theoretical structure of science. Foucault insists that the object of a science 'does not await in limbo the order that will free it and enable it to become embodied in a visible and prolix objectivity'.[54] The task of the archaeology of knowledge is to account for the constitution of such objects 'without reference to the *ground*, the *foundation of things*, but by relating them to the body of rules that enable them to form as objects of discourse and thus constitute the conditions of their historical appearance'. Its central assumption is that 'discourse is not a slender surface of contact or confrontation between a reality and a language, the intrication of a lexicon and an experience.'[55]

This exclusion of any relation between theory and experience leads to serious difficulties in the work of both Foucault and Althusser. In Althusser's case the 'symptomatic point' at which these difficulties become apparent is in his account of the historical emergence of the Marxist 'science of history'. *For Marx* and *Reading Capital* treat this emergence almost purely as an intellectual event, as a break from ideology to science within the domain of theory. This treatment is reinforced by the theory of philosophy which Althusser espouses in these works. He suggests that 'philosophical revolutions' follow on the heels of major scientific developments: Platonism after the discoveries of the early Greek mathematicians, Cartesianism after Galileo. Such revolutions may be seen as 'the "reprise" of a basic scientific discovery in philosophical reflection, and the production by philosophy of a new form of rationality' (RC, 185). Accordingly, Althusser's own task will be to elucidate and formalize the new form of rationality which is contained in a 'practical state' in Marx's work, to provide the 'Theory (dignified with a capital letter) of (Marx's) theoretical practice'. Such a theory will perform a task similar to that of Bachelard's 'psychoanalysis of objective knowledge'. It will protect established sciences from the ideological lures which constantly surround them, expose 'scientific ideologies' which have illicitly occupied the 'continent of history' opened up by Marx, and establish new branches of Marxist research on the correct conceptual foundations. Soon after the publication of *Reading Capital*, however, Althusser began to abandon this conception. And in his *Éléments d'autocritique* (1974) it is denounced as a 'rationalist' and 'theoreticist' deviation, the essence of which is the flaw characteristic of his early work in general: a neglect of the reality and effectivity of the class struggle. The recognition of this effectivity poses one of the central problems of Althusser's later work. For he must do so without reducing Marxism to a theorization of the experience of class stuggle: such a reduction would return him to the framework of historicism.

Althusser's answer to this problem is a new view of the nature of philosophy. The role of philosophy is still to trace a line of demarcation between the scientific and the ideological, but it no longer does so in the positivist guise of a 'science of the scientificity of the sciences'. Rather, philosophy must be seen as a representation of 'the class struggle in theory' – a political battleground on which materialist and idealist tendencies mark out their ever-shifting positions. Philosophy possesses no 'theoretical object' of its own, but acts as a kind of go-between, representing politics in the domain of science and scientificity in the arena of politics. To defend the scientific status of Marxism, therefore, now amounts to adopting a class position in philosophy, to the issuing of 'materialist' theses which may be *justifiable*, but which are not demonstrable, as are the propositions of a science. Furthermore, a shift in philosophical position now precedes and makes possible the emergence of a new science, since philosophy works by 'modifying the *position* of the problems, by modifying the relations between the practices and their object'.[56] On this basis Althusser attempts to provide an historically denser account of the emergence of Marx's discoveries. He argues that, on Marx's road towards historical materialism, 'it is politics that is the determinant element: the ever deeper engagement in the political struggles of the proletariat'.[57] Marx first had to adopt a proletarian political position, which was then 'worked out into a theoretical (philosophical) position', in order to effect the displacement on which the emergence of a science of history depended.

It is in this way that Althusser attempts to preserve the non-positionality of science ('all scientific discourse is by definition a subject-less discourse, there is no "Subject of science" except in an ideology of science'),[58] while admitting the importance of the class struggle and of class viewpoints. But this attempt cannot be consistent. For, however mediatedly, Althusser is still obliged to admit the possibility of a knowledge which is not the knowledge of a science. In order to found his theory of history Marx had to adopt 'a position from which these mechanisms (of class exploitation and domination) become visible: the proletarian standpoint'.[59] Yet if the mechanism of society is already – in a reinstatement of that crucial metaphor – visible from the standpoint of the dominated class, then Althusser's whole project, whose core is a defence of the priority and indispensability of Marxist theory, begins to falter. It is as a result of this contradiction, among others, that Althusserianism rapidly faded as a political and theoretical force in France in the 1970s.

Like Althusser, during the 1960s Foucault attempts to produce a theory in which subject and object are seen as merely effects of the field of discourse, rather than as its origins or causes. Just as the objects of a science are a product of the discursive patterns of that science, so 'the subject (and its substitutes) must be stripped of its creative role and analysed as a complex and variable function of discourse.'[60] In order to explain the appearance of discourses, therefore, we need no recourse to existential or psychological considerations: this appearance is governed purely by 'codes of knowledge', or *epistemes*, or 'rules of formation'. Yet, in making this recommendation, Foucault, who appears to equate the psychological subject or the transcendental subject of phenomenology with the subject *tout court*, entirely overlooks the importance of the moment of enunciation in discourse. His position rests on the characteristic structuralist confusion between the 'conditions of possibility' and the causes of an event. In isolating what – in reference to *The Order of Things* – he terms the 'formal laws' which govern a domain of statements, Foucault is not thereby enabled to explain why any particular statement should be produced on a particular occasion, just as Lévi-Strauss' isolation of a putative grammar of mythology does not explain specific instances of the production of myth, but only the rules in accordance with which such production must take place. Any structural analysis of this kind must be supplemented by a causal explanation of the individual event.[61]

In *The Archaeology of Knowledge* Foucault attempts to overcome this problem by denying that he is seeking to achieve a formalization in the structuralist sense. His aim is rather to describe the immanent regularities of precisely those statements which have historically been produced. But this change fails to resolve the difficulty for a number of reasons. Firstly, Foucault himself admits that the description of regularities is an endless task, since there are innumerable ways in which statements may be said to resemble and differ from each other: no definitive 'theory' can be achieved. Secondly, even if such a theory were possible, it would still have no explanatory force. Such a *post hoc* reconstruction would only be of use in a hermeneutic perspective; but, since Foucault is relentlessly critical of projects of interpretation, this possibility is excluded. Thirdly, the concentration on the immanent 'rules of formation' of discourse distracts attention from the fact that on many occasions (for example, the generation of a science in a climate of religious or political terror) even the internal configuration of discourse requires explanation in terms of 'external' factors. One may conclude that what Foucault sees as the central question of 'archaeology' – 'for what reason did a certain statement appear and no other in its place?'[62] – has been left unanswered.

Foucault's portrayal of the objects of scientific discourse as entirely constituted by that discourse contributes to the same impasse. Clearly, there is an important element of truth in Foucault's claim that 'one cannot speak of anything at any time; it is not easy to say anything new; it is not enough for us to open our eyes, to pay attention, or to be aware, for new objects suddenly to light up and emerge out of the ground.'[63] This insight into the priority of frameworks has become a commonplace of recent philosophy of science. But, in arguing for a total discursive determinism, Foucault takes a crucial step beyond both his contemporaries in the English-speaking world, and even such an important influence on his work as Georges Canguilhem. It is true that, in *La Connaissance de la vie,* Canguilhem affirms: 'theories never emerge from facts. Theories only emerge from previous theories, often of great antiquity.'[64] Yet he immediately goes on to offer a vital qualification of this statement which reinstates the role of empirical reference: 'Facts are merely the path, rarely direct, by which theories emerge from each other.' In general, Canguilhem's Nietzsche-influenced philosophy of the value of the aberrant and the exceptional forbids any determinism of the Foucauldian variety. He speaks of: 'a certain anteriority of intellectual adventure over rationalization, a presumptuous overstepping (*dépassement*), resulting from the demands of life and action, of what it is already necessary to know and to have verified.'[65] For Foucault even 'discoveries' are rule-determined.

Part of Foucault's – and of Althusser's – mistake consists in making the not uncommon leap from the discrediting of the idea of naked, pre-theoretical facts to the conclusion that there can be *no* discrepancy between the empirical implications of a theory and the actual course of events. (This assumption is reinforced, in Foucault's case, by a concentration on the taxonomic and descriptive – rather than the predictive – aspects of systematic knowledge, and in Althusser's case by his Spinozist conception of science.) But the fact that the description of events is always *relative* to the vocabulary of a particular theory, does not entail that such events must always be *consonant* with the implications of such a theory. Much recent philosophy of science in the English-speaking world has been concerned with precisely such discrepancies: with the fact that they continue to occur even in well-'tested' theories; with the *ad hoc* strategems which are devised to disarm their implications; with those moments of scientific crisis which are provoked by the accumulation of such discrepancies; and with the problem of the point at which it becomes rational to abandon such a contradiction-burdened theory. In the work of Foucault and Althusser, however, no such problems can be posed. In *For Marx* Althusser takes care to stress that even pre-scientific ideologies are coherent, unified by a problematic, thereby excluding an intensifying consciousness of contradiction as a factor in the transition from one theory to another. Similarly, Foucault's narratives of epistemic shifts communicate little sense of crisis. In *The Order of Things*, for example, the contemporary discoveries of palaeontology are attributed no role in the transition from the fixism of Natural History to nineteenth-century evolutionary biology. And when Foucault does discuss a moment of scientific crisis, as in the tenth chapter of *The Birth of the Clinic,* he is careful to emphasize ('the difficulty of reaching an understanding when one was in agreement as to the facts') that what is at stake is a pure clash of theoretical frameworks ('two incompatible types of medical experience'), and not a situation in which one theory began to appear increasingly inadequate in the light of another.[66]

As the preceding discussion has indicated, theories of the coherence of systems of scientific concepts are closely linked with theories of continuity and discontinuity in the history of science. If each proposition of a science is seen as capable of facing the tribunal of experience independently, then science will be seen as a gradual process of alteration and accumulation. If, on the other hand, the propositions of a science are seen as so closely interrelated that none can be changed without altering the sense of all the others, then each theory will determine its own set of 'facts' and there will be no common world of reference shared by different theories. Since both Althusser and Foucault emphasize the rigidity and solidarity of problematics, or *epistemes*, or 'regimes of discourse', the concept of discontinuity plays a central role in their respective accounts of the history of science. Again the theme may be traced back to Bachelard, who was concerned throughout his career to expose the notion of 'an abstract and invariable system of reason' which would underlie both 'common sense' and the successive stages of science. In contrast to this assumption, Bachelard affirms that 'thought is modified in its form if it is modified in its object.'[67] The history of science is characterized by 'epistemological discontinuities', after the occurrence of which a science is concerned with new objects, conducts its research according to new principles, and even adopts a new logic. There can be no simple linear accumulation of truths.

A number of commentators have pointed to a similarity between the innovations introduced into epistemology in France by Bachelard and his successors, and a similar transformation of philosophy of science in the English-speaking world, initiated by the work of Kuhn, Hanson and others in the early 1960s.[68] In Kuhn's *The Structure of Scientific Revolutions* the history of science is seen as divided up into a succession of what he terms 'paradigms', theoretical frameworks which are discontinuous in their background assumptions, the kinds of entities which they posit, and their assessment of which phenomena call for explanation. For Kuhn the transformation between one paradigm and its successor is so comprehensive – his favoured analogy is that of a Gestalt-switch between two irreconcilable images – that he is led to argue: 'In so far as their only recourse to [the] world [of their research engagement] is through what they see and do, we may want to say that after a revolution scientists are responding to a different world.'[69] This may be compared with Bachelard's affirmation that: 'contemporary science, in inviting [the mind] to a new form of thought, conquers for it a new type of representation, and hence a new world.'[70] In both cases theoretical frameworks appear to determine the very nature of reality.

However, this convergence is far less close than it at first appears. In Kuhn's case, at least in his early statements of his position, the theory of paradigm changes leads towards relativism. Kuhn argues that, since there can be no paradigm-independent access to reality, there can be no neutral standpoint from which to access the comparative verisimilitude of different paradigms. Consequently, the history of science can no longer viewed as the epic of cognitive progress: 'We may . . . have to relinquish the notion, explicit or implicit, that changes of paradigm carry scientists and those who learn from them closer and closer to the truth.'[71] None of these considerations apply to the work of Bachelard. Indeed, Bachelard's conception of the transition between scientific theories is a remarkably traditional one. It is true that he affirms an initial disjunction between common experience and the reality posited by science ('The world in which one thinks', states *The Philosophy of No*, 'is not the world in which one thinks'),[72] but within the history of science itself Bachelard refers far more frequently to a 'rectification' or 'recasting' of the organizing principles of a branch of science, rather than to a further process of rupture.

One of the comparatively rare occasions when Bachelard employs the term *rupture épistémologique* to refer to a break in scientific development, rather than to the initial break with the lived world, is to be found in *The Philosophy of No*, in a passage concerned with the discovery of the atomic substructure of chemical elements. Yet even here Bachelard emphasizes that 'a non-Lavoisian chemistry . . . does not overlook the former and present usefulness of classical chemistry. It tends only to organize a more general chemistry, a panchemistry.'[73] In the final chapter of the book Bachelard extends this observation: 'Generalization by the "no" should include what it denies. In fact, the whole rise of scientific thought over the last century derives from such dialectical generalizations, which envelop what is negated.'[74] Behind its Hegelian phraseology, this account of scientific development differs little from the traditional realist conception of earlier scientific theories as 'limiting cases' of later theories, as approximately true or true given certain additional initial conditions. Such developments may involve a major reorganization of scientific knowledge – and in this sense there may be said to be 'discontinuity' – but there is no hint in Bachelard's work of what English-speaking philosophers of science have come to refer to as 'incommensurability'. As a result, Bachelard has an extremely forthright view of science as an enterprise of cognitive progress. In a lecture given in 1951 he affirmed: 'The temporality of science is a growth of the number of truths, a deepening of the coherence of truths. The history of the sciences is the story of this growth and of this deepening.'[75]

Althusser's relation to this aspect of Bachelard's work is highly ambiguous. On the one hand, he wishes to affirm the objectivity of science, yet his general opposition to 'philosophies of history' makes him extremely suspicious of the use of the concept of progress, in whatever domain. Thus in *Reading Capital* Althusser suggests that 'the real history of the development of knowledge appears to us today to be subject to laws quite different to this teleological hope for the religious triumph of reason. We are beginning to conceive this history as a history punctuated by radical discontinuities . . ., profound reorganizations which, if they respect the continuity of the existence of the regions of knowledge (and even this is not always the case), nevertheless inaugurate with their rupture the reign of a new logic, which, far from being a mere development, the "truth" or "inversion" of the old one, literally takes its place' (RC, 44). However, if scientific change does consist in one theoretical space being substituted for another, if it involves 'a transformation of the *entire* terrain and its *entire* horizon' (RC, 24), incommensurability must follow, and with it relativism. Althusser's argument that 'every ideology must be regarded as a real whole, internally unified by its own problematic, so that it is impossible to extract one element without altering its meaning' (FM, 62), appears to point in the same direction: it would be impossible to challenge ideological propositions except by employing *their* terms in precisely their sense, and this would require already having accepted the problematic of the ideology in question as a whole. Althusser, however, draws back from these implications of his own positions. In *For Marx*, for example, he speaks of the transition from 'Generality I' to 'Generality III' in Bachelardian terms as the production of 'a new scientific generality which rejects the old one even as it "englobes" it, that is, defines its relativity and the (subordinate) limits of its validity' (FM, 185). At other times, although careful to substitute the term 'process' for that of 'progress', Althusser is prepared to admit an accumulation of knowledge. In his 'Philosophy Course for Scientists' he refers to 'a double "dialectic": the total elimination of "errors" and the integration of earlier findings, still valid but transformed, into the theoretical system of the new insights'.[76] At a deeper level, Althusser's view of the emergence of Marxist science as being also the emergence of the science of its own ideological pre-history indicates a realist commitment (relativism can have no theory of the social function of error); yet this commitment is never reconciled with the relativist implications of many of his own formulations.

[. . .]

Undoubtedly, one of the reasons for the failure of the Althusserians to note the relativist implication of Foucault's histories of knowledge is that a similar ambiguity is deeply embedded in the work of Althusser himself: it clings to the terms 'objectivity' and 'autonomy' which are central to Althusser's account of science. When Althusser writes that: 'It is not individuals who make the history of the sciences, but its dialectic is realized in them and in their practice',[77] this statement may be taken as indicating the kind of view of science put forward in the English-speaking world in the later work of Karl Popper. For Popper, too, has attacked empiricist theories of knowledge and the view that the statements of science can be seen as symbolic or linguistic expressions of mental states, resulting from encounters between a subject and the world of perception; he has called for an 'epistemology without a knowing subject'.[78] Such an epistemology would be based on the 'sheer autonomy and anonymity' of what Popper terms 'the third world', the world of propositions, theoretical systems, problem-situations, errors and solutions, which exists independently of the consciousness and volition of human individuals. However, Popper's third world can only exist on the presupposition that its elements are linked not by causal sequences, but by chains of argument, whose validity can only be assessed by reference to the contemporary problem-situation in the third world, and not by recourse to any psychological or sociological considerations. Such a view is also hinted at by Bachelard when, in a lecture such as *L'Actualité de l'histoire des sciences*, he argues for an autonomous temporality of science on the basis that: 'In the history of the sciences – besides the link from cause to effect – there is established a link from reason to consequence.'[79]

There are a number of points in Althusser's work at which this appears to be the sense of 'objective' which is intended, although this sense and this intention are never adequately clarified: for example, when Althusser mysteriously affirms that science is not part of the superstructure (RC, 133); or insists on the distinction between historical and dialectical materialism, despite the fact that the latter, as 'the discipline which reflects on the history of the forms of knowledge and on the mechanism of their production' (RC, 157), appears to be simply one region of the former. In these cases Althusser seems to be groping towards a definition of the special autonomy and historicity of science as that of 'an axiological activity, the quest for truth'.[80] His reluctance to formulate this autonomy clearly may be attributed to the fact that such a conception appears to concede an unacceptable effectivity to ideas; it seems to ignore the rootedness of the theoretical practice of science in determinate social and historical conditions. Thus there appears in Althusser's discussions of science a second type of formulation in which theoretical practice is seen as autonomous, but only in the sense of 'autonomy' which is applied to all forms of practice within the Althusserian social formation. In *Reading Capital* Althusser writes: 'we have paid great attention to the concepts in which Marx thinks the general conditions of economic *production* . . . not only to grasp the Marxist theory of the *economic* region of the capitalist mode of production, but also to ascertain as far as possible the basic concepts (*production, structure* of a mode of production, history) whose formal elaboration is equally indispensable to the Marxist theory of the production of knowledge, and its history' (RC, 44). In short, what Althusser does is to confuse the objectivity of a process with the 'process of objectivity'. The epistemological independence of the development of science from the consciousness of individual knowing subjects is confused with the independence of social process from human consciousness and volition assumed by Althusser's determinist social theory, while the 'rational autonomy' of science is not distinguished from the 'relative autonomy' of an instance within the Althusserian social formation.

One of the few commentators to notice this ambiguity in Althusser was

Alain Badiou, the author of an influential review of *For Marx* and *Reading Capital*. In this essay, 'Le (Re)commencement du matérialisme dialectique',[81] Badiou noted a tension in Althusser's work between '[a] philosophy of the concept which strongly resembles an exhibition of the structured field of knowledge as multi-transcendental and subjectless', and a Spinozist theory of 'causality without negation'.[82] The first of these allows for an autonomy of logical relations, but at the price of introducing the 'dangerous' notion of the transcendental; while the second eliminates transcendence at the cost of presenting scientific statements as purely causally determined. Althusser is faced with the 'difficult combination of a regional, regressive and historical epistemology and a global theory of the effects of structure'. This difficulty is clearly reflected in Althusser's changing position on the status and nature of Marxist philosophy. In *For Marx* and *Reading Capital* Marxist philosophy is presented as being simply the theory of theoretical formations and of their history, yet at the same time – at least in *Reading Capital* – Althusser realizes that this definition alone is inadequate, since it treats 'knowledge as a *fact*, whose transformations and variations it treats as so many effects of the theoretical practice which produces them' (RC, 61). In other words, a 'scientific' history of knowledge, based on the Marxist conception of the social formation, cannot in itself provide the means of distinguishing theoretical ideologies from scientific theories: astrology would be treated with the same impartiality as astronomy. Thus what is needed, in addition to a history of knowledge, is an account of the 'mechanism' by which the object of knowledge produces the cognitive appropriation of the real object, since ultimately 'the relation between . . . the object of knowledge and the real object . . . constitutes the very existence of *knowledge*' (RC, 52). Althusser, of course, is unsuccessful in supplying such an account, since the description of such a 'mechanism' already presupposes a criterion for the identification of knowledges. Furthermore, in posing the question as one of 'appropriation' of the real (the notion of correspondence is not far away), Althusser not only cancels all the daring of his account of science as a form of production, he also denies himself the central insight of the Bachelardian tradition: that objectivity is not an ahistorical relation, but must itself be progressively and historically constituted.

Althusser's revised conception of philosophy as a kind of theoretico-political go-between fails to ameliorate this position, since Althusser still does not question the division between an 'objective' history of science and the philosophical justification of science. Rather, philosophy becomes simply a process of issuing theoretical *diktats* on the objectivity of the sciences, while the history of the sciences is now consigned entirely to historical materialism. As late as his *Essays in Self-Criticism*, Althusser continues to affirm the 'idealism or idealist connotations of all Epistemology' considered as a speculative discourse concerned with the furnishing of 'justifications' of science, and to suggest that 'if Epistemology is based on Historical Materialism (though naturally possessing a minimum of concepts which are its own and specify its object), then it must be placed within it.'[83] This viewpoint has been taken up and elaborated in works by the Althusserian Dominique Lecourt. In his book *Bachelard: le jour et la nuit* Lecourt argues that Bachelard has opened the way to 'a theory of the history of scientific practice, of its conditions (historical and material) and of its forms'.[84] However, Bachelard himself remained the victim of the 'epistemological illusion', and continued to employ the traditional vocabulary of the theory of knowledge even as he opened up new problems. He may be read as attempting, in the 'speculative' and 'idealist' mode of philosophy, to answer questions which in fact belong to 'the *science* of the process of scientific practice, a canton of historical materialism'.[85]

Both Althusser and Lecourt fail to recognize that their original error lies in the supposition that discussion of the sciences must be divided between an objective and materialist history, and a 'speculative' epistemology. Althusserianism never takes cognizance of the fact that – in the domain of the sciences – history and philosophy are complementary and intertwined, that, in Canguilhem's phrase, 'without relation to the history of the sciences, an epistemology would be an entirely superfluous double of the science of which it claimed to speak';[86] while, without a philosophically normative dimension, the history of science cannot even identify its object. This is the position of Bachelard, who argues, at the beginning of *La Formation de l'esprit scientifique*, that 'The epistemologist must . . . sift the documents collected by the historian. He must judge them from the point of view of reason, indeed from the point of view of a reason which has evolved.'[87] It is also the position of Canguilhem, lucidly proposed in the lecture which serves as an introduction to his *Études d'histoire et de philosophie des sciences*, where he argues that the relation of the *history of science* to its object cannot be equated with the relation of a *science* to its object. The object of a science is determined by the ensemble of verified propositions which have been established about that object at a specific moment. There may well be changes in this ensemble of propositions, but these changes do not concern the science itself, whose object may be considered – in this sense – as non-temporal. The history of the sciences, however, is concerned precisely with the transformations of the concepts which define the objects of the sciences. But concepts are not objects. Since the boundaries and transformations of a concept are always relative to a specific interpretation of that concept, the history of the sciences cannot itself be 'objective' in the scientific sense: it can only be written from a definite philosophical standpoint. For Canguilhem the history of the sciences is not a description of discourses or practices, but 'a representation of meanings'.[88]

Yet even if these assumptions be granted, there still remains the problem

of the epistemological viewpoint from which the history of the sciences should be written. In Bachelard's work this problem is resolved by the introduction of the concept of 'recurrence'. Bachelard assumes that the only possible point from which to begin is the scientific values and attitudes of the present, since to deny these values would be to deny the rationality of the development of science itself. Once this viewpoint has been adopted, the mass of documentation on the history of a science can be divided into what is 'lapsed' and what is 'ratified', between those results which must be consigned to the pre-history of scientific knowledge, and those which can be integrated into the sequence of the 'progressive formations of truth'.[89] This choice of standpoint does not imply any form of dogmatism, however. The relation between what is lapsed and what is ratified is labile, since such a 'recurrent' history of the sciences appreciates that the values and results on which it is based are themselves destined to be replaced by unforseeable future discoveries and developments, and that therefore the history of the sciences must be continually re-written. Canguilhem, who adopts the Bachelardian conception of recurrence, expresses the distinctiveness of this position in the following way: 'One sees the whole difference between recurrence, understood as a critical judgement of the past by the present of science, assured, precisely because it is scientific, of being replaced and rectified, and the systematic and quasi-mechanical application of a standard model of scientific theory exercising a kind of epistemological policing function over the theories of the past.'[90] The scientific present does not represent immutable truth, but it offers the only plausible perspective from which to judge the scientific past.
[. . .]

Althusser's central concern is to establish the conceptual foundations of a Marxist science of history, and to ensure that this science is not itself threatened with relativism and historicism by being portrayed as the product of historical experience or historical forces. To achieve this end he affirms an absolute disjunction between history as subjectively apprehended and spontaneously theorized, and the 'theoretical object' of a Marxist science of history, which is constructed entirely in thought, according to a rational necessity. This conception obliges him, at certain points, to take his distance from Marx himself. In *The German Ideology*, for example, Marx and Engels repeatedly affirm that their aim is to set out from 'real active men and on the basis of their real life-process': only in this way can the illusions of ideology and philosophy be exposed. But for Althusser this appeal to 'real history' and to 'real active men', to life against consciousness, is itself ideological, a Feuerbachian residue in the works of the 'epistemological break'. In *For Marx* he argues that 'The critique which, in the last instance, counterposes the abstraction it attributes to theory and to science and the concrete it regards as the real itself, remains an ideological critique, since it denies the reality of scientific practice, the validity of its abstractions and ultimately the reality of that theoretical "concrete" which is knowledge' (FM, 187). However, as we have already seen, Althusser's own position leads to intractable problems in its attempt to construct a purely deductive 'science' of history. Later Althusserian texts acknowledge this error. In his essay 'Sur la dialectique historique', Étienne Balibar admits that *Reading Capital*, despite its critique of reductionism, had remained wedded to economism insofar as the other instances of the social formation were seen as ultimately determined by the requirements of, and therefore definable in terms of, the conditions of reproduction of the mode of production. Balibar concedes that it is impossible to determine *a priori* the essence of any social instance independently of its combination with other instances within a given social formation. Furthermore, it is now the social formation, understood as a particular system of class struggles, which reproduces or fails to reproduce a given mode of production, rather than it being the mode of production which defines the relations of a hierarchy of subordinate instances.[91] However, this concession to what would formerly have been termed 'empiricism' does not lead to any revision in the fundamental assumptions of Althusserian epistemology. Unable to accommodate the real without abandoning its own principles of scientificity, Althusserianism simply collapses into inconsistency.

With Foucault the situation is quite different. Indeed, one of the deepest principles of his work is precisely that return from 'metaphysics' to real history which Althusser denounces in the Marx of *The German Ideology*. In Foucault's case, of course, the source is Nietzsche, who writes at the beginning of *Human, All-too-Human*: 'Lack of historical sense is the hereditary defect of all philosophers . . . Many of them take man automatically as he has most recently been shaped by the impression of a particular religion or even of particular political events . . . But everything has become; there are neither eternal facts nor eternal verities.'[92] Thus, where Althusser seeks to neutralize empirical history in order to make way for the philosophically-accredited object of Marxist science, Foucault considers that real history has already exposed the vagaries of philosophy. It is for this reason that, whereas Althusser criticizes the authors of the *Annales* school for having inadequately theorized their object, Foucault argues in the introduction to *The Archaeology of Knowledge* that the history of disjunct temporalities and chronological series discovered by the *Annales* historians has in itself exposed the illusions of totalizing philosophies. Foucault's position is well summed up by a remark he makes at the end of *The Archaeology of Knowledge:* 'If you recognize the rights of empirical research, some fragment of history, to challenge the transcendental dimension, then you have ceded the main point.'[93]

The contrast in the status of knowledge itself which these opposing positions imply is perhaps even more striking. Althusser appreciates that in discussing the history of science in terms of modes of theoretical production he is running a great risk. For such a history 'takes knowledges for *what they are*, whether they declare themselves knowledges or not, whether they are ideological or scientific etc.: for *knowledges*. It considers them solely as *products*, as results' (RC, 61). In other words, the objective history of science which Althusser supposes possible fails to provide a normative criterion for knowledge. And however much he twists and turns, Althusser cannot avoid the need for such a criterion. In Foucault's case, however, this is precisely the effect which he wishes to achieve: his aim is to treat knowledge in an objective, third-person manner as simply a form of social practice like any other, without making any epistemological judgement. It is for this reason that, whereas Bachelard and Canguilhem take the scientific present as the unavoidable vantage-point of historical epistemology, Foucault attempts to distance himself from every presupposition of contemporary science. However, this does not mean that Foucault has attained a philosophical neutrality, as he himself often supposes. Rather, during the 1960s, he adopts a position which, although not identical with that of Nietzsche – who views knowledge as a pragmatic 'invention', the product of a play of unconscious drives, biological contingencies and moral imperatives – nevertheless has the same effect. In describing modes of rationality as determined by structures which are themselves historically contingent, Foucault adopts the Nietzschean view of the 'irrational' origin of reason itself. In this way, even in those of Foucault's works in which political struggle has all but disappeared from view, the ground is being prepared for the account of knowledge which emerges during the 1970s. For if forms of scientific discourse cannot be seen as *accepted by* subjects on rational grounds, it becomes possible to construct a theory in which such forms are *imposed on* subjects by the operation of power. The way is open for a 'politics of truth'.

NOTES

1 Jean-Paul Sartre, *Between Existentialism and Marxism*, New Left Books, London, 1974, p. 55.
2 See Bernard Pingaud, Introduction to *L'Arc* 30, 1966 (special issue on Sartre).
3 *Critique of Dialectical Reason*, New Left Books, London, 1976, p. 125.
4 Ibid., p. 126.
5 Ibid.
6 Claude Lévi-Strauss, *Structural Anthropology* 2, Penguin, Harmondsworth, 1978, p. 330.
7 *The Savage Mind*, Weidenfeld and Nicolson, London, 1966, p. 262.
8 *Critique of Dialectical Reason*, p. 74.
9 *Structural Anthropology* 2, p. 36.
10 *The Savage Mind*, p. 253.

11 See 'Claude Lévi-Strauss: A Confrontation', *New Left Review* 62, July/August 1970.
12 *Structural Anthropology*, Penguin, Harmondsworth, 1972, p. 21.
13 *The Savage Mind*, p. 262.
14 *Du Miel aux cendres*, Librairie Plon, Paris, 1966, p. 408.
15 *Critique of Dialectical Reason*, p. 75.
16 *The Savage Mind*, p. 262.
17 See the remarks on 'Structuralism and Literary Criticism' in 'Answers to Some Investigations', *Structural Anthropology* 2, pp. 274–76.
18 Ibid., p. 274.
19 *L'Homme nu*, Librairie Plon, Paris, 1968, p. 574.
20 *Structural Anthropology* 2, p. 349.
21 *L'Homme nu*, p. 569.
22 'Entretien avec Claude Lévi-Strauss', in Raymond Bellour and Catherine Clément, eds, *Claude Lévi-Strauss*, Paris, 1979, p. 160.
23 Louis Althusser and Etienne Balibar, *Reading Capital*, New Left Books, London, 1970, p. 17. Further references to this work will be indicated in the text in parentheses by the abbreviation RC, followed by a page number.
24 *Structural Anthropology*, p. 121.
25 *The Savage Mind*, p. 117.
26 Ibid., p. 130.
27 'Introduction à l'oeuvre de Marcel Mauss', in Marcel Mauss, *Sociologie et anthropologie*, Paris, 1950, p. xix.
28 For a representative statement of this position, see Carl G. Hempel, 'Reasons and Covering Laws in Historical Explanation', in Sidney Hook, ed., *Philosophy and History: A Symposium*, New York, 1963 (reprinted in Patrick Gardiner, *The Philosophy of History*, Oxford University Press, Oxford, 1974).
29 *Structural Anthropology*, p. 35.
30 *For Marx*, Allen Lane, London, 1969, p. 208. Further references to this work will be indicated in the text in parentheses by the abbreviation FM, followed by a page number.
31 *Ethics*, Part 2, Proposition XVIII.
32 Quoted in Urs Jaeggi, *Theoretische Praxis*, Frankfurt/M., 1976, p. 105.
33 *Politics and History: Montesquieu, Rousseau, Hegel and Marx*, New Left Books, London, 1972, p. 99.
34 *Tristes Tropiques*, Penguin, Harmondsworth, 1976, p. 71 (translation modified).
35 Gaston Bachelard, *Le Nouvel esprit scientifique*, Presses Universitaires de France, Paris, 1978, p. 178.
36 *L'Activité rationaliste de la physique contemporaine*, Presses Universitaires de France, Paris, 1951, p. 10.
37 *L'Engagement rationaliste*, Presses Universitaires de France, Paris, 1972, p. 36.
38 This statement requires a qualification. Bachelard oscillates between constructivism and the tacit assumption that scientific theories do refer to an underlying reality. But since he tends to equate 'naive' realism with realism *tout court*, he is unable to give a theoretical status to such a reality.
39 *Essai sur la connaissance approchée*, Librairie Philosophique J. Vrin, Paris, 1928, p. 43.
40 *La Poétique de la rêverie*, Presses Universitaires de France, Paris, 1960, p. 46.

41 *Politics and History*, p. 38.
42 See 'Archaeology and Knowledge (Michel Foucault)', in Dominique Lecourt, *Marxism and Epistemology*, New Left Books, London, 1975.
43 Stanislav Andreski, ed., *The Essential Comte*, London, 1974, p. 32.
44 Ibid., p. 22.
45 Michel Foucault, 'La Pensée du dehors', *Critique* 229, 1966, p. 526.
46 *The Birth of the Clinic*, Tavistock, London, 1973, p. 108.
47 Ibid., p. xii.
48 *Le Rationalisme appliqué*, Presses Universitaires de France, Paris, 1975, p. 38.
49 Ibid., p. 2.
50 *The Archaeology of Knowledge*, Tavistock, London, 1972, p. 191.
51 *Structural Anthropology* 2, pp. 231–32.
52 *The Birth of the Clinic*, p. 90.
53 *The Archaeology of Knowledge*, p. 191.
54 Ibid., p. 45.
55 Ibid., p. 48.
56 *Essays in Self-Criticism*, New Left Books, London, 1976, p. 58n.
57 Ibid., p. 168.
58 *Lenin and Philosophy and Other Essays*, New Left Books, London, 1971, p. 160.
59 *Essays in Self-Criticism*, p. 161.
60 *Language, Counter-Memory, Practice*, Basil Blackwell, Oxford, 1977, p. 138.
61 For discussion of this point, see Charles Taylor, 'Force et sens', in G. B. Madison, ed., *Sens et existence*, Paris, 1975.
62 'Réponse au Cercle d'épistémologie', *Cahiers pour l'analyse* 9, Summer 1968, p. 17.
63 *The Archaeology of Knowledge*, pp. 44–45.
64 Georges Canguilhem, *La Connaissance de la vie*, Librairie Philosophique J. Vrin, Paris, 1965, p. 50.
65 *Idéologie et rationalité*, Librairie Philosophique J. Vrin, Paris, 1977, p. 56.
66 *The Birth of the Clinic*, p. 174.
67 *Le Nouvel esprit scientifique*, p. 56.
68 It should be noted that the French term *épistémologie* has a narrower connotation than its English equivalent, being closer to the English term 'philosophy of science' than to 'theory of knowledge'.
69 Thomas Kuhn, *The Structure of Scientific Revolutions*, Chicago University Press, Chicago, 1974, p. 111.
70 *La Philosophie du non*, Presses Universitaires de France, Paris, 1975, p. 122.
71 *The Structure of Scientific Revolutions*, p. 170.
72 *La Philosophie du non*, p. 110.
73 Ibid., p. 65.
74 Ibid., p. 167.
75 'L'Actualité de l'histoire des sciences', *L'Engagement rationaliste*, p. 139.
76 *Philosophy and the Spontaneous Philosophy of the Scientists and Other Essays*, Verso, London, 1990, p. 122.
77 *Politics and History*, p. 168.
78 See Karl Popper, *Objective Knowledge*, Oxford University Press, Oxford, 1972, especially chapters 3 and 4. The suggestion of an affinity between Althusser

and Popper on this point has been made, among others, by Ian Hacking, 'Imre Lakatos's Philosophy of Science', *British Journal for the Philosophy of Science* 30, 1979, p. 394, and Paul Patton, 'Althusser's Epistemology', *Radical Philosophy* 19, Summer 1978, p. 8.

79 *L'Engagement rationaliste*, p. 46.

80 Georges Canguilhem, *Etudes d'histoire et de philosophie des sciences*, Librairie Philosophique J. Vrin, Paris, 1970, p. 19.

81 *Critique* 240, May 1967.

82 Ibid., p. 466.

83 *Essays in Self-Criticism*, p. 124n.

84 *Bachelard: Le jour et la nuit*, Grasset, Paris, 1974, p. 95.

85 Ibid., p. 101.

86 *Etudes d'histoire et de philosophie des sciences*, p. 12.

87 *La Formation de l'esprit scientifique*, Librairie Philosophique J. Vrin, Paris, 1977, p. 17.

88 Georges Canguilhem, *La Formation du concept de réflexe au XVIIe et XVIIIe siècles*, Presses Universitaires de France, Paris, 1955, p. 158.

89 See *L'Activité rationaliste de la physique contemporaine*, chapter 1.

90 *Idéologie et rationalité*, p. 21.

91 *Cinq études du matérialisme historique*, François Maspero, Paris, 1974, pp. 203–45. For an English version, see Etienne Balibar, 'Self Criticism: An Answer to Questions from "Theoretical Practice"', *Theoretical Practice* 7/8, January 1973.

92 Friedrich Nietzsche, *Human, All-Too-Human*, I/i, paragraph 2.

93 *The Archaeology of Knowledge*, p. 203.

6

THINKING WITH BORROWED CONCEPTS: ALTHUSSER AND LACAN

David Macey

The reference to psychoanalysis, sometimes overt, sometimes covert, so imbues the Althusserian project of founding and elaborating a science of modes of production and social formations that it appears almost natural. No doubt it always seemed rather less than natural to many in the French Communist Party, which had officially denounced psychoanalysis as a 'reactionary ideology' in 1949.[1] No significant revision of that condemnation had taken place when 'Freud and Lacan' was first published in 1964 and Althusser's public gesture of theoretical sympathy for Lacan was a courageous one. Yet the presence of psychoanalysis in Althusser's discourse does, with hindsight, begin to look distinctly unnatural, though not because psychoanalysis is to be rejected as a reactionary ideology in favour of Pavlov. To go back to Althusser's references to Freud, Lacan and psychoanalysis is to return to texts which were once a familiar part of the intellectual landscape on both sides of the Channel, due allowance being made for the remarkably slow migration of concepts across that stretch of water. Going back can often be an unsettling experience: the familiar begins to look uncannily strange, natural allies to look like unnatural bedfellows.

In France, the mid-1960s saw the cementing of what Michel Pêcheux nicely termed a ' "Triple Alliance" in theory' between the names of Althusser, Lacan and Saussure.[2] Saussure appears to have been of no great interest to Althusser himself, but the Triple Alliance was very much a theoretical reality. It could, on occasion, be tactically expanded to include Foucault – and especially the Foucault of *The Order of Things* and *The Archaeology of Knowledge* – and it could drift towards a flirtation with a more generalized structuralism, though Althusser would later admit that his cardinal sin had been Spinozism and not structuralism.[3] The origins of the Triple Alliance are, however, to be found in the Rejection Front unilaterally declared by Althusser in 1963.

In an article on philosophy and the human sciences written in 1963, Althusser remarks that 'Marx based his theory on the rejection of the myth of the "*homo oeconomicus*", Freud based his theory on the rejection of the myth of the "*homo psychologicus*" ', adding that Lacan 'has seen and understood Freud's liberating rupture'.[4] In correspondence with Lacan, Althusser is more expansive and tells the psychoanalyst: 'You are . . . the first thinker to assume the theoretical responsibility of giving Freud the real concepts he deserves. . . . It was at the point where I realized that I was capable of giving Marx's thought . . . its *theoretical form*, that I found myself on the threshold of understanding you.'

Lacan and Althusser had, in the latter's view, the 'same adversaries', namely the 'pseudo-psychologists and the other philosophers of "the human person" and of "intersubjectivity" ', the 'technocrats' of structuralism, with their pretentions, homilies and their amateurism, 'in short, their theoretical imposture'. The Freudian and Marxist revolutions are analogous in that their respective theorists were obliged to think in a 'non-philosophical form' because the historical constraints of the day had reduced their thought to a 'wild' [*sauvage*] state. To that extent, neither revolution was complete, but Althusser feels justified in prophesying its victory and speaks of the joy of 'a reason which has at last "come home" to its most disconcerting and nearest objects. I prophesy: we have, largely thanks to you, entered a period in which it is possible to be prophets in our own country. I do not have the merit of running any risk in making this prophesy; we now have the right to make it, as we have the means to do so in this country, which has at last become *ours*.'[5] Lacan replied that he had read the copy of 'On the Materialist Dialectic' sent him by Althusser, adding, in the characteristic tone that combines flattery of his reader with a self-assurance bordering on arrogance, 'I recognize my questions in it.'[6] Preoccupied with his own battles and with psychoanalytic politics, Lacan did not become a major participant in the project that was being tentatively outlined by Althusser.

The Rejection Front and the subsequent Triple Alliance had enemies in common rather than a shared project, and their primary enemies were humanism and eclecticism. Once more, Althusser's undoubted courage has to be noted. There is a real and tragic grandeur to his proclamation in April 1965 that the development of Marxist science is 'a *duty* for Communists' and his claim that 'the party wants to unite theory with its practical application.'[7] This, surely, was always the voice of a prophet crying in the wilderness of his own land, of an intellectual in the wilderness of his own party. Arguing the case for theoretical anti-humanism in the PCF was never going to be easy. This was the party which, since the Popular Front of 1936, had insisted that the proletariat was the rightful heir to a national culture which was being debased by the bourgeoisie. And a major part of that heritage was precisely the humanism of the Enlightenment. It was also the party which, according to Althusser, had been born into a theoretical void.[8]

There were many reasons, in Althusser's view, to stress the need for ideological struggle and 'theoretical formation' – not least the ideological effects of the widening Sino-Soviet split, as reflected in the long-standing tensions between the 'Italians' (proto-Eurocommunists) and the 'Chinese' (proto-Maoists) in the PCF and its student organization. Hence the further 'analogy' between resistance to psychoanalytic and political 'revisionism'. Althusser speaks of the need to combat 'psychoanalytic revisionism' and the 'fall into ideology [that] began . . . with the fall of psychoanalysis into biologism, psychologism and sociologism'.[9] The return to Freud and the return to Marx are, that is, both struggles against revisionism. One is a struggle against the Marxist humanism of, say, Garaudy; the other a battle against 'the reduction of a distinguished practice to a label suitable to the "American way of life"' and a 'theology of free enterprise'.[10] The perversion in question is of course ego-psychology, or the theory that analytic treatment should promote and strengthen a 'conflict-free' zone within the ego. Ego-psychology is anathema to Lacan's insistence that the ego itself is an illusory and alienating construct; there is no therapeutic gain to be had in strengthening an illusory construct. The thrust, if not the letter, of Althusser's call to arms deflects the argument away from any clinical context and establishes a further analogy. At some level, he implies, the struggle against psychoanalytic and theoretical revisionism are one and the same. At a more banal, but no less real level, Lacan's scornful reference to the 'American way of life' would have touched an anti-American chord in many a French Communist (and not a few Gaullists). The allusion to a 'pact of peaceful coexistence' between psychoanalysis and psychology[11] – which, as will become apparent, is probably borrowed from Georges Canguilhem – was also highly cathected with political connotations at a time when peaceful coexistence between the 'super-powers' was regarded in pro-Chinese circles as a prime symptom of revisionism. Political signifiers are being used here to connote the existence of a conceptual parallel between Althusser's Marxism and Lacan's psychoanalysis.

At no point is there a real attempt on the part of the Triple Alliance to 'articulate' psychoanalysis and historical materialism, probably because it would be doomed to failure – not least because of the incompatibility between their respective emphases on intrapsychic reality and socio-economic reality. Balibar, for example, speaks rather circumspectly of the possibility of discovering or detecting 'epistemological analogies' between the theoretical work of Marx and Freud, and explains them in terms of the similiar 'ideological situation' of the two theorists.[12] Psychoanalysis is not a partner in an articulation but, rather, a provider of concepts. There is an obvious irony at work here. Althusser describes Freud as having been forced to think with imported concepts, with 'concepts borrowed from the thermodymamic physics then dominant'[13] (thereby avoiding the difficult issue of whether or not Freud's reference to thermodynamic physics is a metaphor, a borrowed conceptual framework, or an integral part of his descriptions of the libido and the primary processes), and then borrows psychoanalytic concepts for a variety of purposes.

When allied with Mao's essay *On Contradiction* (1937), psychoanalysis supplies the concept of overdetermination, originally elaborated in *The Interpretation of Dreams* to describe the manner in which every element of the dream-content is expressed many times in the dream-thoughts. It provides the protocols for the practice of symptomatic reading, modelled on the manner in which Marx reads the texts of classical political economy, exposing the second text which exists in their slips and silences, and reproduced in the reading that allows Althusser to detect the epistemological break divorcing the mature Marx from the young humanist of the 1844 Manuscripts.[14] The model is the suspended or evenly-poised attention with which the analyst listens to his or her analysand, refusing to reject or privilege any verbalization, just as the analysand follows the fundamental rule of saying all and omitting nothing. Having had years of personal experience of analysis, Althusser was well aware of just what the analytic situation involved and, as if to forestall the obvious objection that analysts listen rather than read, he again argues in terms of tacit analogies: since Freud, we have begun to understand what is meant by speaking; since Marx we have begun to suspect what reading means.[15] In a slightly more mysterious way, psychoanalysis provides the raw materials for the construction of the idea of metonymic or structural causality, which describes the effects of a structure on its component elements. Here, the import process is less clear than it might be; the reader tends to be referred by Althusser to Jacques-Alain Miller,[16] and thence to Lacan.

More conspicuously, psychoanalysis will feed into the theory of ideology, classically the most difficult area for any variety of Marxism seeking to escape the antinomies of false and true consciousness or the simplicities of economic determinism. Althusser displaces debates about ideology in two directions in the influential essay on ideology and ideological state apparatuses.[17] The two directions are not easy to reconcile. On the one hand, Althusser moves towards a sociological account centred on the reproduction of the conditions of production, effectively reviving certain of Gramsci's comments on the distinction between state and civil society,[18] or those apparatuses which function 'by ideology' as opposed to the repressive agency of the state itself. On the other, he moves towards psychoanalysis and a theory of the constitution of subjects and even subjectivity.

In 'Marxism and Humanism' (1964) ideology is described as being 'a matter of the *lived* relation between men (*sic*) and their world'.[19] The canonical and slightly different formulation is from 1969: 'What is expressed in ideology is . . . not the system of the real relations which govern the existence of individuals, but the imaginary relation of those individuals to the real relations in which they live.'[20] Initially, no specifically Lacanian connotations appear to attach to the notion, and imaginary is effectively synonymous with false, the antonym of science or Theory. It is also made synonymous with lived experience.

Highly positive terms in any variant of the phenomenological tradition, 'lived' and 'lived experience' (*le vécu*) are, for Althusser and his associates, negatively connoted. As a bitterly self-critical participant in the *Lire le Capital* project was to note after the event, an exclusive concentration on theory and theoretical formation made it possible to 'relegate everything else, all the petty academic, financial or sexual miseries of students to the domain of illusion which, in our discourse, was designated by a concept: *le vécu*.'[21] *Le vécu* was to take a bitter revenge. One of the omens of May '68 was the situationist pamphlet entitled *De la misère en milieu étudiant* (*On the Poverty of Student Life*), and the issues raised in May certainly pertained to *le vécu*. As a slogan of the day proclaimed, 'Structures do not take to the streets.' Another and more *ad hominem* slogan was yet more cruel: *Althusser à rien* ('Althusser no good/Al, you're useless' [*tu sers à rien*]). Perhaps it is significant that the ISAs essay, which places so much stress on the role of the educational apparatus, makes no mention of the fact that that apparatus had recently ground to a halt. And that the praise for the efforts of schoolteachers and masters should be innocent of any reference to the rebellion of students. It is also striking that no mention is made of the Ecole Normale Supérieure – the 'amniotic fluid' in which Althusser lived for so long – or of its undoubted role in the reproduction of a social and intellectual élite.[22]

'Freud and Lacan' originally appeared in *La Nouvelle Critique* in 1964. When it appeared in English translation in *New Left Review* five years later, Althusser prefaced it with a letter to his translator and a note. Arguing that certain of his earlier theses required expansion or correction, Althusser made some strange suggestions that were never followed up. On the one hand, 'the unconscious' should be 'rechristened' as soon as a better term could be found. Further discussion should be devoted to 'forms of familial ideology' and the 'crucial role they play' in initiating the function of the instance of the unconscious. Their elucidation was a task for historical materialism, and one that could not be undertaken by Lacan, 'given his theoretical formation'. Althusser concludes that '*no theory of psychoanalysis can be produced without basing it on historical materialism* (on which the theory of familial ideology depends, in the last instance).'[23] 'Familial ideology' remains sadly unspecified, as does the reference in the ISAs essay to the 'other' (non-ideological) functions of the family. Lapsing into near-banality and frustrating the hope that his work might have something to offer feminism, Althusser merely remarks in a footnote that '[t]he family . . . intervenes in the reproduction of labour power. In different modes of production it is the unit of production and/or the unit of consumption.'[24] The formulation provides little ammunition for struggles against a male-dominated society (or party).

The project that is being outlined here clearly reveals the hegemonic ambitions of historical materialism as it aspires to the role of epistemological High Court or even meta-science. Although he speaks in general terms of the need for ideological criticism and epistemological elucidation – a labour at least initiated by Lacan – if the specificity of Freud's discovery is to be grasped, and if it is to be defended against 'psychoanalytic revisionism', the comments added in 1969 introduce a disquieting note. The 'rechristening' of the unconscious would be revisionist indeed, and the implication that the kernel of psychoanalysis must somewhow be separated out from 'familial ideologies' would be no less far-reaching. It would at least appear to imply some recasting of the Oedipal complex, which seems to be the referent for Althusser's portmanteau allusion to 'the ideology of paternity-maternity-conjugality-infancy'.[25]

More astonishing is the use of familial metaphors in 'Freud and Lacan' itself. Arguing that Western Reason has always paid great attention to births, Althusser continues: 'When a young science is born, the family circle is always ready for astonishment, jubilation and baptism. For a long time, every child, even the foundling, has been reputed the son of a father, and when it is a prodigy, the fathers would fight at the gate if it were not for the mother and the respect due to her.'[26] The nineteenth century, however, saw the birth of three 'natural' or illegitimate children: Marx, Nietzsche and Freud. No more will be heard of Nietzsche (or of mothers). Foundlings and illegitimate children are, of course, the principal figures in Freud's 'family romances' – the myths invented by children in their attempt to negotiate Oedipal difficulties by saying 'these are not my real parents.' A strange family romance appears to be at work in Althusser's text, and especially in the claim that 'fathers in theory [Freud] could find none' and that he had 'to be himself his own father, to construct with his own craftsman's hands the theoretical space in which to situate his own discovery'.[27] If a family romance is at work here, the implications of the Young Marx/Mature Marx dichotomy and of references to a return to the Freud of 'his *maturity*'[28] begin to look like elements in a complex network of fantasy. Illegitimacy, or the fantasy of being one's own father, would seem to be the precondition for the legitimacy of concepts and theory. The theoretician must not only be his own father; he must also deny ever having been a child.

The loneliness of the innovative theoretician is a recurrent motif in Althusser: Marx, Freud, Machiavelli and Spinoza together make up a pantheon of lonely individuals struggling in theoretical solitude to give birth to their concepts.[29] In 1964, it was not difficult to add Lacan to the pantheon. He had recently been removed by the International Psychoanalytic

Association from its list of approved training analysts, and had openly likened his situation to that of Spinoza when he was expelled and excommunicated from the synagogue on 27 July 1656.[30] Althusser clearly identifies with his pantheon and would later speak with nostalgia of the 'marvellous times' when he at last achieved his one desire: 'Being alone and right in the face of all'.[31] Theoretical work obviously does not suspend the working of the imaginary.

At the end of 'Freud and Lacan', Freud is credited with the discovery 'that the human subject is decentred, constituted by a structure which has no "centre" either, except in the imaginary misrecognition of the "ego", i.e. in the ideological formations in which it "recognizes" itself.'[32] The formulation occurs after a reference to Freud's comparison of his discovery of the unconscious to the Copernican Revolution, that *locus classicus* of his heroic history of the sciences and a crucial element in his self-image (or self-misrecognition). Freud speaks of the realization that 'the ego is not master in its own house', meaning that the unconscious has reasons of which the reason of the ego knows nothing.

Althusser is projecting onto Freud Lacan's theory of the mirror-stage, as described in two of the best-known *écrits*.[33] The mirror-stage describes that crucial stage of development in which a child of approximately eighteen months recognizes its own image in a looking-glass. The image is unified and presents a level of co-ordination that the child has yet to achieve in its actual life; it is therefore greeted with jubilation. It also represents, however, an imaginary other – and an image of the other – and the child's identification is therefore an alienation, a misrecognition. Identification, alienation and misrecognition combine to produce a characteristic pattern of behaviour: the child identifies with others, crying when it sees another child fall, and complaining that it has been struck when it is in fact the aggressor. Lacan finds in this pattern the origins of all subsequent alienations and identifications: the identification of master with slave, of seduced with seducer. It is the prototypical situation that will lead to man's desire being defined as the desire of/for the other. This is the mirror to which Althusser turns in his description of ideology as an imaginary order.

Whilst he draws on Freud's theory of narcissism and the description of the *fort-da* game in *Beyond the Pleasure Principle*, Lacan's text also makes it clear that his sources are not confined to the psychoanalytic tradition. The behaviour of a child is contrasted with that of a chimpanzee of similar age – an animal with better motor coordination and no lasting interest in mirror-images. Primate ethology provides the contrasting model, and its findings are combined with those of child psychologists such as Wallon.[34] Far from signalling a rejection of *homo psychologicus*, the mirror-stage represents the introduction of elements of psychology and ethology into psychoanalysis.

As the child-chimpanzee comparison suggests, Lacan is also concerned with a human-animal contrast or differentiation; the same concern appears in his frequent references to Lévi-Strauss' nature/culture transition. And his concern here is overdetermined by his most powerful and lasting philosophical influence – namely, Hegel – for whom the break-up of a collectivity of individuals associated as 'a community of animals' is a major moment in the development of individuality, and according to whom 'self-consciousness . . . only has real existence so far as it alienates itself from itself.'[35] The Hegel in question is the creation of Alexandre Kojève, whose seminar, held at the Ecole Pratique des Hautes Etudes from 1933 to 1939 and regularly attended by Lacan in the years 1933–37, influenced a generation.[36] (A renewed interest in it recently triggered a debate about the 'end of history'.[37]) It was Kojève who provided the particularly violent reading of the *Phenomenology of Spirit* and the concentration on the master-slave dialectic that so marks Lacan. Kojève and not Hegel himself supplies, for instance, the notion of a struggle for recognition and pure prestige, and virtually every mention of the name 'Hegel' in the *Ecrits* should in fact read 'Kojève'.[38]

Althusser speaks of Lacan's 'paradoxical resort' to 'philosophies completely foreign to his scientific undertaking (Hegel, Heidegger)'.[39] That he has misrecognized a vital element in Lacan can be simply demonstrated by means of two quotations pertaining to the phenomenology of 'the basic category of the unconscious': desire.[40] The first is from Kojève himself: 'Desire is human . . . only if it is directed towards an other *Desire* and towards the Desire of an *other*.'[41] The second, from probably the greatest of France's post-war Hegelians, illustrates the ease with which a Lacanian-sounding formula can appear in a reading of Hegel: 'The desire for life becomes the desire for an other desire or rather, given the necessary reciprocity of the phenomenon, human desire is always a desire for the desire of an other.'[42] In his inaugural lecture at the Collège de France, Foucault described the recent history of French philosophy as being the history of an attempt to escape Hegel, via either logic or epistemology, and added that appeals against Hegel might be 'one more of the ruses he uses against us, and at the end of which he is waiting for us, immobile and elsewhere.'[43] Lacan's mirror is the 'elsewhere' in which Hegel waits for Althusser.

The existence of the Hegelian-Kojèvean strand in Lacan is not the only problematic area. Althusser's theses on ideology are dualistic, operating with a science/ideology, real/imaginary dichotomy, whereas Lacan introduces a triadic or trinitarian structure of Real, Symbolic and Imaginary. The orders interact rather than being opposed to one another, and there is certainly no question of the subject's escaping their combined actions. And although the differences between Lacan and Althusser may appear verbal, they are conceptual. For the Marxist theoretician, 'real' is presumably synonymous with 'actually existing'; for Lacan it refers to that which lies forever outside discourse, that which is unamenable to analysis and akin to the deity of negative theology: susceptible to description only in terms of what it is not. 'Imaginary' is not synonymous with 'fictive', and designates the ability to create and identify with images or imagos. Lacan's use of the term 'imaginary' is no doubt affected by the characteristic tendency of twentieth-century French philosophy to think the problem of the other in purely visual terms, a classic example being Sartre's theory of 'the gaze' [*le regard*]. Insofar as it is synonymous with the realm of culture, it would seem that it is in fact the symbolic which is closest to most definitions of ideology. The identification of the symbolic with ideology is not, however, an option open to Althusser, since it would create an opposition between science and not only ideology, but also the whole of human existence.

The operation of ideology and its constitution of subjects ('[a]ll ideology hails or interpellates concrete individuals as concrete subjects, by the functioning of the category of the subject'[44]) is illustrated by a primal scene of Althusser's devising: an individual walking down the street is hailed – 'Hey, you there?' – and turns around. He thus becomes a subject, 'because he has recognized that the hail was "really" addressed to him. . . . Experience shows that the practical telecommunication of hailings is such that they hardly ever miss their man: verbal call or whistle, the one hailed always recognizes that it is really him who is being hailed.'[45] That an element of humour may be in play here is suggested by the footnote in which Althusser alludes to the 'special' form of 'the policeman's . . . hailing of "suspects" ', but it unwittingly signals a flaw in the argument: the workings of ideology are illustrated by a state repressive practice. A sardonic Michèle Barrett raises a further objection when she notes that interpellation's supposed universality is unlikely to apply to women, for whom the 'experience of being hailed (especially by whistling!) on the street more often has the opposite effect of denying their individual identity and interpellating them in unnervingly generic terms.'[46] Nor is it likely to apply to the young blacks whose interpellation on the streets of Paris is more likely to result in a beating (or even death) than in recognition. In terms of the relationship with psychoanalysis, it is, however, the superimposition of a structure of recognition upon one of misrecognition that is so disastrous. The subject of Lacan's mirror-stage does not recognize himself through the verbal interpellation of an other; he (mis-)recognizes himself in an image of the self as other.

The interpellation thesis relates to a sort of primal scene, in keeping with the argument that 'ideology' (as opposed to 'ideologies') is eternal and has no history. The suggestion is tentatively related to 'Freud's proposition that the *unconscious is eternal*, i.e., that it has no history'.[47] No reference is given for this allusion, but it is probably to Freud's description of the 'timelessness' of the unconscious. Timelessness is, however, merely one characteristic of the unconscious, which is also typified by exemption from mutual contradiction, the dominance of primary processes, and the replacement of external by psychical reality.[48] Whether or not the unconscious (of an individual) has or does not have a history is in fact the subject of considerable psychoanalytic debate, with some arguing that it is a phylogenetic heritage transmitting a universal content, and others that it is constituted by a process of primal repression, mythical or otherwise. Once more, an epistemological analogy proves to be misleading in the extreme.

The supposed eternity of the formal structure of ideology, and the primal scene that demonstrates its gender- and race-bound operations, indicates the direction in which Althusser's essay seems to be moving: towards a symbol-based theory of ideology and, ultimately, towards Durkheim. Significantly, an earlier essay specifies that 'the first form of this ideology, the reality of this bond, is to be found in *religion* ("bond" is one of the possible etymologies of the word *religion*).'[49] This is far removed from the *Communist Manifesto*'s insistence that the history of all hitherto existing society is the history of class struggles. That history would appear, on the contrary, to have been preceded by the establishment of elementary forms of ideological life. Hence, perhaps, the near-tautology: 'Ideology has always-already interpellated individuals as subjects . . . individuals are always-already interpellated as subjects . . . individuals are always-already subjects.'[50]

Althusser's borrowings from Lacan are marked by a number of important misrecognitions, the most crucial being the failure to recognize the relevance to Lacan of the Hegelian tradition. Althusser attempts to recruit Lacan for purposes of his own, and the form of the recruitment (or interpellation?), reveal much more about the Marxist philosopher than the psychoanalyst. Founded on the basis of opposition to a host of adversaries, the Rejection Front provides the starting-point for a new project: the epistemological liberation of Freud from the ideologies that beset him, just as they beset Marxism. Lacan is the vital ally here because he defends the 'irreducibility' of psychoanalysis and its object (the unconscious),[51] and because he 'thinks nothing but Freud's concepts, giving them the form of our scientificity, the only scientificity there can be'.[52] This is wishful thinking on Althusser's part. As I have argued elsewhere, Lacan thinks a good deal more – and less – than Freud's concepts. He also 'thinks' surrealism, the lessons of the classical psychiatry in which he trained (and to which he owed his clinical and diagnostic acumen), the distinctive version of Hegelianism bequeathed him by Alexandre Kojève, elements of phenomenology . . .[53] The wishful thinking does, on the other hand, help to locate Althusser's reading of Lacan/Freud within a specific tradition.

In an essay originally published as the preface to an American translation of George Canguilhem's *Le Normal et le pathologique*, Michel Foucault describes the post-war history of French philosophy as being characterized by a division between 'a philosophy of experience, of meaning and of the subject' and 'a philosophy of knowledge, rationality and of the concept'. The former tendency is associated with Sartre and Merleau-Ponty, the latter with Jean Cavaillès, Gaston Bachelard, Alexandre Koyré and Canguilhem himself.[54] The representatives of the philosophy of consciousness include the main shared 'adversaries' of the Lacan-Althusser front. In a survey of the academic field of the 1950s, Pierre Bourdieu outlines a very similar intellectual typology, and speaks of the 'almost universal cult' of Canguilhem. The historian of science who, in the 1950s, had been a symbol of serious-mindedness and rigour at a time when existentialism was triumphant, later came to be an almost totemic figure or tutelary deity for those rejecting dominant models in philosophy.[55]

Canguilhem is a major representative of the epistemological tradition within the history of the sciences. His history is one of discontinuities – of breaks, ruptures and conceptual shifts – in which the sciences do not evolve in linear fashion; whilst his concept of scientificity is a matter of the constitution of a theoretical object, and neither of some empirical adequation to the real nor of a complacent reference to 'experimental method'. The normal/pathological distinction, without which modern medical practice and thought would be incomprehensible, is not, for instance, an empirical 'fact', but a way of organizing knowledge about the body. It results from the existence of a knot of concepts.[56]

Canguilhem was Cavaillès's successor at the Institut d'Histoire des Sciences et des Techniques. Logician, historian of the sciences, and victim of the Gestapo, Jean Cavaillès argued in uncompromising terms that science was a matter of logic and therefore that '[I]t is not a philosophy of consciousness, but a philosophy of the concept that can supply a doctrine of science.'[57] In his posthumously published autobiography, Althusser would admit to knowing relatively little about Cavaillès and to having contented himself with 'a few formulations'.[58] The constantly self-deprecating tone and mood of the autobiography make it difficult to know just what value should be attached to the disclaimer, but Althusser had certainly borrowed 'formulations' that would mean a great deal to the younger theorists working with him.

Canguilhem himself was a figure of enormous importance to those who pursued the implications of the Althusser/Lacan alliance. In the period leading up to the publication of *Lire le Capital*, Canguilhem's work and that of Althusser's team overlap to a high degree. The *Lire le Capital* seminar held at the ENS in 1964–65 coincided with Canguilhem's seminar on the problematic of the history of the sciences at the Institut d'Histoire des Sciences et des Techniques. A detailed comparison of Althusser's meditations on 'the object of *Capital*' and of Canguilhem's on 'the object of the history of the sciences' would no doubt be illuminating, but will not be undertaken here.[59] In 1967–68, the current of influences would be reversed when Canguilhem began to re-read and reformulate Bachelard in the light of the work of Althusser and Foucault. The result was a short-lived enthusiasm for the topic of 'scientific ideologies'.[60] In the preface to the second edition of the relevant essays, Canguilhem enigmatically remarks that '[T]o err is human; to persist in error is diabolical' and leaves it to his reader to decide whether or not his work of this period was 'aberrant'.[61]

Although Lacan does refer to the Canguilhem tradition, and was later to adopt the 'mathematization' model of scientificity associated with some representatives of the epistemological school (notably Alexandre Koyré), he was in fact notoriously hostile to rigorous conceptualization and objected, for instance, to the eminently conceptual *Language of Psychoanalysis* produced by Laplanche and Pontalis – Laplanche describes it as 'a critical reflection on every concept' – on the grounds that it was 'too scholastic'.[62] For a long time, Lacan's concepts remained fairly fluid, and were subject to a constant and tactical process of redefinition. The highly conceptual index appended to *Ecrits* is, of course, the work of Jacques-Alain Miller and not Lacan.

Althusser himself did not pursue the tasks he had set historical materialism vis-à-vis psychoanalysis. They would be taken up by *Cahiers pour l'analyse*. The journal of the 'Epistemological Circle' of the ENS began publication in January 1966 and continued to appear until 1968, with Jacques-Alain Miller as its principal editor. The 'Avertissement' to the first issue – devoted to 'Truth', no less – announced that it would publish texts dealing with logic, linguistics and psychoanalysis, with a view to constituting a 'theory of discourse'. That dialectical materialism would be of major importance to the *Cahiers* went without saying, but the possibility of a science of social formations soon became largely irrelevant. Nothing in the project related to the 'particularity of a doctrine'; the aim was to '[f]orm ourselves, following the example of our masters, in accordance with the rigour of concepts'.[63] As with the original Rejection Front, there was a marked tendency to make analogies serve as arguments. Thus, it could be claimed that psychoanalysis, like Marxism, provides the principle for 'a new organization of the conceptual field',[64] but the analogy was now between the field of the statement [*énoncé*], defined as the field of logic, and psychoanalysis, defined as the field of speech.[65] The philosophy of the concept was to be given a new incarnation.

To the extent that the *Cahiers* was a quasi-Marxist project, it is a distinctly odd one. Categories such as class are almost totally absent; the economic and the political disappear. As formal logic is increasingly brought to bear on psychoanalysis, Lacan is read in terms which obliterate his philosophical-psychological past and promote the image of a psychoanalyst born purely of an encounter between Freud and a formal theory of discourse. Far from being a specific discourse, Lacan's work now becomes part of a general instance of conceptuality. Whereas Althusser and Balibar began by looking for 'epistemological analogies', the *Cahiers* group would search for a logic of the signifier that typified the discourse of Science, and not of the plural *sciences* of which Canguilhem was the historian. The emphasis on logic overrode the vision of a plurality of 'continents' common to Canguilhem and Althusser.[66] From the early 1970s onwards, Lacan was to internalize this reading via the theory of the 'matheme' – a supposedly formal system of notation designed to ensure the integral transmission of his teachings.

The second issue of *Cahiers pour l'analyse* (March-April 1966) was devoted to 'What is psychology?' The title reproduces that of an article by Canguilhem, originally read to the Collège philosophique in 1956 and published in the *Revue de Métaphysique et de morale* two years later.[67] The answer to the question is not favourable: psychology is a philosophy without rigour, an ethics that makes no demands, a medicine without controls.[68] Most modern psychology is 'a professional practice, the whole of whose "science" is inspired by the search for the "laws" of adaptation to a socio-technical environment'.[69] The original target had been Daniel Lagache, former professor at the Sorbonne, a long-term associate of Lacan's and the author of an unsuccessful attempt to 'unify' clinical psychology and psychoanalysis.[70] In Canguilhem's view the alleged unity of psychology represented no more than a peaceful coexistence pact between heterogeneous practices.[71] Lagache was not particularly relevant in 1966, and the target of Canguilhem's polemic is displaced. By implication, it becomes a defence of Lacan's psychoanalysis, which is not discussed by Canguilhem in this article.

At this point, it is authority, rather than concepts, which is being borrowed by the *Cahiers* group. Its opposition to psychology usually remains remarkably ill-defined in that specific theories are rarely invoked. Canguilhem's criticisms of a specific project become part of a generalized anathema and contribute to the creation of a climate in which Thomas Herbert (i.e., Michel Pêcheux) can quite casually dismiss Melanie Klein and object-relations theory as an empiricist concept of the relation between signifier and signified grounded in an account of 'the pseudo-genesis of the order of the symbolic within the biological order'.[72] By now, Frege was more likely to be the theoretical mentor than either Althusser or Canguilhem.

Althusser's sole written contribution to the *Cahiers* was a reading of Rousseau on the Social Contract which looked rather out of place, if not simply archaic, in the context of the proposed 'genealogy of the sciences'.[73] The ultimate heritage of the Rejection Front of 1963 would lie not in historical and dialectical materialism, but in the formalized Lacanianism that was to emerge in the 1970s. Althusser would view it with a certain dismay, referring to it as a mere variant of a logical formalism.[74] In 1977, Althusser's reading of Freud himself was not dissimilar to what it had been in 'Freud and Lacan', and he still referred to the need to relate the theory of sexuality to ideological agencies and apparatuses. The dream of scientificity was still a possibility. Freud's concept of fantasy, Althusser concluded, was not a *scientific* concept because it was a metaphor, 'but *for us*, on the other hand, it may be the concept of the limit that separates a theoretical formation which has not yet become a science, from a science that is to come. For there is, thank God, a little bit of fantasy between theoretical formation and science: the illusion of having attained scientificity and, given that fantasy is contradictory, perhaps a bit of a true desire to attain scientificity.'[75] Maybe it is the dream of scientificity that is eternal.

NOTES

1 'La Psychanalyse, idéologie réactionnaire', *La Nouvelle Critique*, June 1949.
2 Michel Pêcheux, *Language, Semantics and Ideology*, Macmillan, London, 1982, p. 211.
3 Louis Althusser, *Eléments d'auto-critique*, Hachette, Paris, 1974, p. 65.
4 Louis Althusser, 'Philosophie et sciences humaines', *Revue de l'enseignement philosophique*, June-July 1963, cited in 'Freud and Lacan' in *Lenin and Philosophy and Other Essays*, New Left Books, London, 1971, p. 181n.
5 Louis Althusser, letter of 26 November 1963 to Lacan, reproduced in *Magazine Littéraire* 304, November 1992, p. 50.
6 Jacques Lacan, letter of 1 December 1963 to Althusser, reproduced in ibid.
7 Louis Althusser, 'Theory, Theoretical Practice and Theoretical Formation: Ideology and Ideological Struggle', *Philosophy and the Spontaneous Philosophy of the Scientists and Other Essays*, Verso, London, 1990, pp. 19, 41.
8 Louis Althusser, 'Introduction: Today', in *For Marx*, Allen Lane, London, 1969.
9 'Freud and Lacan', p. 179.
10 Jacques Lacan, 'Subversion du sujet et dialectique du désir dans l'inconscient freudien' (1960), *Ecrits*, Seuil, Paris, 1966, pp. 808–09; 'Variantes de la cure-type' (1955), ibid., p. 335, n. 1.
11 'Freud and Lacan', p. 186.
12 Étienne Balibar, 'Sur les concepts fondamentaux du matérialisme historique', in Althusser and Balibar, *Lire le Capital*, Maspero, Paris, 1968, vol. 2, p. 137.
13 Althusser, 'Freud and Lacan', p. 182.
14 Louis Althusser, 'Du "Capital" à la philosophie de Marx', in Althusser and Balibar, *Lire le Capital*, Maspero, Paris, 1968, vol. 1, pp. 12–13; cf. pp. 28–29, where Althusser refers to 'a reading which we might dare to call *symptomatic* insofar as it detects in a single movement what is undetected in the text it is reading and relates it to *another text*, present in a necessary absence in the first text'.
15 Ibid., pp. 12–13.
16 Jacques-Alain Miller, 'Action de la structure' (1964), *Cahiers pour l'analyse* 9, Summer 1968, pp. 93–105. See also Jacques Rancière, *Lire le Capital* vol. 3, Maspero, Paris, 1973.
17 Louis Althusser, 'Ideology and Ideological State Apparatuses (Notes Towards an Investigation)', in *Lenin and Philosophy*, pp. 121–76.

18 Ibid., p. 136n.
19 'Marxism and Humanism', in *For Marx*, p. 233.
20 'Ideology and Ideological State Apparatuses', p. 155.
21 Jacques Rancière, *La Leçon d'Althusser*, Gallimard, Paris, 1974, p. 88.
22 Louis Althusser, *L'avenir dure longtemps, suivi de Les faits: Autobiographies*, Stock/IMEC, Paris, 1992, p. 155: 'What did the Ecole become? . . . a substitute for a maternal environment, for the *amniotic* fluid.'
23 'Freud and Lacan', pp. 177–78.
24 'Ideology and Ideological State Apparatuses', p. 137 n. Cf. the note to 'Freud and Lacan', p. 194: 'It is not enough to know that the Western family is patriarchal and exogamic . . . we must also work out the ideological formations that govern paternity, maternity, conjugality and childhood: what are "husband-and-wife-being", "father-being", "mother-being" and "child-being" in the modern world? A mass of research remains to be done on these ideological formations. This is a task for *historical materialism*.'
25 Ibid., p. 177.
26 'Freud and Lacan', p. 181.
27 Ibid., p. 182.
28 Ibid., p. 185.
29 See Gregory Elliott, 'Althusser's Solitude', in E. Ann Kaplan and Michael Sprinker, eds, *The Althusserian Legacy*, Verso, London, 1993.
30 Jacques Lacan, *The Four Fundamental Concepts of Psychoanalysis*, The Hogarth Press and the Institute of Psychoanalysis, London, 1977, pp. 3–4.
31 Louis Althusser, *L'avenir dure longtemps*, p. 177.
32 'Freud and Lacan', p. 201.
33 Jacques Lacan, 'Le stade du miroir comme formateur de la fonction du Je telle qu'elle nous est révelée dans l'expérience psychanalytique' (1949), *Ecrits*, pp. 93–100; 'L'aggressivité en psychanalyse', ibid., pp. 101–124.
34 See, in particular, Henri Wallon, *Les Origines du caractère chez l'enfant*, Presses Universitaires de France, Paris, 1949.
35 G. W. F. Hegel, *The Phenomenology of Mind*, tr. J. B. Baillie, Harper and Row, New York and Evanston, 1967, p. 514.
36 On Kojève's very odd career, see Dominique Auffret, *Alexandre Kojève: La philosophie, l'état et la fin de l'histoire*, Grasset, Paris, 1990.
37 Francis Fukuyama, *The End of History and the Last Man*, Hamish Hamilton, London, 1992.
38 Kojève is never mentioned in *Ecrits*. Lacan refers to him as a 'master' in a paper delivered in 1967 ('La méprise du sujet supposé savoir', *Scilicet* 1, 1968, p. 33); cf. *Le Séminaire. Livre XX: Encore*, Seuil, Paris, 1975, p. 97.
39 Althusser, 'Freud and Lacan', p. 188.
40 Ibid., p. 195n.
41 Alexandre Kojève, *Introduction à la lecture de Hegel*, Gallimard, Paris, 1979, p. 169.
42 Jean Hyppolite, 'Situation de l'homme dans la "Phénomènologie" hégélienne' (1947), in *Figures de la pensée philosophique*, Presses Universitaires de France, Paris, 1991, p. 115.
43 Michel Foucault, *L'ordre du discours*, Gallimard, Paris, 1971, pp. 74–75.
44 'Ideology and Ideological State Apparatuses', p. 162.

45 Ibid., p. 163.
46 Michèle Barrett, 'Althusser's Marx, Althusser's Lacan', in *The Althusserian Legacy*, p. 174.
47 'Ideology and Ideological State Apparatuses', p. 152.
48 Sigmund Freud, 'The Unconscious', in *The Pelican Freud Library. Vol 11: On Metapsychology: The Theory of Psychoanalysis*, Harmondsworth, 1984, p. 191.
49 'Theory, Theoretical Practice and Theoretical Formation', p. 25.
50 'Ideology and Ideological State Apparatuses', p. 164.
51 'Freud and Lacan', p. 187.
52 Ibid., p. 198.
53 David Macey, *Lacan in Contexts*, Verso, London, 1988.
54 Michel Foucault, 'La Vie: l'expérience et la science', *Revue de métaphysique et de morale* 90, January/March 1985, p. 4. First published as the preface to *On the Normal and the Pathological*, Riedel, Boston, 1978.
55 Pierre Bourdieu, 'Aspirant philosophe: un point de vue sur la champ universitaire dans les années 50', in *Les enjeux philosophiques des années 50*, Centre Georges Pompidou, Paris.
56 Georges Canguilhem, 'Le normal et le pathologique' (1951), in *La connaissance de la vie*, Vrin, Paris, 1989, p. 155.
57 Jean Cavaillès, *Sur la logique et la théorie de la science*, 4th edn, Vrin, Paris, 1987, p. 78.
58 Louis Althusser, *L'avenir dure longtemps*, p. 75.
59 The gist of Canguilhem's arguments will be found in his 'L'objet de l'histoire des sciences', *Études d'histoire et de philosophie des sciences*, fifth edn, Vrin, Paris, 1989, pp. 9–23.
60 Georges Canguilhem, 'Qu'est-ce qu'une idéologie scientifique?', in *Idéologie et rationalité dans l'histoire des sciences de la vie*, second edn, Vrin, Paris, 1988, pp. 33–46.
61 Ibid., p. 10.
62 Jean Laplanche, *Seduction, Translation, Drives*, John Fletcher and Martin Stanton, eds, Institute of Contemporary Arts, London, 1992, p. 3.
63 Jacques-Alain Miller, 'Avertissement', *Cahiers pour l'analyse* 1, January/February 1966.
64 Jacques-Alain Miller, 'Action de la structure', p. 93.
65 Ibid., p. 100.
66 Cf. Elisabeth Roudinesco, *Jacques Lacan & Co.: A History of Psychoanalysis in France 1925–1985*, Free Association Books, London, 1990, pp. 398–99.
67 For the background and context, see Elisabeth Roudinesco, 'Situation d'un texte: "Qu'est-ce que la psychologie?" ', in the collective volume *Georges Canguilhem: Philosophe, historien des sciences*, Albin Michel, Paris, 1983, pp. 135–44.
68 Georges Canguilhem, 'Qu'est-ce que la psychologie?, *Cahiers pour l'analyse* 2, March-April 1966.
69 Ibid., p. 89.
70 Daniel Lagache, *L'unité de la psychologie*, Presses Universitaires de France, Paris, 1949.
71 Canguilhem, 'Qu'est-ce que la psychologie?', p. 89.

72 Thomas Herbert, 'Pour une théorie générale des idéologies', *Cahiers pour l'analyse* 9, Summer 1968, p. 81.
73 Louis Althusser, 'Sur le Contrat Social (Les Décalages)', *Cahiers pour l'analyse* 8, February 1968, pp. 5–42.
74 Louis Althusser, 'La Découverte du docteur Freud' (1977), in Léon Chertok, ed., *Dialogue franco-soviétique sur la psychanalyse*, Privat, Toulouse, 1984, p. 86.
75 Ibid., pp. 96–97.

7

MESSAGE IN A BOTTLE: ALTHUSSER IN LITERARY STUDIES

Francis Mulhern

Writing books is like sending messages in bottles, Louis Althusser was once heard to remark, in sorrowful reaction to the international phenomenon of 'Althusserianism': you can never tell who will come upon your words or what they will make of them.

In literary studies, which were neither first nor last among Althusser's interests, these messages were soon found and read. The experience (a newly fateful word) was a daunting one, but there was also elation; it felt, for many, like the definitive moment of liberation. But like all such moments, it was only a beginning, and, after nearly three decades of commentary and elaboration, its meaning has come to seem more ambiguous and elusive, nothing so simple as the revelation it once appeared to be.[1]

Althusser's theoretical intervention 'for Marx' bore upon both the substance and the status of historical materialism.[2] Marx's revolution had entailed more than a materialist inversion of Hegel's dialectic, he maintained. The new theory abandoned the supposed expressivism of the old philosophy, substituting the idea of an inherently complex social whole whose political and ideological instances were 'relatively autonomous', 'specifically effective', determined only 'in the last instance' by the economic. Determination, in this conceptual scheme, was likewise complex: not singular yet not merely plural, it was, so to say, typically exceptional in its workings. Any contradiction was as a rule internally marked by the contradictions that formed its conditions of existence, in irreducible states and processes of 'overdetermination'. A complex whole and thus complex time: history so conceived could not move according to a single, regular beat; rather, it must be seen as possessing a 'differential' temporality, yielding an arhythmic succession of unique conjunctures.

These, for Althusser, were the elements of historical materialism proper, after its critical disengagement from historicism and humanism. Against the first, it proposed a decentred, non-expressive process; against the second, it asserted the primacy of structures and practices over the concrete individuals who were, rigorously conceived, their bearers; and in both respects it broke decisively with the problematic of 'the subject' as author or source of history. 'The subject' was the pivotal category in Althusser's main specific undertaking in historical materialism, the exploration of the concept of 'ideology'. This term and its associated meanings had led an irregular, mercurial life in Marxist tradition; in Althusser's thought, it assumed a constant and overwhelming role. Ideology here was a relatively autonomous practice whose principal function was to secure the reproduction of the relations of production; yet received notions of illusion, mystification, false consciousness and spiritualized interest conveyed little of its existential sway. Not the work of subjects, ideology worked *them*, 'interpellating' the social singularities called individuals '*as* subjects', into the identities that qualified them as social agents. These identities sustained an 'imaginary' relation to real conditions, and yet were indispensable, now and in any human future. To live at all was to live in ideology.

Knowledge, strictly speaking, was *scientific* knowledge, the fruit of a non-subjectivist theoretical labour upon the heterogeneous data of experience, that is, ideology. Here was Althusser's complementary claim – the second aspect of his intervention – concerning the *status* of Marx's innovation. As a science, historical materialism founded itself in a break with ideology, constructing its theoretical objects, and elaborating analyses that would be governed by the protocols of theoretical practice itself, not by the (ideological) indications of the empirical world.

Althusser's prospectus for theoretical practice must seem overweening, and in important respects it really was. Like Karl Popper, whose fallibilism is not the most distant of comparisons, Althusser not only accorded unique cognitive privilege to science but invested it with the pathos of heroism. It was not surprising that suspicions of neo-positivism and Stalinist dogmatism should so readily have arisen. Yet notwithstanding the leitmotiv of Marxist triumphalism in his writing, Althusser's 'return to Marx' was not an intellectual reversion to party type. His insistence on the integrity of science did not entail a claim of exclusivity for historical materialism. The theoretical field within which he situated Marx's science was not the old 'dialectical materialism' but the human sciences – specifically, the new 'quadrivium' of history, ethnology, psychoanalysis and linguistics, and their lingua franca, 'structuralism'.[3] The pursuit of scientificity here meant the repudiation of intellectual autarky.

The general themes and orientations of Althusser's Marxism were in themselves sufficient to establish his appeal for the Left in English literary studies, among whom a sense of intellectual illegitimacy was deep and persistent. From the classics, they inherited the synopsis of a general theory, and a few famous fragments concerning Ancient art or Balzac's politics or realism in the novel and drama. The great systematizers of the Second International, irrespective of their individual cultural complexions, tended to see art mainly as a prestigious test case for their general explanatory claims; they brought it down to earth, but then left it there. The Bolshevik generation – notably Lenin and Trotsky – found occasions for ideological intervention in literary life, but wrote little that might serve more general purposes. The British Marxism of the 1930s – represented by Alick West, Ralph Fox and, above all, Christopher Caudwell – was a collective embarrassment.[4] Its direct inheritors sponsored an uncompelling Communist variant of familiar literary-academic procedure. The eventual scope of Raymond Williams's long revolution was as yet undiscerned. Georg Lukács's work furnished the inescapable point of contemporary reference, with his successor Lucien Goldmann an increasingly conspicuous second. And what both thinkers offered were lines of analysis that, though strong and sophisticated, were incorrigibly schematic in their treatment of history and texts, and – notoriously in Lukács's case – prone to aesthetic dogmatism. The Frankfurt School, or what was known of it in Britain at that time, offered a richer and crucially more modern intellectual culture, but was not exempt from the general suspicion of summary totalizing constructions. Thoroughly as such Marxist styles might be learned, scrupulously though they might be practiced, the internalized reproach of the dominant tradition, with its watchwords of fidelity to the empirical record and the detailed life of the text, would not be stilled.[5]

Then came Althusser ('Contradiction and Overdetermination appeared in English in 1967, the entire *For Marx* in 1969; *Reading Capital* followed in 1970) and the prospect of a new departure. Thanks to the new historical concepts, the determinist and schematizing tendencies apparently ingrained in Marxist literary studies could be criticized and overcome in uncompromisingly Marxist terms. The new understanding of ideology, with its crucial revaluation of 'experience', discomposed the first principle of conduct in the dominant critical tradition. Beyond the complementary errors of Marxist 'historicism' and liberal-humanist 'empiricism', it was possible and necessary to broach the scientific, historical-materialist concept of art as an irreducible social practice, to imagine a properly Marxist theory of an unambiguously specified object.

Althusser's personal interest in this project inspired two compelling occasional essays, one on Strehler's Paris production of *El Nost Milan*, the other on the paintings of Cremonini.[6] Beyond their engagement with particular cases, these texts display keen awareness of general questions of theory and method. Both accord analytic primacy to the material event (the play, the canvas) and the practice it instantiates. The 'subjects' of these practices (author, director, painter, spectator) are registered but displaced: the reading of Cremonini's canvases is not controlled by the evidence of the painter's intentional project; the Brechtian reflection on empathetic theatre explores a non-psychologistic understanding of audience response. And both essays are framed as polemics against critical 'gastronomy', the established obstacle to criticism as knowledge.

Yet they cannot be taken as pilots of such a criticism. Althusser seizes upon Strehler's Bertolazzi because its strange dual tempo dramatizes something like his own understanding of the ideological. Cremonini's verticals and circles excite him because he sees in them a figuration of his own anti-humanism. Both texts are, as it were, moments of counter-ideological 'recognition' (the indispensable word), the more euphorically articulate for that, but the less instructive as adumbrations of a new theory and practice.

However, Althusser's only programmatic declaration concerning aesthetics, the letter to André Daspre, appeared to underwrite this conflation of theoretical specification and aesthetic preference. Althusser's goal was 'a real knowledge of art'; his means – 'there is no other way' – a 'rigorous reflection on the basic concepts of Marxism'. For now, he would elaborate 'a first idea'. Art is categorially distinct from science; it does not produce knowledge in the strict sense. Yet it is not an indifferent mode of the ideological. For art sustains a differential relation to knowledge; it can 'make us see' the 'reality' to which it 'alludes', and this by virtue of the 'internal distance' it establishes *within* ideology. He was, of course, talking here about 'authentic art, not works of an average or mediocre level'. . . .[7] If this was a call to a new theoretical quest, it seemed that the likely route would be circular. 'First ideas' are always awkward (Althusser wrote movingly about the unequal struggle to innovate in received idioms), but this one seemed all too settled. Art as categorially distinct from science, rooted in everyday language yet capable of privileged insight; aesthetics as, in effect, the elucidation of artistic greatness, not the knowledge of a specific practice but an elaborated protocol of discrimination – these were the commonplaces of the literary academy. It was not easy, at this point, to see how Marxist self-reflection (which was not encouraged, on this occasion, to communicate with other critical knowledges) would transmute them into science.

The declared context of the letter to Daspre was the work of Althusser's young collaborator Pierre Macherey, whose *Pour une théorie de la production littéraire* (appearing in the same year, 1966) was the inaugural statement of Marxist theoretical practice in the field of the literary.[8] Macherey's book was, in two senses, a study in morphology. Its first concern was to determine the characteristic shape of received literary criticism – the forms of its attention – and to assert the contrasting protocols of a scientific alternative; its emerging theme, elaborating the founding thesis of this science, was the action of literary form in ideology. Received criticism acted as if to regulate writing and reading in the 'domain' of literature. As a 'normative' practice, it judges comparative achievement; as 'interpretation' it offers to resolve and mediate meaning; and in both modes it proceeds fallaciously, actually 'replacing' what it claims to analyse with ideal others – the work as it might have been or in its 'full' meaning. A scientific criticism, in contrast, would be a discourse of knowledge, a systematic inquiry into the 'laws' of a theoretically specified object: literary 'production' as a determinate material practice in ideology.

The results of literary production, Macherey went on to claim, were the opposite of those affirmed in critical tradition: not composure and fullness but incompleteness, discrepancy and absence. These were the effects of literary form. For although literature was not science, it 'naturally scorn[ed] the credulous view of the world'; held within ideology, its 'determinate insufficiency' nevertheless parodied and caricatured ideology, thus offering an 'implicit critique' of it.[9] The task of a Marxist criticism was to trace the workings of this productive disorder and to explain it.

Macherey's theoretical excursion was in all relevant senses Althusserian, but it was not in any ordinary sense Marxist. The official inspiration of the book was Lenin – invoked here as elsewhere with unstinted ceremony – but its more substantial, though tacit, intellectual debt was to a thinker whose example had become canonical in Althusser's circle: Freud. The imago of text and critic in Macherey's discourse was the symptom and its (psycho)analyst. Literary works could be understood as the dreams, jokes and parapraxes of a divided collective subjectivity. The analogy is a powerful one (indeed, a little further meditation upon it might have refined Macherey's undiscriminating critique of interpretation), but it does not license the further assumption concerning the differential critical value of the literary. Freud's symptomatic texts are valuable as evidence for analysis; in themselves they are modes of unknowing, denial, confusion. But according to Macherey, cognitive privilege belonged to the literary as such, and not only to the theory that could explain its figurations. Like Althusser, he conceded literature a place of co-primacy with science in the hierarchy of culture.

Macherey would subsequently take quite different bearings,[10] but, for now, a distinctive Althusserian problematic remained in force: the object proper to Marxist theoretical investigation was 'ideology and literary form'. This was the title of the first English-language initiative under Althusser's general aegis, Terry Eagleton's pilot essay for his *Criticism and Ideology*.[11] The model of theoretical practice was evident in the shape of Eagleton's inquiry. A probing review of the received critical culture in its liberal and socialist forms (Leavis and Williams respectively) led to a general theoretical construction of the place of the literary in the social whole, and thence towards the summit, a 'science of the text'. The central propositions of the book were in the main familiar: 'materialist criticism' as an anti-humanist, anti-historicist practice forwarded in a break with ideology; literature as ideology 'raised to the second power'; Freud as the exemplary theorist and reader of self-divided textual production. Yet as well as elaborating and varying these themes, Eagleton lodged punctual criticisms of Althusser and Macherey. He noted the tendentious reservation in the letter to Daspre, and insisted, in opposition to Macherey, that the literature-ideology relationship was not necessarily subversive. It was, he observed, as if literature must be spared 'the shame of the sheerly ideological', as if 'the aesthetic must still be granted mysteriously privileged status, but now in embarrassedly oblique style'.[12] Exactly so. But Althusser and Macherey were not alone in the hour of their temptation. What Eagleton feared in their texts he was in the end unable to banish from his own. The central chapter of *Criticism and Ideology* recorded a struggle in process, here assigning special powers to literature, there reserving them to the (duly rigorous) reader, and never surrendering the conviction, which was also secure in Althusser and Macherey, that there existed a stable entity named 'literature' (or 'form') to be known, a real object awaiting its adequate concept.

This undischarged essentialism found its counterpart in the closing chapter of Eagleton's study, an attempt without precedent in Althusser or Macherey to theorize differential literary value. Rightly affirming the necessity of such a theory (differential judgement is for many strictly analytic purposes irrelevant or even diversionary, but in the ordinary world of culture it is ineluctable), Eagleton also maintained that a Marxist account of value would be relational or transitive: a text is valuable, that is, not in itself, but for certain users in specific conditions (the presiding spirit here was Brecht). Yet his discussion gravitated towards the opposite conclusion, seeking value in the historical conditions of production of the text, and so suggesting an originary and lasting endowment of distinction or banality; literary value was, after all, the immanent variation of an essential category.[13]

In these texts, the project of an Althusserian Marxist theory of the aesthetic was boldly launched and as surely frustrated. Their governing problematic was, as Althusser might have said, 'amphibological': an old category refigured as a new concept, an attempt to furnish a scientific answer to an unsurmounted philosophical question.[14] Macherey himself went on to reject the question 'what is literature?' as an unwarrantable intrusion into sovereign theoretical space. His later work at once redrew the theoretical image of literature to emphasize its role in the production of ideological compromise, and, more radically, turned from literature as text to literary culture as an institutionalized ideological practice – to 'the literary effect' as it is deployed in the educational apparatus of the class-divided nation.[15] Eagleton noted the possibility of such modified lines of analysis, but chose not to pursue them; his subsequent work turned away from the architectonic prospectus of *Criticism and Ideology* in favour of an interventionist, 'political' criticism that, though not less theoretically engaged and still emphatically Marxist, could not be called 'Althusserian'.[16]

Meanwhile, another initiative had sprung into vigorous life. Taking early shape in the years of Althusser's greatest productivity, the collaborative work of the *Tel Quel* circle centred on Phillipe Sollers and Julia Kristeva developed rapidly, reaching a critical moment of self-definition – so history was pleased to have it – a few months after the events of May-June 1968.[17] Althusser's affiliates maintained a pointed distance from *Tel Quel*, as if in awkward consciousness of eager but unsought company.[18] Althusser was a canonical reference in the journal – like Lacan, an acknowledged *levier*, lever or influence, in its work.[19] But its closer mentors were Barthes, Derrida and Foucault, who led off the collective volume, *Théorie d'ensemble*.[20] Above all other things a resumption of French avant-garde traditions in the arts, and at this time devoted to an anarcho-Maoist programme of cultural revolution, *Tel Quel* set its theoretical bearings in an intellectual network (*réseau* was a favoured metaphor) that included Althusser and partly sustained him, but with very different intellectual and political priorities. Althusserian Marxism was thus at once valorized and displaced, functioning here as a privileged citation in a context at once familiar and alien.

The more sanguine, less defensive evaluation of this development was that *Tel Quel* offered a possible realization of Althusser's vision of a non-autarkic Marxism developing as a science among others, in the space of cultural theory. This, indeed, was the spirit animating a kindred project that took shape in Britain, in the work of *Screen*.

'The *Screen* project' is a familiar way of evoking a collaborative enterprise that eludes simple summary. The magazine never was intellectually homogeneous, in large part because of the discrepant interests in play in its parent organization, the Society for Education in Film and Television. Its dominant intellectual tendency, in the critical passage of the 1970s, was itself unstable, in part because of the quick tempos and syncopated rhythms characteristic of an import-dependent vanguard culture, and in part also because there was no pre-established harmony among the theoretical interests that now came to the fore. 'The *Screen* project' is not a true singular, and there is no definitive version of it. However, with such qualifications made, there was no mistaking the difference between this and the other, more strictly canonical reading of Althusserian possibilities.

There was, to begin with, a weighty difference of circumstance. It cannot have been unimportant that *Screen*'s given field of activity was cinema rather than literature. The sheer materiality of cinema as industry, technical practice and experience was less easily spiritualized than that of the literary institution – whose conservative devotees, indeed, would affirm just so much, knowing full well the difference between a conventicle and a crowd. The strategic *topoi* of modern critical culture were not settled truths here: auteurism may have reiterated traditionalist notions of composition and reading, but it also helped to undo the disciplinary segregation of 'art' and 'entertainment'; and while essentialist theories of 'film' were advanced, they encountered stubborn resistance in the objective complexity of the developed filmic repertoire, with its multiple and variably ordered matters of expression. Furthermore, the availability of a diverse oppositional film-making culture, in which some of the journal's editors were directly involved, was bound to inflect all theoretical reflection – as Benjamin was aware, any object appears differently in the perspective of production.

Althusser's demand for the analysis of specific, relatively autonomous practices and his construction of ideology as institutionalized material practice furnished the general terms legitimating an unconstrained exploration of cinema in its full historical and structural complexity; at the same time, the whole history of both dominant and critical cinema acted against the kind of conceptual inertia that patterned the letter to Daspre. *Screen*'s inquiry into the formation, functioning and tendential effects of cinematic practices was pursued along lines at first parallel and soon convergent with that of *Tel Quel*, in an inter-theoretical discourse on ideology, subject and text.

Semiotics, developing through a critical ingathering of modern scientific initiatives in poetics and linguistics – formalist, structuralist and other – offered concepts and taxonomies that bore the promise of a post-aesthetic, materialist analysis of textual forms and functions. Psychoanalysis appeared not merely as a potent analogy but as a decisive contributor to the understanding of subjectivity. Marxism furnished terms of historical understanding and defined the politics of text and subject. There was more than one summary of this theoretical conjunction. Peter Wollen identified a meta-theoretical unity of purpose: 'each concerns itself with an area of human activity that articulates natural with social history' – signs, labour and sexuality. Stephen Heath, more tentative, spoke of 'the encounter of Marxism with psychoanalysis on the terrain of semiotics'.[21] There was, equally, no regularity of proportion in the work produced under its aegis. Wollen's work did not (and does not) take the totalizing course that his general formulation might be taken to indicate, rather moving from topic to topic with unruffled flexibility of emphasis and theoretical reference. Heath was, in practice, the more concerned to probe the sense of the general strategy in particular settings of analysis. In the *Screen* circle generally, variations multiplied. Consistent with its own critical themes, this was an 'impure' project, lacking an essence.[22] The yield was very impressive, but it furnished the evidence that this second version of Althusserian initiative – all at once broader, bolder and more modest – was scarcely better insured than the first. The renunciation of Marxist autarky in favour of a dialogic theoretical discourse enhanced productivity, but not, therefore, predictable analytic output. This was not a story of scientific progress from incompleteness into notional sufficiency. Marxist cultural theory had need of that critical contact, but, dialogue being what it is when not a pious simulation, theories have a way of talking back – and with results that owe something to rational debate but rather more to force of circumstance.

Throughout the 1970s, Althusser remained an inspirational reference. The intensifying and increasingly influential work of the Birmingham Centre for Contemporary Cultural Studies was indebted to him. The names of Eagleton and Macherey identified a whole critical tendency. Marxist-feminist writers – Cora Kaplan and Penny Boumelha, for example – looked to Althusser's historical concepts as a means of articulating class and gender determinations in textual analysis.[23] Tony Bennett set out to liquidate Marxism's deep dependence on essentialist notions of literature and value in a line of investigation that, though inevitably divergent from the prior analyses of Macherey and Eagleton and critical of them, was nevertheless plainly Althusserian in spirit.[24] It was easy to believe, looking around, that the outlook for theoretical practice was good.

In retrospect, however, the 1970s may be seen as the years of the great Althusserian inflation, a *trompe l'oeil* sequence in which ever-greater discursive circulation concealed a draining of conceptual value. There were at least three agencies at work in this. One was the banalizing process to which any influential idea is vulnerable. Another, more substantial, was the progress of Althusser's leading British exponents, whose quest for rigour led them to press one after another of their mentor's philosophical proposals to the point of self-destruction.[25] The third, and much the weightiest, was more general, and strictly political: a relative decline of all Marxisms, attendant upon the frustration, reversal or decomposition of the historical tendencies that had seemed to vindicate them. Marxism commanded the attention of a whole gallery of intellectual and political interests because, irrespective of its theoretical or programmatic cogency in any given area (which, indeed, might not impress at all), it seemed the inescapable context of radical thought and activity. As the ideological banner of a practical movement, it had a record of achievement (however mixed), a social constituency actual or potential (the labour movement), and immediate prospects in every global theatre. Given such historical endowments, Marxist theory could survive any particular challenge. The corollary – that without these practical supports, the theory would have far less intuitive appeal – was not much dwelt upon, but there was no evading the force of the eventual demonstration.

The course of the 1980s, in every part of the world, mocked every conventional socialist expectation. Social democracy, Communism, anti-imperialism and revolutionary socialism – all were visited by counter-finalities that could be said to falsify them as general formats of political advance. The very name of socialism, long the site of fierce discursive rivalry, now seemed too monologic for some left-wing sensibilities. Historical materialism – the appropriately general theory of historical processes as dynamic wholes – fared no better. Appearing no longer to answer to common-sense estimates of the probable or the practical, it suffered a co-ordinate loss of critical authority. The stronger radical political trends of the eighties were particularist; and in the radical academy, above all in its departments of literary and cultural studies, matching styles of analysis appeared – perspectivist, and agnostic or hostile towards totalizing thought. It was this great ecological shift, rather than any newly discovered problem or any pre-given outcome of intellectual arbitration, that redrew the pattern of selection pressures, to the disadvantage of Marxism and in favour of the counter-enlightenment thematics that now proliferated as post-structuralism, or post-modernism, or – a hybrid for the times – post-Marxism.[26]

But even now, in a milieu increasingly indifferent to Marxism and ever more ignorant of it, the name of Althusser continued to be invoked. For he it was whose concept of relative autonomy had cautiously opened the transition to a social theory no longer inhibited by the dogma of a closed totality with a determining economic ground. He it was whose theory of ideology, once relieved of its functionalist embarrassment, had recentred cultural analysis on the question of the subject and its constructions. He it was who had helped to nurture the inter-theoretical dialogue that was now entering its maturity. In truth, or so some theorists persuaded themselves, Althusser really *was* a post-structuralist, the Monsieur Jourdain of the avant-garde. One veteran of the theory wars, Antony Easthope, discerned in the whole sequence a grand narrative of anti-humanism. Easthope's *British Post-structuralism*, a serial review of the seventies and eighties, is generous, pleasingly worldly, and firmly socialist in spirit. Yet as a construction of theoretical history it is shaped by a Whiggish evolutionism that assimilates all pre-existing virtue to Althusser, and then forwards it to the culminating moment of post-structuralism. *New Left Review*'s Gramscian theses on Britain are glossed in the light of the journal's later interest in Althusser, who is now accredited with sole authorship of a theme (relative autonomy) as old as Engels. 'Althusser', we are told, 'imported into Britain at least three lines of thought . . . which can be validly regarded as post-structuralist: the account of the historical formation as decentred; the assertion that knowledge as proceeding from theoretical practice is discursively constructed; the account of the subject as effect rather than cause.' So much, then, for Darwin (the first 'line') or Popper (the second), or Freud (the third). And so much for Althusser, whose work, for all its self-interpellation as Marxist, 'is best regarded now as a structuralism passing over into post-structuralism'.[27] Excess of hindsight, teleological reversion, rationalization: Easthope's rendering provokes any or all of these objections. However motivated, it is untenable as a summation of the left theoretical culture of the past thirty-odd years. But it does, in its way, confirm the poignant impression that, by the end of the eighties, Althusser's name, enfolding certain vestiges of his ideas, survived as little more than a souvenir in a culture that had largely forgotten his intellectual and political projects.

The transition to post-structuralism, in the sense of a generalized thematics now current in a post-Marxist academic Left, was not so much an autonomous critical process, more the effect of manifold political disenchantment – not a working out, however unforeseen, of Althusser's logic but an abandonment of it. To say so is not to deliver a summary judgement on the diverse thinkers that found the post-structuralist canon, or on the varied work now proceeding in their joint and several names: the new culture of subversion is a whole far less than the sum of its parts. Neither is it to claim that there exists a pristine theoretical practice, obscured but not annihilated by years of misappropriation, to which, like Althusser to Marx, we must now return. The matter is more difficult and the prospect far less clear. In conclusion – though that is not the ideal word – it may be worthwhile to dwell a little on some of Althusser's key ideas, and to offer a provisional latter-day assessment of them.

Ideology was the theme for which Althusser became celebrated in radical literary and cultural studies; and the course of his thinking marked it as his most ambiguous theoretical venture. Althusser's view was in one respect familiar: the concept of ideology implied a determinate relationship between cognitive deficiency and social interest; it was, in the authorized words of his English translator, a mode in which 'the practico-social predominates . . . over the theoretical, over knowledge'.[28] But the discrepancy between knowledge and the practico-social had never been so insisted upon. Ideology was pervasive, the spontaneous knowing-unknowing of human experience in this and all possible societies.[29] Without relinquishing the first, more familiar sense of the concept, Althusser then pursued his elaboration of the second. The 'imaginary relation' of ideology was the mode in which the ideo-affective life of humans assumed its socially viable form as identity: ideology 'interpellates the individual as a subject.' In arguing thus, Althusser effected a drastic and damaging conflation of two distinct problems: the functioning of ideology in its more familiar sense, as a socially motivated differential relation to knowledge, and the general mechanism of human subject-formation. How, in this perspective, could ideology be known or displaced? Althusser's established response was: by science and art. But if ideology was now identical with the anthropological constant of identity-formation, how could these be conceptualized as ordinary historical practices? And if, contrariwise, they could be retained only as quasi-miraculous interventions in the imaginary – if, that is, they could not be retained at all, but must rather be discarded as rationalist and romantic mystifications – what would remain of ideology as a critical concept? These and kindred objections came from sympathetic and hostile commentators alike, and most influentially from post-structuralist quarters, where a counter-construction had already taken shape. Althusserian 'science' was implicated in the characteristic disavowal of meta-discourse, which exempted itself from the conditions of existence that it stipulated for its objects. The account of subject-formation was either false, and hence inadequate, or valid, and therefore subversive of its own pretensions to final rationality. In either case, the ideal of scientificity was unfounded, as also was its putative other, the supporting fiction of ideology. 'Science' was a gambit in 'the politics of truth', a power-play in the contention of discourses and their subjects.

This destructive response has proved most attractive to contemporary taste, but there were others, including at least one of Althusserian inspiration. Göran Therborn proposed a mechanism internal to ideology, such that the fatalistic unity subjectification-subjection could pass into self-contradiction, generating crises of identity and belief with uncertain outcomes – in other words, a material 'dialectic of consciousness' of the kind that Althusser tended to resist.[30] The limitation of Therborn's analysis, taken over from Althusser, was its bracketing of science (along with art) as a special case. Just as Althusser's formalist analysis of subjectification occluded the fact that all ideology advances truth-claims, so Therborn encouraged the specular inference that knowledge-bearing discourse is somehow not implicated in the formation of subjects. There is no such division of labour in the real world of discourse, where logics and rhetorics act indissociably, and seldom according to a rule of inverse proportions. If the theory of subject-formation holds at all, it must hold for all discursive practice. Yet Althusserian reason seemed unable to secure its legitimate philosophical defence of scientificity without abstractions of this kind, so provoking agnostic and irrationalist counter-attack. This predicament had a strictly epistemological ground in an anti-realist account of science, which then found self-destructive confirmation in a false reduction of culture to ideology.

Raymond Williams has been seen as the humanist antithesis of the Althusserian sensibility, but his developed theory of culture, far from incompatible with the science/ideology distinction, may prove its safer setting. Culture, in Williams's sense, is the integrally historical making of sense and of subjects, always both.[31] Its substance is the work of material practices – rhetorics, institutions. Culture does not constitute an expressive totality: its antagonisms are complex, its times differential, and its meanings discrepant and changeable. Ideology (restored to a stricter sense as socially determined mystification) and science (understood, less heroically, as fallible rational inquiry into the real) are present, but as contingent faculties of cultural practice, not its primordial essences. Literature is present too, of course, but now in a role more evident to the later Macherey than to Althusser, as an ideological formation in the history of writing and reading. However, Macherey's analytic shift from text to institution, though productive in itself, was less a resolution of his earlier theoretical difficulty than an escape from it. Inquiry into the forms and functions of textuality, however formalist it must often appear, will remain central to any literary theory deserving its name. It seems to me very striking, in retrospect, that Williams's understanding of literary form was from earliest days free from the essentialism that hobbled Althusser and Macherey, as indeed it has frustrated most Marxist aesthetic theorizing.

Ideology enjoyed *relative autonomy* within a complex whole determined only in the last instance by the economic. This was probably the most immediately appealing of Althusser's messages, legitimating as it did the elaboration of 'regional' theories and analyses uninhibited by the snap totalizations for which mechanistic and Hegelian styles of Marxism had become notorious. The rich yield of work done under its sign is a tribute to its intellectual worth. But as a concept, it too displayed a propensity to develop by its bad side. 'Relative autonomy' soon came under suspicion as a compromise formation mediating the antagonism between a dogmatic philosophy of history and a properly critical and materialist concept of practice. Proposed as a resolution of Marx's social topology, it was increasingly exploited as a passage into alternative theoretical space. Here again this unsought outcome was facilitated by problems in Althusser's theoretical formulations, though these were not nearly so grave as those besetting the concept of ideology. It is true that the term 'relative' often serves as an *ad hoc* lubricant of inter-prepositional friction. But the objection, delivered with an air of unsparing materialist rigour, that ideology is *either* determined *or* autonomous – no third way – was ill-founded.[32] Conditional autonomy (a more precise designation) is the typical status of complex systems; only the humanist assumption that social life is utterly distinct from the rest of reality lent credence to the confident disjunctions of Althusser's progeny. It is also true, or so I would maintain, that Althusser's formulation of 'the last instance' was deficient, conflating the temporal and structural meanings of the concept with unfortunate results.[33] But there is no great difficulty in amending this aspect of the analysis, in a plainly Marxist sense. Indeed, it seems odd that 'relative autonomy' and 'the last instance' should have attracted so much attention when, arguably, the more original contention of Althusser's discussion lay elsewhere. The titular concept of his essay was not either of these, after all, but *overdetermination*. Althusser's purpose was not – or not merely – to loosen the bad wholes of mechanist or expressivist reasoning, redistributing causal resources upwards from base to superstructure, but to substitute an alternative conception of the social *as a whole*. The concept of overdetermination did not merely designate the resultant of relatively autonomous effectivities; it offered to specify the typical form of *unity* of the social process, to show how any practice was internally marked by the other practices that constituted its conditions of existence, and thus – 'Hegelian' though it must seem – to rethink, not to discard, the notion of the presence of the whole in all its parts.

If 'relative autonomy' was the licence Althusser granted to radical literary and cultural studies, 'overdetermination' was the corresponding obligation or challenge. It was scarcely limiting, in an operational sense: this was a conceptual instrument suited equally to localized textual analysis and to large-scale historical constructions of period and genre. It legitimated productive working relations with psychoanalysis (the source of the term, indeed) and semiotics, where such concepts as Kristeva's 'intertextuality' provided support and specification; and it cleared a conceptual space within which key social determinations other than class could be explored in a non-reductionist manner. But it was the distinctively Marxist element in Althusser's scheme – unlike its associated concepts, which might be accommodated within any laodicean sociology of culture – and was not spared the general devaluation of the times. 'Overdetermination' was the first word of many of Althusser's English-speaking offspring; its meaning remains under-explored.

This short story of a concept and its fortunes may serve as a parable concerning the status of historical materialism in a wider theoretical culture. Althusser's restrictive definition of dialectical materialism and his revised account of Marx's concept of history were complementary aspects of a single, fundamental decision to renounce the vision of Marxism as a cosmology in the making, and therewith to renounce theoretical autarky. The return to Marx would be rational only if practiced as a turning out into critical solidarity with scientific inquiry in general. Althusser's defence of Lacan – theoretically, against the Zhdanovist traditions of his own party and, practically, against psychoanalytic officialdom – furnished the strongest imaginable warrant of his commitment to this revised ethics and politics of culture. (It is now common knowledge that experience had granted him a terrible cognitive advantage in the understanding of 'differential temporality' and 'specific effectivity' in psychic life.) His great theme of 'reading' as work on the materiality of texts, which drew inspiration from psychoanalysis and also from the structuralism of the day, was the appropriate practical form of a critical and self-critical mode of intellectual conduct.

This was Althusser's most important single contribution to a Marxist culture, but because it was not merely pious it was not merely a gift. There was here a difficult – and increasingly unwelcome – demand. It was possible to believe, in more euphoric moments, that a new theoretical synthesis was in prospect: an anti-humanist materialism. But this favoured locution was actually so weak ('materialism' specifies nothing about the material world, 'anti-humanism' is a crude polemical theme) that in practice it sponsored the opposite of synthesis: a new, or not so new, perspectivism. It has always seemed to me that Althusser's orientation was less than the first but more than the second of these.

A project of synthesis can hardly help but rekindle the old cosmological dream, and in doing so, inhibit rather than assist theoretical inquiry. Historical materialism claims that human formations of sense and subjectivity are organized by determinate modes of production and their associated class relations. Psychoanalysis claims that these formations register the enduring effects of the primal entry into sociality, in patterns that are at once more and less variable than economic systems. Neither can fully account for the textual evidence; yet it seems difficult to take these claims seriously and at the same time to believe that some higher resolution awaits them. A small illustration may concretize the issue. It is true, let us grant, that *L'Education sentimentale* dramatizes and validates the process of a certain bourgeois political disappointment, after the failure of the 1848 revolutions. It seems true, too, that Flaubert's figuration of persons and their relations is governed by the imago of the mother. The novel condenses these distinct matters in such a way that they can be neither separated nor co-ordinated in a relationship of essence and expression. Flaubert's textual space is as it were occupied twice over, staturated at once by the social meanings of French society in a certain period and by a certain pattern of unconscious desire. In this, we might say, it epitomizes the condition of all culture, where social and psychodynamic meanings are always jointly active, not only in their shared semiotic space but within each other, and according to logics that neither exclude patterns of co-ordination nor depend on them.

To reason so is not, however, to offer simple support for a notion of 'pluralism', a word in which a damaging ambiguity has flourished for too long. As an institutional principle affirming the rights of all intellectual tendencies, pluralism is a necessary condition of fruitful inquiry. But this meaning of the term is often used, wittingly or not, to valorize a second meaning, which is more clearly registered as relativist or perspectivist. These too have their rights, but they derive no privilege, as intellectual positions, from their simulation of institutional virtue: collective pluralism does not vindicate, let alone enjoin, individual eclecticism. And they are validated least of all by appeal to the name of Althusser. To say that no theory can claim a monopoly on knowledge of the social is not to claim that truth is relative, or parcellized. Althusser affirmed the first proposition but would have rebutted its fallacious sequel. Marxism cannot, in heroic isolation, harvest the yield of our possible social knowledge. Yet in so far as it lodges claims concerning the general structure of the social, it not only opposes alternative conjectures of the same scope, but also exercises a critical check on claims of more limited application. This is a logical entailment, by which Marxism survives or fails as a self-consistent rational theory.[34] Reduced to tending 'class factors' in a perspectivist schedule of analysis, the theory would become precisely the kind of thing against which Lenin famously defined it: a 'trade-union consciousness' in cultural studies.

Renouncing the old cosmology (though his tone sometimes belied the gesture) and resisting the false alternative of perspectivism, Louis Althusser drafted a bold, vulnerable proposal: in his own words, here transposed, an overdetermined unity of theoretical activity, endlessly novel in its configurations but determined in the last instance by Marx's science of history. Just how suggestive that proposal was, and how vulnerable to reduction or rewriting, the past twenty years have shown. Today, it remains, much worn by time and handling but still legible, a message to read, think about and act upon.

NOTES

1 These pages offer what, for want of a better phrase, might be called a theoretical memoir. Laying no claim to the systematic achievement of critical or historical reconstruction proper, they are more personal in background and perhaps idiosyncratic in balance and range. The text is also, and for this reason, somewhat Anglocentric – a limitation I cannot surmount here, but nevertheless wish to acknowledge. My thanks to Gregory Elliott for his encouragement and critical advice.

2 *For Marx*, Allen Lane, London, 1969; *Reading Capital*, New Left Books, London, 1970; *Lenin and Philosophy and Other Essays*, New Left Books, London, 1971, *passim*.

3 Roland Barthes spoke of 'a *quadrivium* of pilot sciences', though listing economics and not psychoanalysis along with the other three (see *Elements of Semiology*, Hill and Wang, New York, 1968, pp. 101–02, n. 55).

4 My own contribution to this culture of embarrassment ('The Marxist Aesthetics of Christopher Caudwell', *New Left Review* 85, May/June 1974) was typical in its 'Althusserian' desire to raze the local theoretical heritage. Though I stand by the destructive analysis proposed there, I have long felt that Caudwell deserved a more generous and more resourceful (that is, more truly critical) reading.

5 Williams's famous judgement on Caudwell epitomized a whole structure of left literary-critical feeling: 'for the most part his discussion is not even specific enough to be wrong' (*Culture and Society 1780–1950*, Penguin, Harmondsworth, 1961, p. 268).

6 'The "Piccolo Teatro": Bertolazzi and Brecht', in *For Marx*, and 'Cremonini, Painter of the Abstract', in *Lenin and Philosophy*.

7 'A Letter on Art in Reply to André Daspre', *Lenin and Philosophy*, at pp. 207, 204.
8 *A Theory of Literary Production*, Routledge and Kegan Paul, London, 1978.
9 *A Theory of Literary Production*, pp. 133, 59.
10 In collaboration with Etienne Balibar: see their 'De la littérature comme forme idéologique', *Littérature* 13, February 1974; translated as 'On Literature as an Ideological Form' (*Oxford Literary Review* 3, 1978) and reprinted in Francis Mulhern, ed., *Contemporary Marxist Literary Criticism*, Longman, London, 1992 (to which subsequent references refer).
11 'Ideology and Literary Form', *New Left Review* 90, March/April 1975; *Criticism and Ideology*, New Left Books, London, 1976.
12 *Criticism and Ideology*, pp. 83–84.
13 See my 'Marxism in Literary Criticism', *New Left Review* 108, March/April 1978, which advanced this critical argument, among others – but which, as a whole, shared with its interlocutor the limiting problematic discussed above.
14 The tendency of Michael Sprinker's work, in the United States, runs counter to this suggestion. For him, the relation between the aesthetic and the ideological forms our 'current horizon of understanding' and, to that extent, 'we remain determinately within the Althusserian problematic.' He would add, however, that the concept of the aesthetic is more elusive than the traditions of bourgeois and Marxist reflection acknowledge (*Imaginary Relations*, Verso, London, 1987, pp. 2, 3). See, for more general interest, E. Ann Kaplan and Sprinker, eds, *The Althusserian Legacy*, Verso, London, 1993, which includes a variety of North American (and other) appreciations of Althusser's work.
15 'On Literature as an Ideological Form', p. 35.
16 *Criticism and Ideology*, p. 56. Eagleton's retrospective assessment of Althusser appears in the preface of his *Against the Grain: Essays 1975–1985*, Verso, London, 1986, pp. 2–4; in the same volume, see also his 'Macherey and Marxist Literary Theory' (1975), pp. 9–21.
17 Tel Quel, *Théorie d'ensemble*, Editions du Seuil, Paris, 1968.
18 Balibar and Macherey associated *Tel Quel* with a vision of art as 'anti-nature' and 'violation of order' – a 'reversal . . . characteristic of conservative ideology' ('On Literature as an Ideological Form', p. 54, n. 10). See also Eagleton, *Against the Grain*, p. 4.
19 *Théorie d'ensemble*, p. 8.
20 See Foucault, 'Distance, aspect, origine'; Barthes, 'Drame, poème, roman'; and Derrida, 'La différance', *Théorie d'ensemble*, pp. 11–24, 25–40, 41–66 respectively.
21 Wollen, *Readings and Writings: Semiotic Counter-strategies*, Verso, London 1982, p. 211; Heath, *Questions of Cinema*, Macmillan, London, 1981, p. 201. Wollen's version of this trinity formula was always firmly grounded in a commitment to science; he was correspondingly more distant from *Tel Quel* than Heath, who was for a time an active collaborator in the journal. Heath's *Signs of the Times: Introductory Readings in Textual Semiotics* (co-edited with Colin MacCabe and Christopher Prendergast, Granta, Cambridge, n.d.) marked the entry of *Tel Quel* into British left culture.
22 Rosalind Coward and John Ellis's *Language and Materialism* (Routledge and

Kegan Paul, London, 1977) was widely received as a synopsis of *Screen*'s thinking, but did not claim that status for itself.

23 See Boumelha, *Thomas Hardy and Women: Sexual Ideology and Narrative Form*, Harvester, Brighton, 1982, and Kaplan, *Sea Changes: Culture and Feminism*, Verso, London, 1986.

24 See his *Formalism and Marxism*, Methuen, London, 1979; also 'Marxism and Popular Fiction', first published in *Literature and History* 7, 1981, and reprinted in *Contemporary Marxist Literary Criticism.*

25 The sociologists Barry Hindess and Paul Hirst were the key figures here; their reading of Althusser quickly rose to quasi-canonical status in *Screen* and its literary-theoretical hinterland.

26 Tony Bennett explains his transition to 'post-Marxism' (not, he stresses, *anti*-Marxism) in his *Outside Literature*, Routledge, London, 1990, part 1.

27 *British Post-structuralism since 1968*, Routledge, London, 1988, pp. 17, 21.

28 *For Marx*, 'Glossary' (composed by Ben Brewster and amended by Althusser), p. 252.

29 The absolute quality of this thesis was confirmed *a contrario* by Althusser's one attempt to qualify it. Ideology, he wrote, is 'an *omni-historical* reality, in the sense [that its] structure and functioning are immutable, present in the same form throughout what we can call history, in the sense in which the *Communist Manifesto* defines history as the history of class struggles, i.e. the history of class societies' (*Lenin and Philosophy*, pp. 151–52). If this purported qualification is valid, then the substantive thesis fails.

30 *The Ideology of Power and the Power of Ideology*, Verso, London, 1980.

31 For one compact summary, see Williams, *Marxism and Literature*, Oxford University Press, Oxford, 1977.

32 See, for example, Paul Hirst, *On Law and Ideology*, Macmillan, London, 1979, pp. 52–53, 71–72 and *passim*, and for the settled retrospect, Easthope, *British Post-structuralism*, pp. 213–14.

33 Cf. the introduction to *Contemporary Marxist Literary Criticism*, p. 25.

34 Stephen Resnick and Richard Woolf appear to me to be trying to evade this unaccommodating conclusion – or to bowdlerize it – when they maintain, first, that for Althusser there can be no one social truth, only a plurality of truths; but, second, that Marxism should accept or reject exogenous theoretical claims following an assessment of their 'social conditions and consequences' ('Althusser's Liberation of Marxian Theory', in *The Althusserian Legacy*, pp. 65, 67).

8

ANALYSIS TERMINATED, ANALYSIS INTERMINABLE: THE CASE OF LOUIS ALTHUSSER

Gregory Elliott

Once everything has been said, everything still remains to be said. . . . Everything still remains to say; everything always remains to be said.
André Gorz, The Traitor

Si au lieu de bénir ou excommunier, on commençait par comprendre?
Louis Althusser, Journal de captivité

In a text read at the funeral of Louis Althusser, Jacques Derrida observed of him that he had

> traversed so many lives . . . so many personal, historical, philosophical and political adventures; marked, inflected, influenced so many discourses, actions, and existences by the radiant and provocative force of his thought, his manner of being, of speaking, of teaching, that the most diverse and contradictory accounts could never exhaust their source.[1]

And yet whilst the 'unique adventure which bears the name of Louis Althusser' was indelibly singular, it has assumed, well beyond the borders of his native country, a representative status, inseparable from the post-war adventures of the dialectic. In a celebrated formula of 1960, criticized for its historicism by Althusser, Sartre accredited Marxism 'the untranscendable philosophy for our time'.[2] According to a pervasive self-image of the age, the historical moment 'expressed' by Marxism has been surpassed, ceding, *circa* June 1968, to Rorty's 'North Atlantic Postmodern Bourgeois Liberal Democracy' as the untranscendable horizon of contemporary thought. In consequence, the post-war thinker who, perhaps more than any other, sought to render Marxism genuinely contemporary, by articulating modernist philosophy and Communist politics, had been laid to intellectual rest well before the official obsequies of October 1990.

If Althusser's effacement from the scene occurred no less rapidly than his rise to prominence within it, this is, in part at least, attributable to his intolerability for a generation in whose 'former philosophical consciousness' he once loomed so large. But the ties that bind are not so easily severed. Where denegation prevails, repression obtains. The 'enormous condescension of posterity', to borrow a phrase from E. P. Thompson,[3] is no more reliable a guide to its object's true worth than the gratuitous adulation of anteriority. Moreover, it is index enough that what Althusser represented – the summation of the 'illusion of the epoch' (Althusserianism, highest stage of Marxism?) – is one component of the theoretical unconscious of the present.

Althusser was not merely a Marxist – sufficient in itself to condemn him to the philosophical equivalent of the Natural History Museum, so far as much of the class of '68 is concerned (having embarked for Beijing in its youth, and landed in Bel Air in middle age).[4] He was a Communist and – what is doubtless worse – a French (not an Italian) one, and is correspondingly susceptible to the tendency to affix the label 'Stalinist' to anything and everything which moves in that complex history. Furthermore – and notoriously – he was Nietzsche's companion in lunacy, compounding the philosophico-political *actes d'accusation* of the late 1970s by the murder of his companion of 35 years and wife of four in November 1980. And such cases are, at best, of pathological curiosity (unless, that is, they enjoy the good fortune of having been edited and introduced by Michel Foucault).[5]

'Neither amnesia, nor disgust, nor irony produces even the shadow of a critique.'[6] In the event, the first option is no longer available to us. As is its wont, the repressed has, to the evident discomfort of some, returned. A vindication of the Althusserian programme across the disciplinary board has recently been attempted; while the papers presented to a conference in 1988 on the Althusserian legacy have now been collected.[7] Above all, the simultaneous publication in April 1992 of the first volume of Yann Moulier Boutang's biography of Althusser, and of the philosopher's 'autobiography' (due to appear in English translation in autumn 1993), has aroused a massive wave of interest on both sides of the Channel.[8] Within months of its release in France, *L'avenir dure longtemps* had sold 40,000 copies, attracting sustained – and, in the main, serious – attention in the French press[9] and prompting a two-hour TV programme. The longest book written by Althusser is set – if it has not already done so – to become the highest-selling; the thinker who endured a living death for the last decade of his life is enjoying a posthumous existence among an audience much of which had probably never heard of, let alone read, *For Marx* or *Reading Capital.*

Predictably, British coverage to date (including a slot on BBC 2's *Late Show* in October 1992) has taken its cue from Althusser's 'confessions' and focused predominantly, if not exclusively, on the sensational dimension of *l'affaire Althusser*. The ritual monotony of the titles prefacing reviews

– 'A Marxist murderer', 'Sex, murder and philosophy', 'Marx and murder' – explains the space devoted to the deceased adherent of an outmoded (and/or iniquitous) doctrine by the mainstream press.[10] If French commentators had, doubtless inadvertently, conveyed the impression that Althusser's murder of his wife weighed less heavily with them than his failure to abjure the God that failed[11] – given Hélène Rytman's biography, morality tales about anti-Communist beauty and the Stalinist beast were implausible – some of their Anglo-American counterparts were readier to insinuate the equation: *fait divers* = *fait philosophique*, or (Althusserian) Marxism = Madness = Murder. It was left to the *Sun*'s Augean stable-mate, *The Times Literary Supplement*, under Murdochite proprietorship and Oakeshottian presidency, to give full vent to the outraged decency of the moral majority, in an article, riddled with errors, that entered an unwitting affidavit against the benevolence of the values it indignantly counterposed to the Parisian contagion of theoretical anti-humanism.[12]

'I am one thing, my writings are another', proclaimed Nietzsche in his putative autobiography.[13] The point applies to Althusser, as to any other thinker: the genesis, the structure, the validity, and the effectivity of a body of thought are analytically distinct issues for any inquiry that aspires to something other than *ad hominem* incrimination or exculpation of ideas. At any rate, the secrets of Althusserian Marxism will not be exposed by edifying inspection of its artisan's adolescent bedclothes (or the glacial improprieties of his parents' marriage-bed, for that matter); 'as a general rule', he once objected to Plekhanov's imprudent speculations on the causes of the French Revolution, 'concepts are not hidden in beds.'[14] By way of variation on a Sartrean theme, it might simply be remarked: Louis Althusser became a manic-depressive murderer, no doubt about it. But not every manic-depressive murderer is Louis Althusser. The heuristic inadequacy of literary supplement psycho-babble is contained in these two sentences.[15]

The first thing to be noted about the occasion for Althusser's renewed celebrity (or notoriety) is that the status of both his texts is no less complex than their character. *Les faits*, written in 1976 and unfinished, was scheduled for inclusion in an abortive journal edited by Althusser's pupil, Régis Debray. *L'avenir dure longtemps*, almost four times the length (some 270 pages), and drafted, characteristically, in feverish haste in the spring of 1985 between bouts of hospitalization, was initially intended for publication, but then simply laid aside. No will having been left by Althusser, his closest surviving relative – a nephew – became his executor and decided to authorize their appearance under the auspices of the Institut Mémoires de l'édition contemporaine and the seemingly scrupulous editorship of Olivier Corpet and Yann Moulier Boutang.[16]

Althusser's unavailing struggle against the psychological torment that predated and punctuated his public career – the 'war without memoirs or memorials' evoked by him in his single most powerful essay, 'Freud and

Lacan'[17] – has finally been granted its memorial and yielded memoirs of a kind. But can the autobiographer's tale of how he became what he was be trusted? That there are reasonable grounds for doubt is suggested, if by nothing else, by the marked discrepancies between *Les faits* and *L'avenir*. The former, under a typically laconic (and ironic) title, is composed in a comic register (it contains, for example, fictional encounters with Pope John XXIII and General de Gaulle [ADL, 338–39]). The latter pertains to the converse mode – its tragic score unrelieved (indeed, intensified) by the falsely optimistic notes it strikes towards its conclusion. Essentially covering the same terrain, they do so quite differently, offering not so much a mutual corrective as alternative perspectives upon the Althusserian destiny.

Where readings have not been flagrantly culpable, they have too often been unduly ingenuous, in pre-Freudian fashion taking Althusser at his word and therewith subscribing to an 'idea of reading which makes a written discourse the immediate transparency of the true, the real discourse of a voice'.[18] As the author of *Reading Capital* insisted at the outset, there is no such thing as an innocent reading. Althusser's own strategy vis-à-vis Marx – the 'symptomatic reading' which sought to reconstruct the latent structural matrix (or theoretical 'problematic') generative of the manifest serial discourse – drew upon the Freudian interpretation of dreams. His analysis of the Althusser case and the reasons for his unreason – the tangled causal skein that culminated in an act of conjoint destruction and self-destruction – requires an analogous operation. The occasionally oneiric discourse of *L'avenir* cries out, almost literally, for a symptomatic reading.

It is immeasurably aided by Moulier Boutang's meticulous reconstruction of Althusser's life up to 1956, which permits informed and properly critical scrutiny of his own tendentious rendition. For there were many Althussers, of whom Althusser's is only one – one who does not exhaust (may even traduce) the plural and contradictory reality commemorated by Derrida and who must, accordingly, be approached *en connaissance de cause*. Yet the problem, baldly stated, is that, despite his biographer's heroic endeavours, such knowledge is not at our disposal and is unlikely to be even when we possess the completed biography. The bare facts of what Althusser once dubbed his 'auto-heterobiographical circumstances',[19] and their concatenation, are in the process of being established; the implacable illogic of his unconscious remains recalcitrant to elucidation. 'Nothing', he justly remarked in one version of those facts from another scene, 'is as simple as the unconscious elements on which analysis works; but nothing is as complicated as their individual combination' (ADL, 354).

Because they appear under his signature Althusser's own disconcerting simplicities have been received as the disclosure of that individual combination in its plenary complexity – as if, *contra* Pascal, the Althusserian heart had its reasons and they were known to Althusser's head. Furthermore, his projection of the shadow of 'Althusser' onto the young Althusser – the construction of his own history in the 'future anterior'[20] – has been accepted as the authoritative (since authorized) version.

L'avenir advertises itself as the public explanation which Althusser was at once excused and denied by the *non-lieu* ('no grounds') decreed, under Article 64 of the French penal code, after the murder of his wife:

> This is why, since everyone has been able to speak in my place and the legal process has prohibited me from any public explanation, I have resolved to explain myself publicly.
>
> I do so first of all for my friends and, if possible, for myself; in order to lift this heavy tomb-stone which weighs down on me. . . . Yes, to free myself from the condition in which [I have been placed] by the extreme gravity of my state . . . my murder, and also – and especially – by the equivocal effects of the decree of *non-lieu* from which I benefited, without being able, in fact or in law, to contest the procedure. For it is under the tomb-stone of the *non-lieu*, of silence and public death that I have been forced to survive and learn to live (ADL, 23).

Reminding us that there was an Althusser before and after – as well as during – Althusserianism, the author stipulates that *L'avenir* constitutes 'neither a journal, nor memoirs, nor autobiography' (ADL, 25), but rather what he once described to his biographer as a 'traumabiography'. He claims to be 'sticking strictly to the facts', but immediately attaches a crucial qualification: 'hallucinations are also facts' (ADL, 74). We are dealing, not with the tranquil recollection of an accomplished life, but the anguished retrospection of a death foreold – one which amply confirms Malraux's observation that what is tragic about death is that it transforms life into destiny. *L'avenir*, in the words of its editors, is an 'inextricable mélange of "facts" and "fantasies"' (ADL, ix).

Derrida had remarked that whilst public discourse about Althusser tended to associate his name with those of Marx or Lenin, his intimates were compelled to invoke other figures: Pascal, Dostoevsky, Nietzsche, or Artaud. Anticipating this insight, Althusser seeks to situate his text by allusion to Foucault's edition of Pierre Rivière's testament and Rousseau's *Confessions* (adding, 'alas, I am not Rousseau'). Other autobiographical writings that come to mind are Sartre's *Words* and President Schreber's *Memoirs of my Nervous Illness*. In effect, this is a fragmentary 'wild (self-) analysis': something akin to the testimony of a Nietzsche in the discourse of a Freud. Just as Althusser can lay claim to Rousseau's privilege and bane – 'I am like no one in the whole world'[21] – so his confessions are literally exceptional, for better and worse alike.

Much of their poignancy, as well as their ambivalence, derives from a fact so blinding as to risk invisibility: *L'avenir* is a symptom of the chronic manic-depressive syndrome which it hopes to exorcize through a public talking-cure. It opens – excruciatingly – with the scene of the crime and closes, after apparent self-detection, with the explanatory commentary of an 'old medical friend' (ADL, 273–79), therewith reinstating the *non-lieu* in conclusion. The first half of the book is given over to the aetiology of its subject's mental illness (or the origins of his madness) in a 'family romance', enacted in Algeria and southern France *entre les deux guerres*, which soon acquires the contours of a familial horror-story. From his maternal aunt Althusser learnt the family secret: that his mother's fiancé had been killed during the First World War; that she had subsequently accepted the marriage-proposal of his brother; and that she had named her only son after the love of her youth – and of her life. Thus informed, Althusser drew a devastating conclusion: he had, so to speak, been born, not made. For inscribed in the infant Louis' Christian name was the true – and other – object of her affections:

> above all, it said: him [*lui*], the third person pronoun which, ringing like the summons of an anonymous third person, deprived me of any personality of my own, and referred to this man behind my back: *Him was Louis* [*Lui, c'était Louis*], my uncle, whom my mother loved, not me (ADL, 34).

As depicted by him, Althusser's mother is a *mater dolorosa* straight out of the pages of de Beauvoir's *Second Sex*.[22] Remembered as a violated wife – 'a martyred mother bleeding like a wound' (ADL, 33) – Lucienne Althusser, née Berger – the maiden name (*proprio sensu*) to which she reverted after her husband's death in 1975 – is portrayed as a castrating mother, impelled by her phobias to enforce a strict regime of social and sexual 'hygiene' upon Althusser and his sister, Georgette. From the domestic milieu in which her uncontested writ ran his father was, literally or metaphorically, absent, inspiring in the son the sense that he had no father. The consequence, so Althusser claims, was a feeling of fathomless solitude, relieved only by his relationship with his maternal grandparents ('my true family, my only family') in the 'infant paradise' of the Bois de Boulogne, overlooking Algiers, or of Larochemillay, in the Morvan, to which they retired (ADL, 56ff.).

As Althusser notes (ADL, 162–65), the related themes of the 'fatherless child' and 'solitude' would recur in his philosophical writings.[23] *Cherchez la femme* is the leitmotif of his case history:

> My mother loved me profoundly, but it was only much later, in the light of my analysis, that I understood how . . . the unhappy woman, she lived as best she could what had happened to her: having a child whom she could not restrain herself from baptizing 'Louis', with the name of the dead man whom she had loved and still loved, in her soul. . . . I am recomposing here what I lived and what I have come to understand of it. . . . In my case death was the death of a man whom my mother loved above all else, beyond me. In her 'love' for me, something paralyzed and marked me from earliest

childhood, fixing for a very long time what was to be my fate. It wasn't a question of a fantasy, but of the very *reality* of my life. Thus it is, for each of us, that a fantasy becomes life (ADL, 48).

Whatever it was, it induced, we are told, the project that structured Althusser's existence: '*to seduce her by realizing her desire*':

> I realized what my mother desired and expected . . . from the person of the other Louis – *and I achieved it in order to seduce her*: wisdom, purity, virtue, pure intellect, disincarnation, scholarly success, and, to crown it all, a 'literary' career . . . and admission to an Ecole Normale Supérieure, not Saint-Cloud – my uncle's – but better still, the rue d'Ulm. Then I became the intellectual whom people know of, who fiercely refused to 'dirty his hands' with the media . . . and, my name on the first page of some books which my mother read with pride, a renowned philosopher (ADL, 51–52).

Thus to win his mother's love, by realizing her desire, was for Althusser simultaneously to realize his own being, by fashioning an ego (psychic and corporeal). The paradoxical effect of his project – as with its repetition in his relationship to his teachers (ADL, 81) – was to exacerbate the perceived original ex-centricity: seduction of others meant Althusser's seduction into his own betrayal. For, 'I always had the impression of not being me, of not genuinely existing, but of existing only by and in *artifices*, namely the artifices of seduction achieved by *imposture* . . .' (ADL, 53).

In 'revelations' onto which critics have latched, Althusser confides that the imposture extended to his philosophical culture (more precisely, the lack of it) (ADL, 157–58). However that may be, his formal education was interrupted, after he had come sixth in the examinations for admission to the Ecole Normale Supérieure, rue d'Ulm, by the advent of war in September 1939. The political option current in the Catholic and monarchist circles in which he had moved at the Lycée du Parc, Lyons – 'rather Hitler that the Popular Front' – materialized with the collapse of the Third Republic. Among those sacrificed to *Travail*, *Famille*, *Patrie* in the 'strange defeat' of June 1940 was Althusser. That the experience of captivity was a formative influence is clear. Notwithstanding the manifold privations it records, his own account stresses the redeeming features: while Sartre had never felt freer than under the Occupation, Althusser had never felt more secure than in his prisoner-of-war camp (ADL, 99). Released from the maternal embrace, he finally discovered masturbation and, in the person of Robert Dael, a friend whom he recalls as 'tender with me like a woman (the genuine mother whom I had not had)' (ADL, 100). Accordingly, liberation in 1945 induced not elation, but disorienation, betokening reversion to the isolation which enhanced that 'nostalgic desire for fusion' (ADL, 88) motivating subsequent attachments.

Post-war, those attachments reduced, in essentials, to three: the Ecole Normale Supérieure – 'it too the substitute for a maternal milieu, the *amniotic* fluid' (ADL, 155) – where Althusser resumed his education and secured an academic post after being received second at the philosophy *agrégation* in 1948; Hélène Rytman – Jewess, *résistante*, ex-Communist, fallen on hard times – whom he met in 1946; and the French Communist Party, to which he adhered in November 1948.

Hélène 'gave me . . . the prodigious gift of a world which I did not know . . . a world of solidarity and struggle, a world of action . . . a world of courage . . .' (ADL, 123). Yet the prospect of redemption so miraculously opened up soon gave way to the threat of perdition. The relationship with Hélène, eight years his senior, to whom, so he claims, Althusser lost his virginity at the age of 28, was traumatic from the outset, plunging him into a deep depression which necessitated the first of a score of hospitalizations, after Pierre Mâle had diagnosed schizophrenia. (But for the reversal of this verdict by Julian Ajuriaguerra, and its replacement by severe melancholia, the affair might have ended there [116–17].)[24] According to Althusser, he and Hélène performed an indispensable maternal and paternal function for one another. While Althusser replaced the parents to whom, terminally ill, she had administered fatal euthanasiac injections, Hélène was everything for which he had yearned:

> simultaneously like a good mother and a good father to me: older than me, loaded with experience and life, she loved me as a mother loves her child, her miraculous child, and at the same time like a father, a good father, since she quite simply initiated me into the real world, this infinite world into which I had never been able to enter. . . . Through her desire for me – pathetic me – she also initiated me into my role and masculinity as a man: she loved me as a woman loves a man! (ADL, 123–24)

Indissolubly linked to these *rites de passage* was Althusser's induction into the world of French Communism, which he embraced, so he narrates, after the loss of his Roman Catholic faith (ADL, 197). As the hopes borne by the Resistance succumbed to the Cold War, and the 'united front' of 1944–47 fractured into the 'two camps' of 1948, Althusser arrived at the PCF's own conviction: paraphrasing St. Augustine, *hors du parti, point de salut politique* (outside the party, no political salvation). Even without accentuating circumstances, the conjuncture would have proved inclement for the new academic recruit. Nizan's Serge Pluvinage may accurately convey the pre-war experience of Communist intellectuals ('the question of original social sin was absolutely never posed');[25] as Althusser's Introduction to *For Marx* attested – possibly in conscious reminiscence (and contradiction) of *The Conspiracy* – during the cultural Cold War imputations of original social sin flourished and prospered.[26] Accentuating circumstances there were, however, in the form of Hélène's exclusion from the party and Althusser's assumption of the mission to secure her readmission. So explosive an issue was this that if no salvation was to be had without the party, damnation beckoned within it.

Althusser basically reiterates the standard account of the affair, attributing his wife's misfortunes to the malevolence of Elsa Triolet, and confirms the details supplied by one of the participants in it, Emmanuel Le Roy Ladurie.[27] Accepting Hélène's version of events, Althusser sought to clear her name of the charge of having been a double agent (to whom rumours of supervising a sanguinary episode of *épuration* attached). Without benefiting her, his zeal merely served to expose him to the inquisition and censure of the PCF cell at the ENS for consorting with a 'Hitlero-Trotskyite' (as the inimitable Stalinist amalgam of the era had it). In a narrative significantly at variance with that supplied in *Les faits* (ADL, 336), Althusser claims in *L'avenir* to have joined the unanimous vote for Hélène's expulsion from the Peace Movement, but to have defied the instruction of his branch to sever relations with his companion (ADL, 194–95). Disconsolate at the temporary ostracism of his comrades, yet consoled by her love, Althusser asserts that this 'veritable Moscow trial in the heart of Paris' induced a realistic appreciation of the PCF and the methods of its adamantine leadership – an assessment confirmed by his experience of overhearing Laurent Casanova, then responsible for subjugating intellectuals to ideological rectitude, berate the biologist, Marcel Prenant, on the subject of 'bourgeois' arithmetic (ADL, 197).

While there is no reason to doubt Althusser's insistence that he never subscribed to the dementia of Lysenkoism, upon the public repudiation of which his own epistemology was based,[28] it is possible that his proclaimed clairvoyance about the PCF is a retrojection of subsequent disillusionment (as memorably expressed in *Ce qui ne peut plus durer dans le parti communiste* in 1978).[29] What is incontestable, as we shall see, is that the comparative equanimity with which he affects to have greeted the sanctions of his comrades is belied by the historical record.

In *Les faits*, discussing his imprisonment in Germany, Althusser recounts a plan which consisted in giving the guards to think that an escape had been effected, and then, some weeks later, when the enemy had failed to recapture the 'escapees', making the genuine attempt. For him it exemplified 'the problem of all philosophical (and political and military) problems: namely, of knowing how to exit from a circle while remaining within it' (ADL, 313). Having identified his attachments, *L'avenir* becomes a tale of a 'circle of circles' – the family, the Ecole, the companionship, the party, the clinic – and their mutual implication and overdetermination to produce, via what he once called the 'necessity of contingency', a singular destiny. Applying his own formula, it might be said that his narrative enacts his inability to find an egress from circles whose arc was inflected, but not designed, by him, and which degenerated from the seemingly virtuous to the intermittently vicious to the ultimately infernal. *Pace* Sartre, Hell is not other people.

By his own admission, Althusser and Hélène constituted a couple who, by the end, could live neither with, nor without each other. Dependent upon her as a mainstay and refuge, his self-destructiveness found expression in courting realization of his greatest terror: abandonment by her. In addition to the burden of anxiety and distress imposed by his recurrent depression, Hélène was subjected to his 'provocations' and humiliations (for example, his relationships with other women) – especially when in the manic phase of his psychosis (ADL, 147ff.). Quite why things deteriorated so inexorably and fatally in 1980 is not adequately explained by Althusser's self-analysis. If it is to be believed, confronted with yet another depression – possibly the most acute to date – Hélène determined to leave him and spoke of suicide, but did not act upon her resolution. What supervened, in Althusser's final harrowing image of November 1980, amounted to the 'Hell for two, behind closed doors, of a deliberately organized solitude' (ADL, 244), terminated only by the murder in which 'my own destruction symbolically passed through the destruction of others – especially my dearest and closest friends, including the woman whom I loved the most' (ADL, 269).

By then, the failure of a plethora of 'treatments' to release Althusser from the unrelenting grip of his madness, which dictated hospitalization at least once every two years, was evident. Althusser is painfully frank about his psychiatric history – from a wrenching account of subjection to ECT at the hands of a hospital orderly whom his patients nicknamed 'Stalin' (ADL, 117–18), through the narcotic analysis undertaken, from 1950–62, with Laurent Stevenin (ADL, 140), to the medical psychoanalysis, dispensing with the indignities of the couch, he embarked upon with René Diatkine thereafter. (Interestingly, Althusser does not linger over the rationale for this option – at the antipodes of his contemporaneous endorsement of Lacan's 'return to Freud' in 'Freud and Lacan'.) The conscious themes of his depression he isolates as the terror of abandonment; the fear of vulnerability to a demand for love of which he was incapable; and anxiety about public exposure as an impostor (this was the source of the 'spectacular depression' he suffered at the height of his celebrity, in the immediate aftermath of publication of *Pour Marx* and *Lire le Capital*, in the autumn of 1965). Whatever their unconscious promptings and significance, tracked down by Althusser to the maternal 'castration' which deprived him of his 'physical and psychic integrity' (ADL, 128), their course invariably involved transition from melancholic depths to manic summits:

> Very rapidly I passed from depression to hypomania, which sometimes took the form of a violent genuine mania. Then I felt myself to be omnipotent over everything – the external world, my friends, my projects, my problems,

> and those of others. Everything seemed to be – and was – incredibly easy.... It will be understood that in this extraordinary facility and pretention there was a massive dose of aggression, which was released ... like a symptom of the fantasy of impotence and hence depression, for it was merely a defence against my tendency to depression and against the fantasies of impotence which nourished it.... My fear of being utterly impotent and my desire to be omnipotent, my megalomania, were simply two sides of the same thing: the desire to possess what *I lacked in order to be a full and free man*, and which I was terrified of lacking (ADL, 135).

Paradoxically, the 'security' of the psychiatric clinic answered to the desire for omnipotence even as it certified Althusser's impotence (ADL, 133). Within the concentric circles of the academy and the party the same drama was played out in the exercise of his public functions. Given that Althusser's characterization of his purpose in the chapters dealing with philosophy and politics has frequently been ignored by commentators, it bears citation:

> ... what I owe my reader, because I owe it to myself, is elucidation of the subjective roots of my specific attachment to my profession of philosophy teacher at the Ecole Normale Supérieure, to philosophy, politics, the party, my books and their impact, i.e., how I found myself ... led to invest and inscribe my subjective fantasies in my objective and public activities (ADL, 152).

In effect, Althusser essays an explanation of how the bearer of the name Louis Althusser became the artisan of Althusserianism. Without conflating questions of genesis and validity, his reflections on the former provide some elements for an understanding of how it was he who arrived at the elaboration of what, as he readily concedes to Raymond Aron, was an 'imaginary Marxism' (ADL, 214).[30]

Althusser's refusal to stage a retraction of Marxism and all its works (including his own) has provoked hostile critics to construe *L'avenir* as a self-detraction. Quite the reverse of engaging in renunciation – a fact which will no doubt irritate some readers and reassure others – Althusser is unapologetic about the philosophico-political 'war of position' conducted by him and his collaborators within the PCF and affirms his enduring commitment to 'the materialist inspiration of Marx', disdaining the thrills and spills of postmodernism (ADL, 215–16). Whilst criticizing the PCF (over its treacherous role in the May Events, for example: ADL, 223), Althusser vigorously defends the rationality of French socialists opting for membership and explains why he persevered in his chosen course:

> When I stayed in the party, I thought ... that by so doing on the basis of an overtly oppositional position ... I could prove, at least formally, that

> oppositional activity inside the party was possible on serious theoretical and political bases, and hence that a transformation of it, maybe in the long run, was a possibility (ADL, 227–28).

In a letter of August 1972 to his former Catholic teacher, Jean Guitton, Althusser had written: 'It is true that philosophy is a battle. No doubt I make many mistakes, but it is a combat which I love. And when I resume the battle it is a sign that I am regaining my health a bit.'[31] After the defeat of the Union of the Left in March 1978, dashing the accumulated hopes of a decade or more, no further such signs were forthcoming from Althusser. In a subsequent letter to Guitton, dated 3 December 1978, he announced: 'My universe of thought has been abolished. I can no longer think. To speak in the language [of my youth], I entreat your prayers.'[32] All intercessions having proved vain, Althusser succumbed to his destiny.

As if in uncanny echo of Nietzsche's exaltation – 'My time has not yet come, some are born posthumously'[33] – the closing pages of *L'avenir* are leavened with a desperate optimism of the will:

> So, despite its dramas, life can still be beautiful. I am 67, but at last I feel – I who had no youth, since I was not loved for myself – I feel young as never before, even if the affair must soon end.
> Yes, the future lasts a long time (ADL, 272).

Perhaps – but not for the author of these lines. With ultimate pathos, what the text cannot know is that, rather than registering the conquest of Althusser's illness, its conclusion betrays the manic phase of his depressive cycle. Within weeks of its completion, persecuted by the French gutter-press, he was back in hospital. Louis Althusser's time had come and gone. Most are not reborn posthumously.

The overwhelming impression conveyed by *L'avenir* is of Althusser's self-destructiveness, extending, in that lonely hour of the last instance, to the destruction of Hélène. Yann Moulier Boutang's exhaustive research, and its riveting first instalment, confirm that this propensity is mimed by the text itself, in a consistent self-denigration – even self-defamation – which conceals a fact warranted by many of those to whom Derrida referred in his eulogy: Althusser was a man with qualities. His own express wish was that his testament would solve his enigma to public satisfaction, thus putting an end to demands for its elucidation and releasing him into an emancipatory anonymity (ADL, 202).[34] *L'avenir* frustrates that aspiration and courts, instead, a further burst of the voyeurism attendent upon the events of 1980–81. For *if* not the 'tissue of lies and half-truths' detected by one of his closest associates,[35] it is, as Moulier Boutang conclusively demonstrates, a re-writing of a life through the prism of its wreckage.

Setting aside comparatively minor issues (such as Althusser's affectation, *à la* Wittgenstein, of ignorance of the history of philosophy), his biographer can claim to have revealed the profundity of Althusser's revisions in five principal respects. Firstly – and crucially – the inversion of the Althusserian family romance can be firmly dated – to July 1964 – and confidently attributed – to none other than Hélène Rytman. She it was, in a letter of 26 July 1964 quoted by Moulier Boutang (LA, 74–75), who advanced the 'wild analysis' of the familial dynamic, as a fatality *ab origine*, faithfully reproduced by her companion. Having, like Althusser's closest male friend of the 1950s – the suicide, Jacques Martin – endured a wretched childhood, Hélène, to put it no higher, abetted Althusser in the projection of the manic-depressive shadow of maturity onto his infancy.[36] Secondly, and relatedly, a central relationship in the young Althusser's existence is underplayed and left largely unexamined in his narrative: his intense bond with his sister, Georgette, whose own history of 'nervous illness' infallibly tracked his own. Suffice it for now to indicate that, some two weeks after receiving Hélène's revelatory letter in the summer of 1964, Althusser had a dream which anticipates the scenario of November 1980. Transcribed by him, and found among his papers, it commenced thus: 'I must kill my sister. . . . Kill her with her agreement, moreover . . .' (LA, 75).[37] Thirdly, Althusser postdates the onset of his recurrent depression to the post-war period, passing over in silence the trials he experienced both during his schooldays and then in captivity. The latter, however, are inscribed in the desolate record of *une vie sans histoire* (JC, 245) he kept at Schleswig.[38]

Moulier Boutang's other main contributions concern Althusser's relationship with Roman Catholicism and the controversy over Hélène's Resistance record. Regarding the former, it is likely that, whilst not politically aligned with Action Française, the pre-war Catholic-Nationalist activist of Jeunesse Chrétienne was considerably further to the right than he is prepared to concede in *L'avenir*. More importantly, his gravitation to the left after the war, and eventual affiliation to the international Communist movement, involved no 'break', epistemological or otherwise, with the faith of the one holy and apostolic Catholic Church into which he had been born. On the contrary, as his first post-war publication suggests,[39] Althusser's involvement with the left-Catholic Jeunesse de l'Eglise reached its peak *after* his adhesion to the PCF (LA, 276ff.). He gradually detached himself from it between 1950–52, terminating his association only when, in 1953, the Vatican anathematized it and the 'worker priests'. Thereafter, the philosopher who quoted Niccolò Machiavelli and Cardinal de Retz with equal facility, who placed the devotional writings of Santa Teresa of Avila alongside the *Collected Works* of Comrade Lenin of Petrograd on his bookshelves, and who reportedly pinned Pascal's evocation of the 'eternal silence' of the Galilean universe, as well as Marx's injunction to change the world, on his study wall, responded with virtual *amor fati* to his ineluctable identity: a lapsed Catholic.

If the organization to which Althusser transferred his allegiances proved so unamenable to the rehabilitation of his companion, it was, so Moulier Boutang gives us to understand, because there was no smoke without fire. Eventual illumination of this obscure episode is promised in the second volume of the biography. In the account to hand, while indicating that Althusser was playing with fire, Moulier Boutang suggests that his claim to have voted for Hélène's exclusion from the Peace Movement amounts to a screen-memory for the catastrophic breakdown which, contrary to his own narrative, he suffered after submitting to the will of the ENS cell on his *liaison dangereuse* (LA, 423ff.)

In sum, it can be said that Moulier Boutang has the virtues of Althusser's vices, putting every reader of the 'autobiography' in his debt by the meticulousness with which he has scanned the return of a repressed history that has yet to be concluded. If he has not (thus far?) resolved the Althusserian enigma, he has sounded it and, in so doing, rendered his work at once indispensable to every student of his subject.

That said, we may return the compliment: when it comes to the questions of Communism and Marxism, Althusser possesses the virtues of his biographer's vices. The second volume may make amends. Its predecessor, however, is marked by an antipathy which does less than justice to Althusser in this respect. However offensive it might sound to anti-Stalinist sensibilities, it needs to be remembered that, in the aftermath of Vichy and Occupation, and given the SFIO's promotion of the Cold War and French colonialism – a record summarized by two critics as *socialisme expéditionnaire*[40] – the PCF, whose role, once it committed itself to the Resistance, was peerless, was an eminently defensible option for anyone on the left in France.[41] Here the few pages devoted to the issue by Eric Hobsbawm are worth infinitely more than Moulier Boutang's many. Writing Althusser's script *avant la lettre* on the dilemmas faced by Communist intellectuals of his generation, Hobsbawm observed in 1964 that

> the communist who cut himself off from the party – and this was long almost the automatic consequence of dissidence – lost all possibility of influencing it. In countries like France, where the party increasingly *was* the socialist movement, leaving it meant political impotence or treason to socialism; and for communist intellectuals the possibilities of settling down as successful academic or cultural figures was no compensation. The fate of those who left or were expelled was anti-communism or oblivion except among the readers of little magazines. Conversely, loyalty left at least the possibility of influence.[42]

Hobsbawm's polarity is too stark, as Sartre's endeavour, during the Korean War, to theorize the political practice of the PCF from outside its ranks testifies.[43] But as Anderson argues, whatever the choice about membership, the likes of Althusser and Sartre were united in their conviction, corroborated by political reality, that the Communist movement represented the only available embodiment of socialist politics.[44] Consequently, they were damned if they did; and damned if they didn't. The price Althusser paid for his party card – submission to the exigencies of the line of the day – was heavy, by any calculation. Yet the opportunity it afforded, in a country in the heart of whose capital Algerians could be murdered in their scores in October 1961 by the guardians of *Liberté, Egalité, Fraternité*, should not be underestimated. Beautiful Parisian souls in the present are unreliable guides to the 'dirty hands' of the not so distant past.

Pending Moulier Boutang's sequel, the theme of 'imaginary Marxism' – Aron's accusation and Althusser's admission – is worth dwelling upon briefly. Raymond Williams once drew a distinction between three varieties of Marxism in post-war Britain: the 'legitimating', the 'operative', and the 'academic'.[45] Assimilation of the Althusserian project into Britain fell, primarily, into the third category. Its motivation in France, by contrast, was predominantly *operative*: a contribution to the transformation of the PCF via theoretical reconstruction of its official ideology. The paradox, of course – conducive to the pervasive reception of Althusserian Marxism as legitimating – was that, in order for the operation to be licit within the PCF, it had to wear the colours of *legitimacy*. Transformation could only proceed by the revindication of tradition: hence the *ruse de guerre*, identified by Althusser, of a heresiarch posing as a defender of the faith (Spinoza made the point long ago: there is no heretic without a text):

> . . . objectively, there existed *no possible form of political intervention in the party other than the purely theoretical*, and, moreover, one based upon the existing or recognized theory so as to turn it back against the party's use of it. And since the recognized theory no longer had anything to do with Marx, but conformed to the highly dangerous inanities of dialectical materialism Soviet- (i.e., Stalin-) style, it was necessary – and this was the only possible route – to return to Marx, to this thought which was politically quite unimpeachable, for *sacred*, and to demonstrate that dialectical materialism *à la* Stalin, with all its theoretical, philosophical, ideological and political consequences, was utterly aberrant (ADL, 188–89).

Althusser's enterprise may have been 'theoreticist' – based upon the wager that political history could be put back on the tracks of October by a conversion to theoretical rectitude; it was far from Marxological, invocations of a reversion to the letter of Marx notwithstanding.

Althusser is both frank and lucid about the tendentiousness of his 'symptomatic reading' of the Marxist canon and reconstruction of the corpus. His purpose, he maintains, accurately divined by his seniors in the

PCF, was to release contemporary Marxism from what he regarded as the false promissory notes issued by them in its name and thereby to 'render it genuinely contemporary':

> I acknowledge it willingly, for I did indeed suppress everything in Marx which struck me as incompatible with his materialist principles, but also such ideology as remained in him – above all, the apologetic categories of the 'dialectic', even the dialectic itself. This, in the shape of its famous 'laws', seemed to me to serve merely as a retrospective apology (justification) vis-à-vis the accomplished fact of the aleatory development of history for the decisions of the party leadership (ADL, 214).

Integral to any redemption of the contemporaneity of Marxism was the conception of it as a developing, 'finite theory' of history, rather than the cosmology, accomplished science of anything and everything 'from protein to poetry',[46] bequeathed to the Third International by the Second. Althusser's intervention was designed, as it were, to salvage 'historical materialism' – the scientific research programme initiated by Marx – from 'historical Marxism' – the institutionalized ideology of political organizations (above all, those of historical Communism).[47] Accordingly, while Althusser preserved the traditional terminology of the sanctioned tripartite division of Marxism into 'dialectical materialism', 'historical materialism', and 'scientific socialism', in his rendition the second of these was emphatically *not* a sub-set of the first, assigned the regional (socio-economic) instantiation of the laws of a dialectic cast, in Plekhanovite or Stalinist fashion, as an ontology of matter-in-movement. Contrary to the materialist metaphysic of Marxist orthodoxy, 'historical *materialism*' connoted no more – and yet no less – than the 'science of history',[48] merely commenced by Marx and in urgent need, after the depredations of decades, of re-commencement – if needs be, by a comprehensive recasting of its theoretical problematic. Althusserian 'imaginary Marxism' aspired to constitute that renovation of historical materialism apt to interpret the contemporary world, thereby arming those, in the main affiliated to the international Communist movement, endeavouring to change it.

The antiquity of Althusserianism – and of Marxism in general – is a ubiquitous article of intellectual faith in these new times (in the words of two commentators from the mid-1980s, Althusser's Marxism 'seems very dated and, like the Beatles' music or Godard's first films, inevitably evokes a recent but vanished past').[49] Progression does not invariably constitute progress and Freud's caution might be erected over the philosophical adventure-playground of postmodernism: 'a contradiction is not a refutation, an innovation not necessarily an advance.'[50] Yet that sense of a 'recent but vanished past' indicates something partially confirmed by *L'avenir*: the complex non/contemporaneity of Althusserianism, or the degree to which it represented a philosophical formation transitional between Marxism and postmodernism, one of whose *effets pervers* was to facilitate intellectual transfer from the one to the other.

In his fine obituary of Althusser, Ted Benton noted that much post-Marxist theorization effects a unilateral, anti-Marxist radicalization of Althusser's own theses.[51] Various examples of this might be cited. But to restrict ourselves to one dimension in which Althusser anticipated the post-Marxist bonfire of metaphysical vanities, we may select an issue on which *L'avenir* and Moulier Boutang's biography offer some fascinating and illuminating material: meta-narratives and the 'end of history'.

A persistent theme of Althusser's discussion of his Marxism is that philosophies of history seduce their partisans into that most hapless of political indispositions: 'telling ourselves stories' (ADL, 203).[52] Althusser's recasting amounted, in effect if not in word, to a revolt against orthodox historical materialism, with its meta-narrative of the advance of the productive forces towards an ineluctable communism, as a pseudo-materialist 'inversion' of Hegelian theodicy – its mystical kernel concealed within a material shell – starring the Ruse of Economic Reason. The abiding sin of all such 'philosophical novels' resided in their incorrigibly 'realist' narrative structure, plotting a story with a hero (e.g., humanity or the proletariat) and an appointed end (e.g., communism), that abstracted from the specificities of the conjuncture which it was the task of an authentically historical materialism to elucidate, therewith furnishing the knowledge of a 'concrete situation' mandatory for any political practice aspiring to transform it for the better. Accordingly, 'philosophical novelists' – among whom Althusser instances Sartre (170) – were no more adequate a 'guide to action' than the 'alchemists of revolution' ridiculed by Marx. *Capital* – the 'Book in which the Second International read the fatality of the advent of socialism as if in a Bible' – supplied, so Althusser insisted, the requisite corrective: the opening up of the 'continent of History' to scientific exploration.[53]

Mention of Sartre reminds us that, in tandem with his rejection of the Stalinist prolongation of the philosophy of history in a 'right-Hegelian' version – economism as Soviet *raison d'état* – Althusser dismissed any 'left-Hegelian' variant – humanism as *raison de la révolution* – by way of anti-Stalinist response. Indeed, by taxing Marxist humanism with instatement of an odyssey of the human essence, from its alienation in capitalism to its reappropriation under communism, Althusser asserted an underlying conceptual affinity between these philosophical symbolic antagonists, whatever their overt political animosity. Furthermore, so the later Althusser would maintain, theoretical Stalinism was marked by a combination of economism and humanism, 'histomat' amounting to what Raphael Samuel has dubbed, in another context, a 'technological humanism'.[54]

De te fabula narratur, we might be tempted to respond. For thanks to Moulier Boutang's research, we now know that the young Althusser was a partisan of an apocalyptic Hegelian Marxism, (mis)construed as the philosophical vindication of a Stalinism at the height of its post-war powers of attraction (and repulsion).[55] Yet before Althusser was Althusser – prior to his own epistemological break with Hegelianism – he declined a central postulate of the Hegelian Marxism nourished in France by Alexandre Kojève's immensely influential lectures on the *Phenomenology* (published as *Introduction to the Reading of Hegel* in 1947), and lately given, via an inversion of the inversion, a new lease of post-Cold War life by Francis Fukuyama: the 'end of history'.[56]

In *L'avenir* (169) Althusser notes the salience of the theme in post-war French intellectual culture, criticizing the 'astounding *bureaucratic* content' with which Kojève, as a self-proclaimed (albeit non-practicing) 'Stalinist of strict observance', endowed it. What Moulier Boutang discloses (LA, 314ff.) is that in an extraordinary 72-page letter of 25 December 1949 – 22 January 1950 to his former teacher, Jean Lacroix, explaining his adhesion to Marxism and the PCF, Althusser reproved both Jean Hyppolite's attribution of the *neo*-Hegelian notion to Marx and the then common deduction from the fashionable equation History = Alienation: i.e., End of Alienation = End of History. Quoting the relevant passage from the 1859 Preface to *A Contribution to the Critique of Political Economy*, Althusser insisted that Marx had projected communism as the end of '*pre*history' – historically determinate economic alienation/exploitation – and not of *history* – some realm from which the dialectic and contradictions would have vanished, ushering in universal harmony among humankind. Consonant with the Cold War times, Althusser's meditations ended on a bureaucratic – philo-Stalinist – note of their own: 'And I believe that we can close this chapter on the end of history, while rejoicing together at the fact that history continues, that Marx was not Hegel, and that Stalin and Thorez are not Hyppolite' (LA, 319).[57]

In his synoptic account of the 'end of history' *topos*, Anderson discusses the part played by the nineteenth–century philosopher, Antoine-Augustin Cournot, in its Gallic transmission. What he understandably neglects is Cournot's possibly equally important role in its *repudiation* by Althusserian Marxism. (Understandably, because Althusser's one – positive – reference to Cournot is made in passing.)[58] Thanks to a recent essay by Althusser's former pupil, Emmanuel Terray, a possible subterranean influence of Cournot upon the Althusserian mutation of historical materialism, and commitment to communism as a quasi-Pascalian wager, has been brought to the surface.[59]

Anderson writes of Cournot's theory of chance and probablility:

> In a famous definition, he declared chance events to be those that were produced by the encounter of two independent causal series. Since the universe

> was not the outcome of a single natural law, but was plainly governed by a variety of different mechanisms, there were both processes governed by more or less linear causal sequences, and occurrences set off by intersections between them. This was the difference between what was regular and what was random, each equally intelligible – the contrast, for example, between the movement of planets and meteors, or of tides and glaciers....
>
> The innovation of his philosophy of history was to be what he called an *aetiology*: a systematic enquiry into the weave of causes that composed the fabric of history. The task of such an enquiry was to trace out the complicated patterns of chance and necessity that had shaped human development, by distinguishing between threads of 'independence' and 'solidarity' within its causal continuum.[60]

Transposed to historical materialism – especially in the Althusserian manifesto of 1962, 'Contradiction and Overdetermination' – the yield is a reconceptualization of any social formation as a decentred 'structure of structures', each possessed of 'relative autonomy' and 'specific effectivity', correspondingly irreducible to an economic first cause or primordial essence, and governed by an (admittedly elusive) 'structural causality'. Consequently, historical materialism was not a philosophy with guarantees – a transcription of historical necessity. But nor was it a ratification of historical chaos. Positing and respecting the complexity of the historical process, as the product of independent causal series and their interlacement, it was the scientific theory of *necessary contingency*. Therein revolution is the (explicable) exception that proves the (implacable) rule.[61]

Historical materialism *à l'*Althusser, then, was not a historicism, economistic or humanist. As a 'process without a subject or goal(s)', to use the specifically Althusserian category, history was neither agonistic alienation – the descent from primitive communism into class society – nor its irenic sublation – the realization of the classless *telos* present in germ at the origin. The political implication was apparent – and drawn (bringing Althusser into disrepute with the leadership of his party, to look no further). To the complexity of history, irreducible to a unique causal mechanism, there corresponded the constitutive complexity of any communist society that might – just might – arise from it. Rejecting some, at least, of the elements of nineteenth-century utopian socialism assimilated by its putatively 'scientific' successor, Althusser advanced an anti-utopian conception of communism. In a conjugation of Durkheimian functionalism and Freudian realism about 'civilization and its discontents', he explicitly contradicted the prospectus of an 'end of ideology', and implicitly dispensed with the projection of an 'end of politics' (the mere Saint-Simonian 'administration of things' envisaged by Engels in *Anti-Dühring* and Lenin in *State and Revolution*).[62]

It is not necessary to endorse Althusser's extravagant claim in *L'avenir* – 'theoretical anti-humanism was the sole [position] that authorized a real practical humanism' (177) – to appreciate the impulse behind it. Rightly or wrongly, Althusser's Communism restricted itself to goals that are modest, and yet sufficiently imperative at a time when the proclaimed end of history has not terminated the problems that brought Communism into being as a political movement: the eradication of Hell from Earth, not the construction of Heaven upon it; or, alternatively put, humanity's entry into its earthly inheritance – one that did not exclude the 'everyday unhappiness' ascribed by Freud to the common human condition (and for which Louis Althusser might readily have exchanged his awesome capacity for suffering). Such a commitment to practical humanism accounts for the presence of some impeccably humanist passages in an oeuvre notorious for its astringent theoretical pronouncements on the 'myth of man'. One of them – quoted by Derrida at Althusser's funeral – beautifully captures the conjunction that imparted something of its singularity to Althusserian Marxism and rendered its author human, all too human:

> Yes, we are . . . united by . . . the same myths, the same themes, that govern us without our consent, by the same spontaneously lived ideology. Yes . . . we still eat of the same bread, we have the same rages, the same rebellions, the same madness (at least in the memory where stalks this ever-imminent possibility), if not the same prostration before a time unmoved by any History. Yes, like Mother Courage, we have the same war at out gates, and a handsbreath from us, if not in us, the same horrible blindness, the same dust in our eyes, the same earth in our mouths. We have the same dawn and night, we skirt the same abysses: our unconsciousness. We even share the same history – and that is how it all started.[63]

NOTES

1 'Louis Althusser', *Les Lettres françaises,* December 1990 (now translated in E. Ann Kaplan and Michael Sprinker, eds, *The Althusserian Legacy*, Verso, London, 1993).
2 Jean-Paul Sartre, *Critique of Dialectical Reason*, Volume 1, New Left Books, London, 1976, p. 822; cf. Louis Althussser and Etienne Balibar, *Reading Capital,* New Left Books, London, 1970, p. 135.
3 Preface (1963) to *The Making of the English Working Class*, Penguin, Harmondsworth, 1980, p. 12.
4 See Régis Debray, 'A Modest Contribution to the Rites and Ceremonies of the Tenth Anniversary', *New Left Review* 115, May/June 1979, pp. 58–59.
5 Cf. Etienne Balibar's observations in 'The Non-Contemporaneity of Althusser', Kaplan and Sprinker, eds, *The Althusserian Legacy*, p. 1.
6 Louis Althusser, *For Marx*, Allen Lane, London, 1969, p. 139.
7 See Robert P. Resch, *Althusser and the Renewal of Marxist Social Theory,* California University Press, Berkeley and Los Angeles, 1992, and Kaplan and Sprinker, eds, *The Althusserian Legacy*. Two further recent publications of

note are Etienne Balibar, *Ecrits pour Althusser*, La Découverte, Paris, 1991, which includes a text read at Althusser's funeral (translated in *Rethinking Marxism*, vol. 4, no. 1, Spring 1991); and Sylvain Lazarus, ed., *Politique et philosophie dans l'oeuvre de Louis Althusser*, Presses Universitaires de France, Paris, 1993, containing papers by Balibar and others presented to a colloquium on Althusser at the University of Paris VIII, (Saint-Denis) in March 1991.

8 Louis Althusser, *L'avenir dure longtemps, suivi de Les faits: Autobiographies*, edited and introduced by Olivier Corpet and Yann Moulier Boutang, Stock/IMEC, Paris, 1992 (henceforth ADL); Yann Moulier Boutang, *Louis Althusser: Une biographie. Tome 1 – La formation du mythe (1918–1956)*, Bernard Grasset, Paris, 1992 (henceforth LA). Subsequently, a second volume in the 'Édition posthume d'oeuvres de Louis Althusser' has appeared, consisting of material utilized by Moulier Boutang in his coverage of the 1939–45 period: Louis Althusser, *Journal de captivité: Stalag XA/1940–1945. Carnets – Correspondances – Textes*, edited and introduced by Olivier Corpet and Yann Moulier Boutang, Stock/IMEC, Paris, 1992 (henceforth JC).

9 See, for example, the reviews by Michel Contat, *Le Monde des livres*, 24 April 1992; Robert Maggiori, *Libération*, 23 April 1992; Didier Eribon, *Le Nouvel Observateur*, 23–29 April 1992; and Jean Lacoste, *Le Quinzaine Littéraire*, April 1992.

10 See, respectively, the accounts by Edward Fox, *Independent Magazine*, 11 July 1992; Gilbert Adair, *Independent*, 2 July 1992; and Mark Lilla, *Times Literary Supplement*, 25 September 1992. The most informed and sympathetic response was that of Martin Bright, *Guardian*, 27 June 1992.

11 A point underlined to me by David Macey (personal communication).

12 In fairness, it should be noted that as regards presentation coverage reached a nadir elsewhere – with the front page of the *London Review of Books*, 17 December 1992, which strove to maintain its reputation, following the departure of its former editor, by featuring a photograph of Althusser beneath the caption: 'The Paris Strangler'.

13 *Ecce Homo: How One Becomes What One Is*, Penguin, Harmondsworth, 1975, p. 69.

14 Althusser and Balibar, *Reading Capital*, p. 112.

15 Sartre's reproof of vulgar-Marxist treatment of Valéry is to be found in his *Search for a Method* (1960), Vintage Books, New York, 1968, p. 56.

16 Perhaps the only immediate cause for regret was the non-inclusion, in an appendix, of three chapters from an earlier draft of ADL, two of them – on Machiavelli and Spinoza – replaced by Althusser's résumé of his 'road to Marx' on pp. 208–13 (in the current chapter xviii), and the third (signalled in chapter xix, p. 233) consisting of reflections which Althusser likewise planned to develop elsewhere (in a work devoted to *La véritable tradition matérialiste*). The Machiavelli and Spinoza chapters have now been published, however, with an introduction by Corpet, under the title 'L'unique tradition matérialiste', *Lignes* 18, Editions Hazan, January 1993, pp. 72–119.

17 See *Essays on Ideology*, Verso, London, 1984, pp. 157–58.

18 Althusser and Balibar, *Reading Capital*, p. 16.

19 *De la superstructure: Droit – état – idéologie*, unpublished manuscript, March – April 1969, p. 138.

20 Cf. *For Marx*, p. 54. For some further reflections, inspired by Freud, on the theme of 'retrospective anticipation', see 'L'unique tradition matérialiste', p. 90.
21 Cf. the opening declaration of Rousseau's *Confessions* (Penguin edition, Harmondsworth, 1953, p. 17): 'I have resolved upon an enterprise which has no precedent, and which, once complete, will have no imitator. My purpose is to display to my kind a portrait in every way true to nature, and the man I shall portray will be myself. Simply myself. . . . But I am made unlike any one I have ever met; I will even venture to say that I am like no one in the whole world. I may be no better, but at least I am different'. Note too his pertinent disclaimer in the introduction to Book Seven (p. 262): 'I may omit or transpose facts, or make mistakes in date; but I cannot go wrong about what I have felt, or about what my feelings led me to do; and these are the chief subjects of my story.'
22 See Simone de Beauvoir, *The Second Sex*, Penguin edition, Harmondsworth, pp. 529–30.
23 See, for example, the opening paragraphs of 'Freud and Lacan', *Essays on Ideology*, pp. 147–48 and my exploration of the theme in 'Althusser's Solitude', *Economy and Society,* vol. 17, no. 4, 1988 (reprinted in Kaplan and Sprinker, eds, *The Althusserian Legacy*).
24 For further details, the reader should consult Elisabeth Roudinesco, *La bataille de cent ans: Histoire de la psychanalyse en France. 2 – 1925–1985,* Editions du Seuil, Paris, 1986, pp. 384–85, 389–90, and especially Moulier Boutang, LA, pp. 365ff.
25 Paul Nizan, *The Conspiracy* (1938), Verso, London, 1988, p. 223.
26 'It is also characteristic of our social history that the intellectuals of petty bourgeois origin who came to the Party at that time [i.e., after the Liberation – GE] felt that they had to pay in pure activity, if not in political activism, the imaginary Debt they thought they had contracted *by not being proletarians*': *For Marx*, p. 27.
27 See, for example, Roudinesco, *La bataille de cent ans*, p. 384 and Emmanuel Le Roy Ladurie, *Paris – Montpellier: P. C. – P. S. U. – 1945–1963*, Gallimard, Paris, 1982, pp. 76–77.
28 See, *inter alia, For Marx*, pp. 21–39 and especially Althusser's forthright preface of 1976, 'Unfinished History', to his pupil Dominique Lecourt's *Proletarian Science? The Case of Lysenko,* New Left Books, London, 1977.
29 Substantially translated as 'What Must Change in the Party', in *New Left Review* 109, May/June 1978.
30 Cf. Raymond Aron, 'Althusser ou la lecture pseudo-structuraliste de Marx', in his *D'une sainte famille à l'autre: Essais sur les marxismes imaginaires*, Gallimard, Paris, 1969. Althusser does not, however, endorse Aron's related reproach (pp. 73, 78–79) that Althusserianism constituted 'Marxism for *agrégés*': quite the reverse.
31 Quoted in Jean Guitton, *Un siècle, une vie*, Robert Laffont, Paris, 1988, Part IV, chapter 4.
32 Ibid.
33 *Ecce Homo*, p. 69.
34 Significantly, in a conversation with Guitton in which he revealed the existence of his memoirs – 'the story of my fearful traumas' – Althusser had

repudiated the pretention of their author: 'I have never achieved transparency. So, like Mallarmé, Alain and Heidegger, I have practised the method of *obscurum per obscurius,* to the obscure via the more obscure.'

35 Pierre Macherey, quoted in Fox, *Independent Magazine*, 11 July 1992.

36 The impact on Althusser of Martin's death, by his own hand, in September 1963 is intimated not only in the moving dedication of *For Marx* to him, but by the obituary notice Althusser wrote for the *Annuaire de l'Association Amicales des anciens élèves de l'Ecole normale supérieure (1967)*, in which he observed that Martin 'had struggled for twenty years – cold, calm, strong, precise – without ever collapsing or giving in, without a single word of complaint: dignified. He chose deliberate death so as not to live another death in the night of an agony without end' (quoted in Moulier Boutang, LA, p. 451).

37 Something of the intimacy of the relationship is conveyed by the letters from brother to sister published in JC, pp. 265–84.

38 See especially JC, p. 88 – Althusser's entry for 12 April 1942, after a gap of several weeks: 'I have just lived one of the most severe trials of my existence, and the most dangerous.' Althusser's prison notebooks also refute the notion that it was contact with Communists in Germany which rallied him to the PCF. A text of 1943 – 'L'espérance', published in the Stalag XA journal, *Le Lien* – does, however, intimate affiliation to a kind of proletarian French nationalism, inspired, no doubt, by his former history teacher, Joseph Hours: see JC, pp. 345–52.

39 'Une question de faits', in *L'évangile captif,* Cahier X of *Jeunesse de l'Eglise*, Paris, 1949.

40 George Ross and Jane Jenson, 'The Tragedy of the French Left', *New Left Review* 171, September/October 1988, p. 18.

41 Just as its sister-parties were for socialists in other countries. Cf. Lucio Magri, 'The European Left between Crisis and Refoundation', *New Left Review* 189, September/October 1991, pp. 6–7: '. . . a historical experience is now ending in painful defeat – an experience which, both materially and in terms of ideas, served sometimes as a model and in any case as a reference point for broad movements of liberation. It is now fashionable in the West, even on the Left, to treat that connection as a thoroughly harmful product of manipulation or folly – that is, to consider the October Revolution and its sequel not as a process which degenerated in stages but as a regression *ab origine*, or a pile of rubble. But the historical reality is rather different. First Stalinism, then the authoritarian power of a bureaucratic, imperial caste, were one side of that historical process . . . but for decades another side also continued to operate: the side of national independence; the spread of literacy, modernization and social protection across whole continents; the resistance to fascism and victory over it as a general tendency of capitalism; support for and involvement in the liberation of three-quarters of humanity from colonialism; containment of the power of the mightiest imperial state.'

42 'Intellectuals and Communism', reprinted in E. J. Hobsbawm, *Revolutionaries*, Quartet, London, 1977: here p. 29.

43 *The Communists and Peace* (1952–54), Hamish Hamilton, London, 1969; cf. André Gorz, *The Traitor* (1958), Verso, London, 1989, pp. 225–29.

44 Perry Anderson, *Considerations on Western Marxism*, New Left Books, London, 1976, p. 44.

45 'Notes on Marxism in Britain since 1945', *New Left Review* 100, November 1976 – February 1977 (reprinted in Williams, *Problems in Materialism and Culture*, Verso, London, 1980).

46 The coinage is Francis Mulhern's, in the Introduction to his anthology, *Contemporary Marxist Literary Criticism*, Longman, London, 1992, p. 6. As Althusser wrote in an essay dating from 1967, 'Marx did not "say everything", not only because he did not have the time, but because to "say everything" makes no sense for a scientist: only a religion can pretend to "say everything". By contrast, a scientific theory, by definition, always has *something else* to say, since it exists only in order to discover, in the very solution of problems, as many, if not more, problems than it resolves' ('On Theoretical Work: Difficulties and Resources', in *Philosophy and the Spontaneous Philosophy of the Scientists and Other Essays*, Verso, London, 1990: here p. 59). The echoes of Popperian epistemology are striking.

47 The formula 'historical Marxism' is adopted from Costanzo Preve, 'La lutte contre le sens commun dans le mouvement communiste "historique" au xxe siècle', in Sylvain Lazarus, ed., *Politique et philosophie dans l'oeuvre de Louis Althusser*, who glosses it thus (p. 130): 'i. e., really, effectively existing [Marxism], incorporated into huge party, state and trade-union apparatuses'. Althusser's most explicit comments on the subject occur in his 'Marxism Today' (1978), in *Philosophy and the Spontaneous Philosophy of the Scientists.*

48 The point is made by Balibar in *Reading Capital*, p. 202 and by Althusser in *Lenin and Philosophy and Other Essays,* New Left Books, London, 1971, p. 43.

49 Luc Ferry and Alain Renaut, *La pensée 68: Essai sur l'anti-humanisme contemporain*, Gallimard, Paris, 1985, p. 200.

50 Quoted in Peter Gay, *Freud: A Life for Our Time*, Macmillan, London, 1989, p. 334.

51 'Louis Althusser', *Indepedent,* 27 October 1990.

52 Indicative of Althusser's heterodoxy here is his citation of the 'revisionist' historian of the French Revolution, François Furet, for repudiating the 'ideology' of 1789 in whose construction and propagation French Communist intellectuals (e.g., Albert Soboul) played a central role.

53 *Reading Capital*, p. 120. As he makes clear (ADL, p. 168), Althusser is referring not to *Nausea* or the *Roads to Freedom* trilogy, when he speaks of 'philosophical novels', but to *Being and Nothingness* and the *Critique of Dialectical Reason.* Whatever the justice of the charge, one thing is certain: the dilemmas confronted by Sartre's fictional biographer, Antoine Roquentin, are not surmounted by Althusser's own autobiographical story-telling. See *Nausea*, Penguin, Harmondsworth, 1983, pp. 61–63.

54 'British Marxist Historians, 1880–1980', *New Left Review* 120, March/April 1980, pp. 83–84. For Althusser's analysis of theoretical Stalinism, see 'Note on "The Critique of the Personality Cult" ', in his *Essays in Self-Criticism,* New Left Books, London, 1976.

55 See LA, pp. 259–76, containing ample quotation from Althusser's 1947 Mémoire de Diplôme d'études supérieures, 'La notion de contenu dans la

philosophie de G. W. F. Hegel'. Thus far, only a brief extract from this key early work has appeared in print, as 'L'esprit d'Iéna contre la Prusse', *Magazine Littéraire* 293, November 1991. Its publication in full is promised in a forthcoming collection of Althusser's philosophical texts by IMEC/Editions Stock.

56 Francis Fukuyama, 'The End of History?', *The National Interest* 16, Summer 1989, and *The End of History and the Last Man*, Hamish Hamilton, London, 1992. Of the many critical responses, readers are referred to Joseph McCarney, 'History under the Hammer', *Times Higher Education Supplement*, 1 December 1989 and 'Endgame of History', *Radical Philosophy* 62, Autumn 1992; Perry Anderson, 'The Ends of History', in his *A Zone of Engagement*, Verso, London, 1992; and Alex Callinicos, 'Is History Really Over?', paper read at the Radical Political Thought Conference, University of Sussex, November 1992. My own thoughts on the controversy are set out in 'The Cards of Confusion: Reflections on Historical Communism and the "End of History"', *Radical Philosophy* 64, Summer 1993, (to be reprinted in Christopher Bertram and Andrew Chitty, eds, *Beyond the End of History*?, forthcoming, Verso, London, 1994).

57 Significantly, in his *Modern French Philosophy* (Cambridge University Press, Cambridge, 1980), which commences with Kojève, Vincent Descombes employs the identical formula to Althusser – 'philosophical novel' – to characterize Kojève's construction of Hegel: 'the austere Hegelian *Phenomenology* turns into a kind of serialized philosophical novel, where one dramatic scene follows another; picturesque characters come face to face, reversals of situation keep up the suspense, and the reader, avid to know the end of the story [*la fin de l'histoire*], clamours for more' (p. 27).

Descombes' analysis of Althusser's subsequent philosophical strategy (p. 118) anticipates Althusser's own:

> ... Marxism was in difficulties on two sides.
>
> 1. In the rear, where it ran the risk of being drawn along in the decline of those philosophies (assembled by Althusser under the heading 'theoretical humanism') with which opinion tended to associate it.
>
> 2. In the front, where its theory of economic determinism (positing a relation of *cause and effect*, rather than one of isomorphism, between infrastructure and superstructure) came under fire from structuralist positions.
>
> Caught between the two, Althusser, a self-acknowledged communist philosopher, might well have described himself in the words that Stendhal gives to Lucien Leuwen: 'I am a cavalry general in a lost battle, who forgets his own interests and attempts to have his cavalry dismount in order to engage the enemy infantry.' It is a difficult manoeuvre that Althusser attempts in abandoning the treacherous ground of *praxis* and the 'dialectic', leaving the existentialist regiments to fight it out alone with the structuralist artillery, siding with the latter himself, taking advantage of the general surprise to consolidate his hold and emerging finally as winner of the day. Such audacious tactics evidently entail certain sacrifices which his ranks must first be persuaded to accept: the entire Hegelian heritage must be repudiated, and likewise all kinship between Marxism and dialectical philosophy of history. The charger of 'contradiction, driving force

of history', on which only a while before the Marxist philosopher was seen to parade, becomes a jaded Rosinante, to be rid of in all haste.

Note, finally, that after the battle had been definitively lost, Althusser's address in Paris was none other than 8, rue Lucien Leuwen . . .

58 In the 1968 lecture 'Lenin and Philosophy': *Philosophy and the Spontaneous Philosophy of the Scientists and Other Essays*, pp. 172–73 ('. . . French philosophy . . . can be salvaged from its own history only by the few great minds against whom it set its face, like Comte and Durkheim, or buried in oblivion, like Cournot and Couturat. . . .').

59 *Le troisième jour du communisme*, Actes Sud, Arles, 1992, pp. 63–68, to which I am indebted for what follows.

60 'The Ends of History', pp. 295–96; see also p. 297.

61 'Contradiction and Overdetermination' can be consulted in Althusser's *For Marx*. For his own retrospective on it, see 'Is it Simple to be a Marxist in Philosophy?', in *Philosophy and the Spontaneous Philosophy of the Scientists*, pp. 213–23. The shrewdness of Terray's account is confirmed by comparing the article in which he first sketched it – 'Une rencontre: Althusser et Machiavel' (in Sylvain Lazarus, ed., *Politique et philosophie dans l'oeuvre de Louis Althusser*, especially pp. 157–58) – with Althusser's own comments on Machiavelli in the posthumous publication, 'L'unique tradition matérialiste', p. 105.

62 Thus, it is no cause for surprise that Althusser is recalled by one of his former students as having rebuked him for the suggestion that 'if people were communists, it was for the sake of happiness. In essence, his reply was: you mustn't say that. It is in order to bring about a change of mode of production. . . .' See Philippe Gavi, Jean-Paul Sartre and Pierre Victor, *On a raison de se révolter*, Gallimard, Paris, 1974, p. 197. In addition to Freud's *Civilization and its Discontents*, see the *New Introductory Lectures on Psychoanalysis* (Penguin edition, Harmondsworth, 1973, pp. 213–19) for a summary statement of his anti-utopianism, specifically aimed at Bolshevism. For some contemporary reflections on these issues by a Marxist influenced by Althusser, see Ted Benton, *Natural Relations*, Verso, London, 1993, pp. 200, 215–21.

Althusser's Freudian affiliations doubtless go some of the way to explain his disdain for Herbert Marcuse (cf. the peremptory dismissal in *Essays in Self-Criticism*, p. 118 n. 13), whose attempted Freudo-Marxist synthesis in *Eros and Civilization* repudiates Freud on this score. As I hope to show elsewhere, Althusser and Marcuse are ultimately less incompatible in certain Freudian respects than they imagined.

63 *For Marx*, p. 150.

BIBLIOGRAPHY OF THE PUBLISHED WRITINGS OF LOUIS ALTHUSSER

Any bibliography of Althusser's work suffers from an in-built (if not planned) obsolescence, given the regular emergence of new material from the philosopher's archives deposited with the Institut Mémoires de l'édition contemporaine, based in Paris, in July 1991. Three more collections of previously unpublished material are currently scheduled for publication by IMEC, in collaboration with Editions Stock: a two-volume selection of philosophical and political texts (including the 1947 thesis on Hegel) and a collection of correspondence. Accordingly, what follows does not claim to be complete, but is as comprehensive (and accurate) as possible, as of November 1993. Items are listed in chronological order of appearance, rather than composition, the date of the latter being provided in brackets when appropriate. Where English translations are available, full details are given on a separate line.

1949

1 'Une question de faits', in *L'évangile captif*, Cahier X of *Jeunesse de l'Église*, Paris, 1949, pp. 13–24.

1951

2 Contribution to the discussion, in 'Journées nationales d'études pédagogiques des professeurs de philosophie' (1950), *Revue de l'Enseignement Philosophique*, vol. 1, nos 1–2, 1951, p. 12.

1953

3 'A propos du marxisme', *Revue de l'Enseignement Philosophique*, vol. 3, no. 4, 1953, pp. 15–19.

4 'Note sur le matérialisme dialectique', *Revue de I'Enseignement Philosophique*, vol. 3, no. 5, 1953, pp. 11–17.

1955

5 'Sur l'objectivité de l'histoire (Lettre à Paul Ricoeur)', *Revue de l'Enseignement Philosophique*, vol. 5, no. 4, 1955, pp. 3–15.

1958

6 'Despote et monarque chez Montesquieu', *Esprit*, vol. 26, no. 11, 1958, pp. 595–614.

Extract from 7.

1959

7 *Montesquieu: la politique et l'histoire*, Presses Universitaires de France, Paris, 1959.

Translated by Ben Brewster as 'Montesquieu: Politics and History', in Louis Althusser, *Politics and History: Montesquieu, Rousseau, Hegel and Marx*, New Left Books, London, 1972, pp. 9–109.

1960

8 'Note du traducteur' (1958), in Ludwig Feuerbach, *Manifestes philosophiques. Textes choisis (1839–1845)*, edited and translated by Louis Althusser, Presses Universitaires de France, Paris, 1960, pp. 1–9.

9 'Les "Manifestes philosophiques" de Feuerbach', *La Nouvelle Critique* 121, December 1960, pp. 32–38.

Reprinted in **24**, pp. 35–43.

Translated by Ben Brewster as 'Feuerbach's "Philosophical Manifestoes"', in Louis Althusser, *For Marx*, Allen Lane, London, 1969, pp. 41–48.

1961

10 'Sur le jeune Marx (Questions de théorie)', *La Pensée* 96, April 1961, pp. 3–26.

Reprinted in **24**, pp. 45–83.

Translated by Ben Brewster as 'On the Young Marx: Theoretical Questions', in *For Marx*, pp. 49–86.

1962

11 Review of Raymond Polin, *La politique morale de John Locke*, in *Revue d'Histoire Moderne et Contemporaine* 36, 1962, pp. 150–55.

12 'Contradiction et surdétermination (Notes pour une recherche)', *La Pensée* 106, December 1962, pp. 3–22.

Reprinted (with appendix) in **24**, pp. 85–116.

Translated by Ben Brewster as 'Contradiction and Overdetermination: Notes for an Investigation', *New Left Review* 41, January/February 1967, pp. 15–35; reprinted in *For Marx*, pp. 87–128.

13 'Le "Piccolo, Bertolazzi et Brecht (Notes sur un théâtre matérialiste)', *Esprit*, vol. 30, no. 12, 1962, pp. 946–65.

Reprinted in **24**, pp. 129–52.

Translated by Ben Brewster as 'The "Piccolo Teatro": Bertolazzi and Brecht – Notes on a Materialist Theatre', in *For Marx*, pp. 129–51.

1963

14 'Les "Manuscrits de 1844" de Karl Marx (Économie politique et philosophie)', *La Pensée* 107, February 1963, pp. 106–09.

Reprinted in **24**, pp. 153–60.

Translated by Ben Brewster as 'The "1844 Manuscripts" of Karl Marx: Political Economy and Philosophy', in *For Marx*, pp. 153–59.

15 'Philosophie et sciences humaines', *Revue de l'Enseignement Philosophique*, vol. 13, no. 5, 1963, pp. 1–12.

16 'Sur la dialectique matérialiste (De l'inégalité des origines)', *La Pensée* 110, August 1963, pp. 5–46.

Reprinted (minus appendix) in **24**, pp. 161–224.

Translated by Ben Brewster as 'On the Materialist Dialectic: On the Unevenness of Origins', in *For Marx*, pp. 161–218.

1964

17 'Problèmes étudiants', *La Nouvelle Critique* 152, January 1964, pp. 80–111.

18 'Teoria e metodo' and 'Gli strumenti del marxismo', *Rinascita*, 25 January 1964, pp. 27–28; 1 February 1964, pp. 28–29.

19 Presentation of Pierre Macherey, 'La philosophie de la science de Georges Canguilhem', *La Pensée* 113, February 1964, pp. 50–54.

20 'Marxisme et humanisme', *Cahiers de l'Institut de Science Économique Appliquée* 20, June 1964, pp. 109–33.

Reprinted in **24**, pp. 225–49.

Translated by Ben Brewster as 'Marxism and Humanism', in *For Marx*, pp. 219–41.

21 'Freud et Lacan', *La Nouvelle Critique* 161–162, December 1964 – January 1965, pp. 88–108.

Reprinted in **78**, pp. 9–34 and in **110**, pp. 23–52.

Translated by Ben Brewster as 'Freud and Lacan', *New Left Review* 55, May/June 1969, pp. 49–65; reprinted in Louis Althusser, *Lenin and Philosophy and Other Essays*, New Left Books, London, 1971, pp. 177–202, and subsequently in Louis Althusser, *Essays on Ideology*, Verso, London, 1984, pp. 141–71.

1965

22 'Note complémentaire sur "l'humanisme réel"', *La Nouvelle Critique* 164, March 1965, pp. 32–37.

Reprinted in **24**, pp. 251–58.

Translated by Ben Brewster as 'A Complementary Note on "Real Humanism"', in *For Marx*, pp. 242–47.

23 'Préface: Aujourd'hui', in Louis Althusser, *Pour Marx*, François Maspero, Paris, 1965, pp. 9–32.

Translated by Ben Brewster as 'Introduction: Today', in *For Marx*, pp. 19–39.

24 *Pour Marx*, François Maspero, Paris, 1965.

Contains **9**; **10**; **12**; **13**; **14**; **16**; **20**; **22**; **23**.

Translated by Ben Brewster as *For Marx*, Allen Lane, London, 1969 (subsequently reprinted by New Left Books and Verso).

25 'Esquisse du concept d'histoire', *La Pensée* 121, August 1965, pp. 2–21.

Extract from **27**.

26 'Préface: Du "Capital" à la philosophie de Marx', in Louis Althusser, Jacques Rancière and Pierre Macherey, *Lire le Capital I*, François Maspero, Paris, 1965, pp. 9–89.

Second, revised edition (François Maspero, Paris, 1968) translated by Ben Brewster as 'Part I: From *Capital* to Marx's Philosophy', in Louis Althusser and Etienne Balibar, *Reading Capital*, New Left Books, London, 1970, pp. 11–69.

27 'L'object du "Capital"', in Louis Althusser, Étienne Balibar and Roger Establet, *Lire le Capital II*, François Maspero, Paris, 1965, pp. 7–185.

Second, revised edition (François Maspero, Paris, 1968) translated by Ben Brewster as 'Part II: The Object of *Capital*', in *Reading Capital*, pp. 71–198.

1966

28 'Théorie, pratique théorique et formation théorique. Idéologie et lutte idéologique' (1965), published in Spanish in *Casa de las Americas* (Havana) 34, 1966, pp. 5–31.

Translated by James H. Kavanagh as 'Theory, Theoretical Practice and Theoretical Formation. Ideology and Ideological Struggle', in Louis Althusser, *Philosophy and the Spontaneous Philosophy of the Scientists & Other Essays*, Verso, London, 1990, pp. 1–42.

29 'Matérialisme historique et matérialisme dialectique', *Cahiers Marxistes-Léninistes* 11, April 1966, pp. 90–122.

30 'Réponse à André Daspre', in 'Deux lettres sur la connaissance de l'art', *La Nouvelle Critique* 175, April 1966, pp. 141–46.

Translated by Ben Brewster as 'A Letter on Art in Reply to André Daspre', in *Lenin and Philosophy and Other Essays*, pp. 203–08; reprinted in *Essays on Ideology*, pp. 173–79.

31 'Cremonini, peintre de l'abstraction', *Démocratie Nouvelle* 8, August 1966, pp. 105–20.

Translated by Ben Brewster as 'Cremonini, Painter of the Abstract', in *Lenin and Philosophy and Other Essays*, pp. 209–20.

32 'Sur le "Contrat social" (Les Décalages)', in *L'impensé de Jean-Jacques Rousseau, Cahiers pour l'Analyse* 8, 1966, pp. 5–42.

Translated by Ben Brewster as 'Rousseau: *The Social Contract* (The Discrepancies)', in *Politics and History: Montesquieu, Rousseau, Hegel and Marx*, pp. 111–60.

33 'Sur la révolution culturelle', *Cahiers Marxistes-Léninistes* 14, November/December 1966, pp. 5–16.

1967

34 'Sur le travail théorique. Difficultés et ressources', *La Pensée* 132, April 1967, pp. 3–22.

Translated by James H. Kavanagh as 'On Theoretical Work: Difficulties and Resources', in *Philosophy and the Spontaneous Philosophy of the Scientists & Other Essays*, pp. 43–67.

35 'Prefazione', in Louis Althusser, *La révolucìon teòrica de Marx*, Siglo XXI, Mexico/Buenos Aires, 1967, pp. ii–xvi.

36 Correspondence with R. Domergue, in Louis Althusser and R. Domergue, *Marxismo segundo Althusser: polemica Althusser-Garaudy*, Signal, Sao Paulo, 1967.

37 Obituary of Jacques Martin, *Annuaire de l'Association Amicales des anciens élèves de l'École normale supérieure* (1967), ENS, Paris, 1967.

1968

38 'La filosofia, la politica et la scienza (Una lettera di Louis Althusser sul pensiero di Gramsci)', *Rinascita*, 15 March 1968, pp. 23–24.

39 'La philosophie comme arme de la révolution (Réponse à huit questions)', interview with Maria Antonietta Macciocchi, *La Pensée* 138, April 1968, pp. 26–34.

Reprinted in 78, pp. 35–48.

Translated by Ben Brewster as 'Philosophy as a Revolutionary Weapon', *New Left Review* 64, November/December 1970, pp. 3–11; reprinted in *Lenin and Philosophy and Other Essays*, pp. 13–25.

40 'An die deutschen Leser' (1967), in Louis Althusser, *Für Marx*, Suhrkamp, Frankfurt M., 1968, pp. 7–15.

41 'La tâche historique de la philosophie marxiste' (1967), published in revised form in Hungarian as 'A Marxista Filozófia Történelmi Feladata', in Louis Althusser, *Marx – Az Elmélet Forradalma*, Kossuth, Budapest, 1968, pp. 272–306.

42 'A Magyar Olvasöhoz' (To My Hungarian Readers), in *Marx – Az Elmélet Forradalma*, pp. 9–15.

Published in French in Saül Karsz, *Théorie et politique: Louis Althusser*, Fayard, Paris, 1974, pp. 315–20.

43 'Avertissement' (1967), in Louis Althusser and Etienne Balibar, *Lire le Capital*, second edition, 2 vols, François Maspero, Paris, 1968, pp. 5–6.

Translated by Ben Brewster as 'Foreword to the Italian Edition', in *Reading Capital*, pp. 7–8.

44 'Lénine et la philosophie', *Bulletin de la Société Française de Philosophie* 4, October/December 1968, pp. 127–81.

Reprinted (minus the interventions of Jean Wahl, Paul Ricoeur, et al.) as *Lénine et la philosophie*, François Maspero, Paris, 1969 and in **60**, pp. 5–47.

Translated by Ben Brewster as 'Lenin and Philosophy', in *Lenin and Philosophy and Other Essays*, pp. 27–68; reprinted in *Philosophy and the Spontaneous Philosophy of the Scientists & Other Essays*, pp. 167–202.

1969

45 'Comment lire "Le Capital"?', *L'Humanité*, 21 March 1969.
Reprinted in **78**, pp. 49–60.

Translated as 'How to Read Marx's "Capital"', *Marxism Today*, October 1969, pp. 302–05.

46 'Avertissement aux lecteurs du Livre I du "Capital"', in Karl Marx, *Le Capital: Livre I*, Garnier-Flammarion, Paris, 1969, pp. 5–30.

Translated by Ben Brewster as 'Preface to *Capital* Volume One', in *Lenin and Philosophy and Other Essays*, pp. 69–101.

47 Letters to Maria Antonietta Macciocchi (1968–69), in Macciocchi, *Lettere dall'interno del P.C.I.*, Giangiacomo Feltrinelli, Milan, 1969, pp. 3–6, 23–26, 53–64, 126–27, 331–61.

Translated by Stephen M. Hellman in Macciocchi, *Letters from inside the Italian Communist Party to Louis Althusser*, New Left Books, London, 1973, pp. 3–5, 21–23, 48–57, 112–13, 295–320.

48 'A propos de l'article de Michel Verret sur "Mai étudiant"', *La Pensée* 145, June 1969, pp. 3–14.

49 'To My English Readers' (1967), in *For Marx*, pp. 9–15.

50 'A Letter to the Translator', in *For Marx*, pp. 257–58.

51 'Lettera a Pesenti', *Rinascita* 32, 1969.

52 'Crise de l'homme et de la société', in 'L'Église aujourd'hui', *Lumière et Vie*, vol. 28, no. 13, 1969, pp. 26–29.

1970

53 'Idéologie et appareils idéologiques d'état (Notes pour une recherche)', *La Pensée* 151, June 1970, pp. 3–38.

Extract from *De la superstructure: Droit-état-Idéologie* (unpublished manuscript, 1969), reprinted in **78**, pp. 67–125.

Translated by Ben Brewster as 'Ideology and Ideological State Apparatuses: Notes towards an Investigation', in *Lenin and Philosophy and Other Essays*, pp. 121–73; reprinted in *Essays on Ideology*, pp. 1–60.

54 'Sur le rapport de Marx à Hegel' (1968), in Jacques d'Hondt, ed., *Hegel et la pensée moderne*, Presses Universitaires de France, Paris, 1970, pp. 85–111.

Reprinted in **60**, pp. 49–71.

Translated by Ben Brewster as 'Marx's Relation to Hegel', in *Politics and History: Montesquieu, Rousseau, Hegel and Marx*, pp. 161–86.

55 'Lénine devant Hegel' (1969), in W. R. Beyer, ed., *Hegel – Jahrbuck 1968/1969*, Meissnheim A. Glan, 1970, pp. 45–58.

Reprinted in **60**, pp. 73–90.

Translated by Ben Brewster as 'Lenin before Hegel', in *Lenin and Philosophy and Other Essays*, pp. 103–20.

1971

56 'Foreword' (1970), in *Lenin and Philosophy and Other Essays*, pp. 7–9.

57 Letter to the translator (on 'Freud and Lacan'), in *Lenin and Philosophy and Other Essays*, pp. 177–78; reprinted in *Essays on Ideology*, pp. 141–42.

58 'Prefazione' (1970), in Marta Harnecker, *Los conceptos elementales del materialismo histórico*, second edition, Siglo XXI, Mexico/Buenos Aires, 1971.

Published in French as 'Marxisme et lutte de classe' in **78**, pp. 61–6.

1972

59 'Sur une erreur politique. Les maîtres auxiliaires, les étudiants travailleurs et l'agrégation de philosophie', *France Nouvelle*, 25 July 1972, pp. 9–12; 1 August 1972, pp. 10–13.

60 *Lénine et la philosophie*, second (expanded) edition, François Maspero, Paris, 1972.

Contains **44**; **54**; **55**.

61 'Reply to John Lewis (Self-Criticism)', *Marxism Today*, October 1972, pp. 310–18; November 1972, pp. 343–49.

Published in French in revised form in **66**, pp. 9–68.

1973

62 'The Conditions of Marx's Scientific Discovery (On the New Definition of Philosophy)' (1970), *Theoretical Practice* 7/8, January 1973, pp. 4–11.

Published in French as 'Sur l'évolution du jeune Marx' in **72**, pp. 103–26.

63 Presentation of Dominique Lecourt, *Une crise et son enjeu*, François Maspero, Paris, 1973.

64 'Note sur "la critique du culte de la personnalité" ' (1972), in Louis Althusser, *Réponse à John Lewis*, François Maspero, Paris, 1973, pp. 69–90.

Translated by Grahame Lock as 'Note on "The Critique of the Personality Cult" ', in Louis Althusser, *Essays in Self-Criticism*, New Left Books, London, 1976, pp. 78–93; reprinted in *Essays on Ideology*, pp. 115–32.

65 'Remarque sur une catégorie: procès sans Sujet ni Fin(s)', in *Réponse à John Lewis*, pp. 91–98.

Translated by Grahame Lock as 'Remark on the Category: Process without a Subject or Goal(s)', in *Essays in Self-Criticism*, pp. 94–99; reprinted in *Essays on Ideology*, pp. 133–39.

66 *Réponse à John Lewis*, François Maspero, Paris, 1973.

Contains 'Avertissement'; **61**; **64**; **65**.

Translated by Grahame Lock as 'Reply to John Lewis', in *Essays in Self-Criticism*, pp. 33–99; reprinted in *Essays on Ideology*, pp. 61–139.

67 Intervention on 'Les communistes, les intellectuels et la culture', *France Nouvelle*, 18 September 1973, p. 11.

1974

68 [Mimeographed text] (1970), in Saül Karsz, *Théorie et politique: Louis Althusser*, pp. 321–23.

69 Letter (1967), in Régis Debray, *La critique des armes*, Editions du Seuil, Paris, 1974, pp. 262–69.

Translated by Rosemary Sheed as 'Letter from Louis Althusser', in Debray, *A Critique of Arms*, Penguin, Harmondsworth, 1977, pp. 258–67.

70 'Justesse et philosophie', *La Pensée* 176, August 1974, pp. 3–8.

Extract from **71**.

71 *Philosophie et philosophie spontanée des savants (1967)*, François Maspero, Paris, 1974.

Abridged and revised version of *Cours de philosophie pour scientifiques: Introduction*, unpublished manuscript, November 1967.

Translated by Warren Montag as 'Philosophy and the Spontaneous Philosophy of the Scientists (1967)', in *Philosophy and the Spontaneous Philosophy of the Scientists & Other Essays*, pp. 69–165.

72 *Éléments d'autocritique* (1972), Hachette, Paris, 1974.

Also contains **62**.

Translated by Grahame Lock as 'Elements of Self-Criticism', in *Essays in Self-Criticism*, pp. 101–61.

73 'Quelque chose de nouveau', *L'Humanité*, 12 October 1974.

Translated by Grahame Lock as 'Something New', in *Essays in Self-Criticism*, pp. 208–15.

1975

74 'Les communistes et la philosophie', *L'Humanité*, 5 July 1975.

75 'Est-il simple d'être marxiste en philosophie? (Soutenance d'Amiens)', *La Pensée* 183, October 1975, pp. 3–31.

Reprinted in **78**, pp. 127–72.

Translated by Grahame Lock as 'Is it Simple to be a Marxist in Philosophy?', in *Essays in Self-Criticism*, pp. 163–207; reprinted in *Philosophy and the Spontaneous Philosophy of the Scientists & Other Essays*, pp. 203–40.

1976

76 Letters to Luis Francisco Rebello (1975), in Louis Althusser and Luis Francisco Rebello, *Cartas sobre a revolução portuguesa*, Seara Nova, Lisbon, 1976, pp. 15–25, 33–36, 41–42.

77 'Avant-Propos: Histoire terminée, histoire interminable', in Dominique Lecourt, *Lyssenko. Histoire réelle d'une 'science prolétarienne'*, François Maspero, Paris, 1976, pp. 7–19.

Translated by Grahame Lock as 'Introduction: Unfinished History', in Lecourt, *Proletarian Science? The Case of Lysenko*, New Left Books, London, 1977, pp. 7–16.

78 *Positions*, Editions Sociales, Paris, 1976.

Contains 'Note'; **21**; **39**; **45**; **53**; **58**; **75**.

79 *La transformación de la filosofia*, Universidad de Granada, Granada, 1976.

Translated by Thomas E. Lewis as 'The Transformation of Philosophy', in *Philosophy and the Spontaneous Philosophy of the Scientists & Other Essays*, pp. 241–65.

1977

80 'The Historic Significance of the 22nd Congress' (1976), in Etienne Balibar, *On the Dictatorship of the Proletariat*, New Left Books, London, 1977, pp. 193–211.

Published in French in revised form as **83**.

81 'Sur Marx et Freud' (1976), published in German as 'Über Marx und Freud', in Louis Althusser, *Ideologie und ideologische Staatsapparate*, VSA, Hamburg, 1977, pp. 89–107.

Published in French in slightly abridged form as 'La découverte du Docteur Freud dans ses rapports avec la théorie marxiste', in *The Unconscious*, vol. I, Metsniereba, Tbilisi, 1978, pp. 239–53; reprinted in **110**, pp. 222–45.

Translated by Warren Montag as 'On Marx and Freud', in *Rethinking Marxism*, vol. 4, no. 1, 1991, pp. 17–30.

82 'Note sur les appareils idéologiques d'état (AIE)' (1976), published in German as 'Anmerkung über die ideologische Staatsapparate', in *Ideologie und ideologische Staatsapparate*, pp. 154–68.

Translated in abridged form by Jeremy Leaman in 'Extracts from Althusser's "Note on the ISAs"', *Economy and Society*, vol. 12, no. 4, 1983, pp. 455–65.

83 *22ème Congrès*, François Maspero, Paris, 1977.

Translated by Ben Brewster as 'On the Twenty-Second Congress of the French Communist Party', *New Left Review* 104, July/August 1977, pp. 3–22.

84 'Alcune parole grosse', *Paese Sera*, 16 April 1977.

85 'Finalmente qualcosa di vitale si libera dalla crisi e nella crisi del marxismo', *Il Manifesto*, 16 November 1977.

Published in French in *Il Manifesto*, ed., *Pouvoir et opposition dans les sociétés post-révolutionnaires*, Editions du Seuil, Paris, 1978.

Translated by Grahame Lock as 'The Crisis of Marxism', *Marxism Today*, July 1978, pp. 215–20, 227; reprinted in *Il Manifesto*, ed., *Power and Opposition in Post-Revolutionary Societies*, Ink Links, London, 1979, pp. 225–37.

1978

86 'Avant-Propos' (1977), Gérard Duménil, *Le concept de loi économique dans 'Le Capital'*, François Maspero, Paris, 1978, pp. 7–26.

87 'La questione dello stato, oggi e nella transizione', interview with Rossana Rossanda (1977), *Il Manifesto*, 4 April 1978.

Reprinted as 'Il marxismo como teoria "finita" ', in Louis Althusser et al., *Discutere lo stato*, De Donato, Bari, 1978, pp. 7–21.

Published in French as 'Entretien', *Dialectiques* 23, Spring 1978, pp. 5–12.

88 'Des intellectuels communistes signent une lettre collective pour réclamer "une véritable discussion politique" dans leur parti', letter from Louis Althusser, Etienne Balibar, Guy Bois, Georges Labica, Jean-Pierre Lefebvre and Maurice Moissonier, *Le Monde*, 6 April 1978.

89 'Ce qui ne peut plus durer dans le parti communiste', *Le Monde*, 25–28 April 1978.

Expanded version published as *Ce qui ne peut plus durer dans le parti communiste*, François Maspero, Paris, 1978.

Translated by Patrick Camiller as 'What Must Change in the Party', *New Left Review* 109, May/June 1978, pp. 19–45.

90 'Al "punto zero" della teoria', interview with Giorgio Fanti, *Paese Sera*, 6 May 1978.

91 'Je ne veux pas être un martyr', interview in *Les Nouvelles Littéraires*, 15 June 1978.

92 'Statt eines Vorworts: Vier Fragen an Louis Althusser', interview with Peter Schöttler, in Louis Althusser, *Die Krise des Marxismus*, VSA, Hamburg, 1978, pp. 7–17.

93 'Il marxismo oggi', in *Enciclopedia Europea*, vol. VII, Aldo Garzanti, Milan, 1978.

Reprinted in Louis Althusser, *Quel che deve cambiare nel partito communista*, Aldo Garzanti, Milan, 1978, pp. 107–26.

Published in French in *M Mensuel, marxisme, mouvement*, 43, January 1991, pp. 7–11.

Translated by James H. Kavanagh as 'Marxism Today', in *Philosophy and the Spontaneous Philosophy of the Scientists & Other Essays*, pp. 267–80.

1982

94 'Lam' (1977), in *Exposicion Antalogica 'Hammaje a Wilfredo Lam', 1902–1982*, Madrid, 1982, pp. 141–42.

1983

95 'La découverte du Dr. Freud' (1976), *Revue de Médecine Psychosomatique*, vol. 25, no. 2, 1983.

Reprinted in Léon Chertok, ed., *Dialogue franco-soviétique sur la psychanalyse*, Editions Privat, Toulouse, 1984, pp. 81–97; and in **110**, pp. 195–219.

1987

96 'Solitude de Machiavel' (1977), published in German as 'Die Einsamkeit Machiavellis', in Louis Althusser, *Schriften, Band 2: Machiavelli, Montesquieu, Rousseau – Zur politischen Philosophie der Neuzeit,* Argument, West Berlin, 1987, pp. 11–29.

Published in French in *Futur Antérieur* 1, Spring 1990.

Translated by Ben Brewster as 'Machiavelli's Solitude', *Economy and Society*, vol., 17, no. 4, 1988, pp. 468–79.

1988

97 *Filosofia y marxismo*, interviews with Fernanda Navarro, Siglo XXI, Mexico, 1988.

Forthcoming in French, Lettres françaises/Mercure de France, 1994.

1990

98 [Dream text], *El semanal*, November 1990.

1991

99 'L'esprit d'Iéna contre la Prusse', *Magazine Littéraire* 293, November 1991, pp. 43–45.

Extract from 'La notion de contenu dans la philosophie de G. W. F. Hegel', Mémoire de Diplôme d'études supérieures, Paris, 1947.

1992

100 *L'avenir dure longtemps, suivi de Les faits: Autobiographies*, edited and introduced by Olivier Corpet and Yann Moulier Boutang, Stock/IMEC, Paris, 1992.

Translated by Richard Veasey as *The Future Lasts A Long Time*, Chatto and Windus, London, and The New Press, New York, 1993.

101 *Journal de captivité: Stalag XA / 1940–1945, Carnets – Correspondances – Textes*, edited and introduced by Olivier Corpet and Yann Moulier Boutang, Stock/IMEC, Paris, 1992.

102 Letter of 26 November 1963 to Jacques Lacan, in *Magazine Littéraire* 304, November 1992, pp. 49–50; reprinted in **110**, pp. 272–5.

1993

103 'L'unique tradition matérialiste', *Lignes* 18, January 1993, pp. 75–119.

104 'Lettres à D . . .' (1966), in Louis Althusser, *Écrits sur la psychanalyse: Freud et Lacan*, edited and presented by Olivier Corpet and François Matheron, Stock/IMEC, Paris, 1993, pp. 57–110.

105 'Trois notes sur la théorie des discours' (1966), in *Écrits sur la psychanalyse*, pp. 117–170.

106 'Sur le transfert et le contre-transfert (Petites incongruités portatives)' (1973), in *Écrits sur la psychanalyse*, pp. 173–186.

107 'Lettre ouverte aux analysants et analystes se réclamant de Jacques Lacan' (1980), in *Écrits sur la psychanalyse*, pp. 249–57.

108 'Remarques complémentaires sur la réunion du PLM-Saint-Jacques du 15 mars 1980' (1980), in *Écrits sur la psychanalyse*, pp. 258–66.

109 Correspondence with Jacques Lacan (1963–69), in *Écrits sur la psychanalyse*, pp. 271–305.

110 *Écrits sur la psychanalyse*: *Freud et Lacan*, edited and introduced by Olivier Corpet and François Matheron, Stock/IMEC, Paris, 1993.

Contains **21**; **81**; **95**; **102**; **104**; **105**; **106**; **107**; **108**; **109**.